ABOUT THE AUTHORS

Victoria Bassetti has worked with legislative and judicial bodies of the U.S. government, including serving as staff director/chief counsel to a subcommittee of the U.S. Senate Judiciary Committee. She has been active in numerous political campaigns and participates regularly in election day voter-protection efforts.

The 2012 documentary *Electoral Dysfunction* is directed by David Deschamps, Leslie D. Farrell, and Bennett Singer, whose credits collectively include multiple Emmy, Peabody, and duPont-Columbia awards.

Mo Rocca is a correspondent for *CBS Sunday Morning* and a panelist on NPR's hit quiz show *Wait, Wait . . . Don't Tell Me!* He is a former correspondent for *The Daily Show with Jon Stewart* and the author of *All the Presidents' Pets: The Story of One Reporter Who Refused to Roll Over.*

Heather Smith is president of Rock the Vote, which, under her leadership during the past two election cycles, has set the highest voter registration records in both midterm and presidential elections in the organization's twenty-year history of mobilizing millions of young Americans to the polls.

ELECTORAL DYSFUNCTION

A SURVIVAL MANUAL
FOR AMERICAN VOTERS

VICTORIA BASSETTI

With a foreword by Mo Rocca

and an afterword by Heather Smith

20 YEARS

THE NEW PRESS

© 2012 by Victoria Bassetti
Foreword © 2012 by Mo Rocca
Afterword © 2012 by Heather Smith
All rights reserved.
No part of this book may be reproduced, in any form, without written permission from
the publisher.

Requests for permission to reproduce selections from this book should be mailed to:
Permissions Department, The New Press, 38 Greene Street, New York, NY 10013.

Published in the United States by The New Press, New York, 2012
Distributed by Perseus Distribution

ISBN 978-1-59558-812-8 (pbk.)

CIP data available.

Now in its twentieth year, The New Press publishes books that promote and enrich public discussion and understanding of the issues vital to our democracy and to a more equi-
table world. These books are made possible by the enthusiasm of our readers; the support
of a committed group of donors, large and small; the collaboration of our many partners
in the independent media and the not-for-profit sector; booksellers, who often hand-sell
New Press books; librarians; and above all by our authors.

www.thenewpress.com
www.electoraldysfunction.org

Book design and composition by Bookbright Media
This book was set in Perpetua

Printed in the United States of America

10 9 8 7 6 5 4 3 2 1

To the memory of my grandfather
Cecil G. Taylor (1909–1999)

CONTENTS

FOREWORD

Pop quiz: Which of the following countries does *not* guarantee its citizens the right to vote?

a) Iran
b) Libya
c) The United States
d) All of the above

If you guessed "all of the above," you're right. Yes, the United States is one of only a handful of nations whose constitution does not explicitly provide the right to vote. (Singapore is another, but they don't even allow you to chew gum on the street.)

I'm guessing you're surprised. I know I was. Think of all the hard work our Founders put in—the revolutionizing, the three-fifths compromising, the having to write the entire Constitution with a quill—and they neglected to include the right to vote. (I know, it was a long hot summer. Hard to stay focused.) It got me thinking: What else don't I know about voting in our country? How does voting really work—or sometimes *not* work—in the U.S. of A.?

So naturally I did what any concerned citizen would do when trying to get to the bottom of things: I took a road trip across

America. Along the way I met all kinds of people at the heart of our nation's elections—voters, election workers, elected officials, even "electors" (you know, the guys and gals who end up picking the President). Of course, no road trip is complete without a bus full of nuns turned away at the polls. (More on that later.)

Spoiler alert: The way we run elections in this country is, as kids today say, totally wacky. What we think of as our "electoral system" is a crazy quilt of local, state, and federal systems. *Thirteen thousand* different voting districts, in fact, each with its own rules and regulations. In Iowa and Minnesota, you can register and cast a ballot on the very same day. In Texas and Pennsylvania, you've got to be on the voter rolls a month before an election. In North Dakota, you don't even have to register—you just vote. In Oregon, there's no actual place to show up and vote—you do it all by mail. And if you live in D.C., you can vote for President, but not for a Representative in Congress. Instead, your "voice" in Congress is called a Delegate, and she's not allowed to vote on the House floor. During my road trip, I met her—Delegate Eleanor Holmes Norton—and she pointed out that taxation without representation remains a reality for 600,000 Americans. Who happen to live in our nation's capital. (Ah, irony.)

Then there's that Electoral College, without question the country's most elite institution. As you probably know, when you and I vote for President, we're actually voting for a select few who vote for President for us. And who are these sage men and women, these stewards of our electoral destiny? They're people like Ben Leatherbury of Salem, Indiana. He's a really nice guy. A really nice guy who was all of *nineteen years old* when he served as an elector.

I also met folks like Tom Tancredo, an outspoken former Congressman from Colorado and onetime presidential candidate. He's not shy about saying that voting isn't a right but rather a privilege to be earned. (He's not shy about much, actually, which is one of the reasons why he's great to talk to.) Tancredo believes that

Americans should have to pass a civics literacy test before being allowed to cast ballots, even if it's not a very tough one: "I don't care
if we publish the test on great big billboards and tell them what the
answers are," he told me. "I don't care. I just want [voters] to know
something about the government that they're voting on!"

Then there are those nuns I was telling you about—a group of
eighty- and ninety-year-old sisters in South Bend, Indiana, who
tried to vote at the same place they'd voted for years, but didn't have
valid state-issued photo identification. Yes, election officials carded
a group of elderly nuns and turned them away. That incident got
me thinking: Do stringent ID laws, on the books now in a growing number of states and upheld by the U.S. Supreme Court, hurt
or help our electoral system? Do they deter voter impersonation, as
proponents argue, or do they make it harder for qualified voters to
actually vote, as critics charge? That's one of the questions we ex-
plore in this book.

But while some people are being turned away from voting, millions of others haven't even managed to register. Guess how many.
Five million? Ten million? Try fifty. That's right—*51 million people*—
or one in every four eligible voters. (And let's take bets on how many
of those vote regularly on *American Idol*, or at least on *The Voice*.) John
Fortier, a scholar with The American Enterprise Institute and the
Bipartisan Policy Center, put it to me this way: "I think both sides
would agree that our registration system is broken." Fortier went on
to share his ideas for how to make the voter registration system un-
broken (or at least a little *less* broken).

One of those unregistered voters—until recently, anyway—was
Flo Perkins of North Vernon, Indiana. After serving her sentence
for a felony conviction incurred several decades earlier, Flo thought
she wouldn't be allowed to vote in Indiana. (That is the case in some
states, like neighboring Kentucky.) After get-out-the-vote organiz-
ers knocked on her door and informed her that she was, in fact,

eligible to vote, Flo registered, and I went with her as she cast a ballot for the first time in her life. It was a very emotional day for Flo, who, as she fed her ballot into the optical scanner, asked: "Does it shred them as they go through?"

The answer is no—at least not when the machines are working. But too often, they don't. Some of us experience voting-machine failures that result in long lines on election day, but that's hardly the most important consequence. As Larry Norden of the Brennan Center for Justice told me, tens of thousands of ballots aren't counted due to problems with voting technology and ballot design. And in some cases, these glitches affect the outcome of elections. So here's a head-scratcher: My iPhone can do just about anything save pick itself up and walk on over to the voting booth, and yet we can't manage to make a voting machine that's consistently reliable?

Did I end up finding a little blue pill to cure America's electoral dysfunction? You'll have to read the book and see the movie to find out. I will tell you that the first step toward fixing the flaws in our voting system is understanding where these problems come from and what their impact really is. And I hope that just as my journey sparked in me a real curiosity about our nation's electoral system, this book will get you and your friends talking about the future of voting and voting rights in America. Because when it comes to constitutional guarantees and such, shouldn't we be keeping better company than Libya and Iran? I mean, sure, they're nice places to visit—but I wouldn't want to get stuck without a vote there.

Mo Rocca
New York, NY
June 2012

ALABAMA STATE TROOPERS CONFRONT TWENTY-FIVE-YEAR-OLD JOHN LEWIS (IN TRENCH COAT) AND SIX HUNDRED OTHER PEACEFUL VOTING RIGHTS MARCHERS AT EDMUND PETTUS BRIDGE IN SELMA, ALABAMA, ON SUNDAY, MARCH 7, 1965. *Minutes later, the troopers assaulted the marchers with billy clubs and fired tear gas at them. Lewis's skull was fractured by the police. Televised images of the melee shocked the nation and helped galvanize Congress to pass the Voting Rights Act of 1965.* **Photo Credit:** *Spider Martin, "Hosea Martin and John Lewis Confront Troopers." Reproduced by permission.*

INTRODUCTION

THE FIRST TIME RYAN DONNELL voted in Philadelphia, he was assigned to vote at an Italian American social club. He was greeted by two poll workers who were smoking cigarettes and eating donuts. Photos of Frank Sinatra and women in bikinis hung on the walls of the club. The voting booths were wedged in-between a ping-pong table and some couches. The experience sent Donnell, a photographer, on a quest to document some of the city's odder voting places. He found polls at roller skating rinks, wallpaper stores, and auto body shops.

In Chicago, some voters go to a taquería or to a bowling alley or to a laundromat.

Voters who live near Yosemite National Park, California, cast their ballots in a small building nestled in the valley amid some very real "purple mountain majesties."

In New Orleans, a nineteenth-century chapel built as a burial place for yellow fever victims houses a polling station. In Kenosha, Wisconsin, sand from Lake Michigan blows up into the beautiful Southport Beach House polling station. In Venice Beach, California, voters go to the lifeguard headquarters to cast their ballots. Throughout the nation, people vote in schools, libraries, and churches.

American democracy is exuberant and messy. America's first "poet of democracy," Walt Whitman, called election day the nation's "powerfulest scene and show." It was more impressive to him than Niagara Falls or the Grand Canyon. He called it our "quadrennial choosing. . . . The final ballot-shower from East to West—the paradox and conflict."

There is still plenty of paradox and conflict today—as much as there was when Whitman wrote his poem "Election Day" in 1884, an era when allegations of vote stealing and voter suppression accompanied almost every election in his home state of New York.

Everyone knows, or thinks they know, that there are problems with twenty-first century voting. If the 2000 presidential election between Texas Governor George W. Bush and Vice President Al Gore didn't prove how disordered American elections can be, then some other local, state, or federal election in the last decade has raised concerns of abuse, mismanagement, fraud, or voter intimidation and suppression.

It isn't supposed to be like that. Most Americans go to the polls filled with a commitment to and idealism about democracy. They know that their role in democracy is vital. They might be angry and fueled with rage at the incumbent party when they go to vote. Or they might be fired with dreams and wishes for better times. But almost all are certain about the fundamental value of democracy and the primacy of voting in our system of government.

So how did we get to the point today where the person who gets the most votes for President can nevertheless lose? Where people are serving time in prison for voting? Where fewer than 50 percent of potential voters participate in the vast majority of elections? Where the administration of the election system is left to people who have a partisan stake in the outcome? Where elections are conducted by more than thirteen thousand administrative bodies operating under disparate rules, with ad hoc budgets and with various levels of professionalism? And—perhaps most surprisingly—where there is no national right to vote?

You might say we didn't plan it that way. Except, we do elect the politicians who write and enforce the laws and who pass the budgets. And so the only solution to our electoral dysfunction is more democracy. The solution to our problematic voting system is . . . voting.

This book and the movie it accompanies are for people who believe in the promise of democracy. It is for the people who walk into their polling stations on a fall day. Sometimes snow is falling. Or it is raining. Or maybe it is 85 degrees outside, and a day at the beach also beckons. They stand in line patiently, often silently, occasionally for hours, with their neighbors. Most of the people in line are strangers to one another, yet on that day they are bound together by their dedication to our great experiment in democracy. This book is also for the people who don't vote, in the hope that even though our system is imperfect, they'll come to see how invaluable their participation is.

In 2008 more people voted for President than watched the Super Bowl. By some estimates, political campaign expenditures for all of America's 2012 elections—from President to local dog catcher—may exceed $6 billion. So don't ever let anyone tell you your vote isn't worth anything.

Today, politicians and political advocates approach our election system divided into two camps: those who cry fraud and those who warn of voter suppression. Members of the two main political parties tend to fall predictably into the camps. Republicans assert that there are massive voter fraud schemes underway. Democrats assert that there are systematic efforts to suppress the vote, particularly the minority and poor vote. (Of course, there are some Democrats who believe that there is fraud and some Republicans who acknowledge that there is voter suppression.)

The 2000 election in St. Louis, Missouri, is a perfect example of the whiplash people can get when they try to untangle whether an election ran rife with fraud or was corrupted by voter suppression efforts, or both.

St. Louis is a majority African American city that votes overwhelmingly Democratic. Before the 2000 election, the city's election board moved approximately 50,000 voters from the active registered voter list onto an "inactive" list. It did so for a number of reasons, such as because according to the city's tax assessment records voters' addresses were on vacant lots or because it had been a very long time since the registered voters had last voted. But none of the prospective voters was notified of his or her change in status. In 1996, only 122,000 people had voted in St. Louis, thus moving 50,000 people off the rolls meant taking potentially as much as 40 percent of the city's voter base out of play.

Before election day, Democratic activists were convinced that there was a methodical effort underway to keep the party's supporters from the polls. On election day, chaos reigned in some neighborhoods. Voters, after standing in line, were told they were not registered. They then had to move to another line in the polling place to appeal the ruling that they could not vote. Then they were told that they could go to the downtown election office and try to vote. By mid-afternoon, hundreds of people crowded into the office desperately trying to cast ballots.

The Democratic Party filed a lawsuit in federal court to keep the polls open longer. It won a ruling to keep them open three extra hours. Forty-five minutes after winning the court case, it lost an appeal, and the polls were closed. One of Missouri's U.S. senators, Republican Kit Bond, called the decision to keep the polls open longer "the biggest fraud on the voters in this state and nation that we have ever seen."

Later, the state's Republican Secretary of State, who was in charge of its elections system, issued a report asserting that there was a conspiracy "to create bedlam so that election fraud could be per-petrated." He argued that the polls were purposefully flooded with ineligible voters on election day and that the election board's office was intentionally overwhelmed to keep it from policing the election. And then he listed a series of fraudulent votes, including some from voters who he said were registered at vacant lots.

Meanwhile, the newly elected Democratic Representative from St. Louis warned that "there was a concerted attempt to suppress votes" and told Republicans that they sounded "like a hot-air balloon losing air."

The local newspaper, the *St. Louis Post-Dispatch*, took up the mat-ter and had reporters go to the two thousand alleged vacant lots used as a reason for striking thousands of voters from the rolls. The re-porters found a building on almost every site. The city's own budget director had been purged from the voter rolls for living at a vacant lot. In fact, he was living in a condominium exactly where he said it was. (The tax assessor leapt on the finding, concerned about poten-tially uncollected taxes.)

Two grand juries, three special investigative panels, and four new election board members later, most felt no closer to knowing what had happened in that election and why. But in trying to unravel the mess, the FBI subpoenaed every single voting and registration re-cord for the city from that year. The U.S. Department of Justice threatened to sue the St. Louis Board of Elections. The board settled the dispute and pledged to institute new procedures.

Was it fraud or suppression in St. Louis in 2000? Or was it nei-ther? Or both? Most likely, the election board and administration officials' mistakes were due to incompetence, coupled with partisan bias, compounded by a failure to follow federal law governing voter registration roll maintenance. As to fraud, in the chaos, a small num-ber of people (likely fewer than a hundred) got to vote who were probably ineligible to vote, but most of them genuinely believed they were entitled to vote. And in any event, follow-up analyses found that they had no impact on the election outcome.

Meanwhile, thousands of people were kept from voting in St. Louis in 2000. No one knows how many because most of them went home discouraged and never reported the incident. But they never got back their chance to vote.

This book tries to take a commonsense approach to the issues. There is some fraud, but it is rarely systematic or effective. Organized, large-scale fraud is mostly a relic of the past. Major election fraud is detected today because it occurs around a highly scrutinized public event, involves many people, and leaves a paper trail. The penalties are so severe, and the likelihood of getting caught so high, that very few people ever attempt to commit organized voting fraud. Still there always have been fools and zealots from both major political parties who get so caught up in an election that they are willing to risk prison by abusing the system. In 2009, in one county in Kentucky, nine Republican officials were caught manipulating electronic voting machines and systematically changing votes. In 2007, a Democratic activist forged ten absentee ballots in Mississippi. They were caught and sent to prison. Most people who try to commit organized voting fraud are found out.

However, voting is a vast, sprawling human enterprise involving millions of individuals who make honest mistakes or who do not know the rules with lawyerlike precision. Their small mistakes are no threat to democracy. While in the wrong, the people who commit these mistakes do not warrant the brutal reaction they are subjected to. And the incidents of fraud do not justify the increasingly restrictive rules and requirements being imposed upon millions of voters. These rules only make voting more difficult and thus more unlikely for numerous people.

Worse, sometimes the new rules on voting are imposed with full knowledge of their disproportionately harmful impact on vulnerable voter groups. The legacy of our nation's century-long suppression of the minority vote makes these efforts all the more reprehensible.

This book explores six ways that the current system sometimes fails or has failed to live up to its highest aspirations. Chapter 1 examines the legal basis for the "right to vote" in America. Chapter 2 recounts the expansion of the American electorate, or who gets to vote at all. Chapter 3 chronicles the reasons people vote or don't vote and what factors go into the decision to vote. Chapter 4 tries to explain our complicated way of electing presidents. Chapter 5 looks at the way we run elections. Finally, Chapter 6 deals with the impact of partisanship on elections.

Fortunately, for most Americans, voting is a good experience. However, those of us who have never had a problem should not ignore the millions who do face problems. We owe them, our fellow citizens, the effort to make sure the system works for everyone.

ELECTORAL
DYSFUNCTION

THOMAS PAINE BY THE SCOTTISH CARICATURIST JOHN KAY, CIRCA 1790. Paine wrote the influential pamphlet, Common Sense, *which is widely believed to have sparked the Revolutionary War. He moved to Paris and became involved in the French Revolution. When he later returned to the United States, Paine was not permitted to vote.* **Photo Credit:** *Library of Congress*

CHAPTER 1

IN SEARCH OF THE RIGHT TO VOTE

*Do Americans Really Have
the Right to Vote?*

"The right of voting for representatives is the primary right by
which other rights are protected. To take away this right is to
reduce a man to slavery, for slavery consists in being subject to
the will of another, and he that has not a vote in the election of
representatives is in this case."

Thomas Paine, Dissertation on First
Principles of Government, *1795*

H E WAS THE PIED PIPER of the American Revolution, a peripatetic
troublemaker. Born in England. Trained as a corsetmaker. At
age 37, Thomas Paine migrated to America with a letter of introduction from Benjamin Franklin in his pocket. Less than two years later,
in 1776, he wrote the transcendent document of the Revolutionary
War, *Common Sense*, the pamphlet that more than anything else
moved our Founders from dissent to revolution.

John Adams, always territorial about his role in the revolution,
sniffed that the pamphlet was "a tolerable summary of the arguments
which I had been repeating again and again in Congress for nine

months." But when push came to shove, he admitted, "History is to ascribe the American Revolution to Thomas Paine."

Paine returned to London the year the U.S. Constitution was drafted and from there traveled to Paris to witness the French Revolution. By 1792, he was preparing to leave London again, indicted for seditious libel after the publication of *Rights of Man*. He fled to Paris, was elected to the French National Convention, was ejected from the convention, and then was arrested and imprisoned in 1793. Released from prison in part due to the intervention of the United States Minister to France (and future President), James Monroe, Paine resumed his role in French politics, rejoining the National Convention. In 1802, he left France during Napoleon's rise to power.

He found refuge once again in the United States. Shortly after the conclusion of the Revolutionary War, the state of New York had recognized his indispensable contribution to the founding of the nation. It had rewarded him for his services with a 320-acre New Rochelle farm and cottage confiscated from a Tory loyalist. Paine returned early in the new century to his New Rochelle farm. But his New World sanctuary was far from idyllic. During his time in Paris and London, Paine had unabashedly proclaimed himself an atheist. En route to New York after his initial stop in Washington, D.C., Paine was assaulted by mobs throwing rocks at him and repudiated by many of his revolutionary friends.

In the fall of 1806, Paine walked into his New Rochelle polling station. He was turned away, denied the ballot. The Tory election inspectors at his polling station rejected him, asserting he was not an American and that he had been renounced by George Washington. Paine objected. He told them they were wrong on both counts. When one of the inspectors threatened, "I will commit you to prison," Paine left without voting. He then pursued the matter in court. He lost. He had no right to vote in the nation that now counts him one of its Founders.

In the years between Paine's traumatic experience at the polls in New Rochelle and today, America's way of voting has changed dramatically. Thirty-three new states have joined the union. Some tried to leave it. A civil war was fought. The Constitution was amended numerous times to address voting issues. But even today millions of American voters can identify with Paine's two-hundred-year-old experience as they walk into the polls and find they cannot vote.

In the decade since the 2000 presidential election, the way America votes has come under almost as much scrutiny and pressure as it bore at the height of the civil rights movement in the 1960s. Billions of dollars have been thrown at the mechanics of voting: the machines we use, the way we register to vote. A rhetorical war has been waged about who should vote and how and when and where we vote. It shouldn't come as a surprise that the simple act of voting should be disputed or that there are sides to this war or that today's political parties align themselves against one another fiercely.

Votes propel parties and people to power. So one side claims to be protecting the integrity of the voting system against fraud and abuse. The other side passionately asserts that it is protecting the heart and soul of our democracy. In the last decade, the result has been a flurry of legislative initiatives in almost every state in the union changing voting laws—from voter identification requirements, to modifications of absentee voting rules, early voting hours, and voter registration rules, to the machines used to count votes. Hardly anything in the system has escaped alteration or power grabs. And voters themselves—hundreds of millions of them—have been the pawns in this battle.

But American voters have been pawns in the battle almost from the beginning. And part of the reason we have been pawns rests on a simple legal fact. From the day Paine walked into his New York polling station to this, one thing has not changed. The startling fact is Americans don't really have a right to vote.

TIME MACHINE

Imagine if contemporary Americans were asked to vote on adoption of the U.S. Constitution, as originally drafted, stripped of all changes wrought over the last two centuries. Our nation of more than 310 million lives in a time and place where, as President George W. Bush pledged in his second inaugural address, "It is the policy of the United States to seek and support the growth of democratic movements and institutions in every nation and culture, with the ultimate goal of ending tyranny in our world." Imbued as we are with that spirit, if we were transported back to the winter of 1787–88 and asked to vote on the Constitution, we might recoil at some of its provisions. The original document establishing our government acknowledges and weaves slavery deeply into our society. Women cannot vote. Two of the three major federal officers, President and Senator, are not voted on by the people.

And there is no right to vote in the Constitution.

The word "vote" appears in the Constitution only in relation to how representatives, senators, and presidential electors perform their duties. Representatives vote. In fact, while they are performing their voting duties in the House, they are immune from arrest for most crimes. But the people's vote is not mentioned. Consequently, an individual's vote is neither protected nor guaranteed. The phrase "right to vote" simply does not appear in the Constitution. And it does not appear in the Bill of Rights.

The Founders wrote a Constitution that gave Congress the right to pass copyright and bankruptcy laws, the right to borrow money, the right to establish post offices. Exactly how long is a mile? Congress is given the power to say, in other words to "fix the Standards of Weights and Measures." Congress was required to keep a journal of its proceedings. Members of Congress were guaranteed a salary.

Amid this wealth of detail, scarcely a word is spent on how the people are to vote or how their consent to be governed is to be assessed.

Even in the wake of the Bill of Rights, which made a slew of individual rights explicit, the Constitution did not mention a right to vote. The right to assemble and petition government was established. The right to keep and bear arms, to a jury trial (in civil disputes where the value exceeds $20), to a speedy trial in criminal cases, to due process of law, to confront witnesses in criminal cases? Yes. Voting rights? No.

It's almost as if in the course of constructing a house, the contractor ordered the refrigerator and stove, the windows and curtains, the roof shingles; bought all the interior paint; and built the swimming pool. But he completely forgot about the foundation.

The Founders were not, of course, so oblivious. And contrary to many common accounts, they were not stiff necked, antidemocratic elitists hostile to the swarm of unwashed voters. But during that hot summer in Philadelphia in 1787, when they were writing the Constitution, the old adage that politics is the art of the possible held sway. The decision not to address voting rights in the Constitution was not an oversight. It was a pragmatic decision. It was not politically practicable to impose uniform suffrage (i.e., voting) laws across the original colonies. If the Founders had tried to do so, they would have ignited a conflict among states, each of which had distinct traditions and approaches to voting. A uniform federal approach to voting would have overridden some states' traditions and inflamed a substantial number of the states needed for the document's ratification. Was the new, fragile federal government really going to tell South Carolina that free blacks could vote? Or was it going to have to do the opposite and tell Massachusetts, which did allow blacks to vote, that it would have to bar their voting?

A uniform federal voting system was a bridge too far. Easier to let state laws and provisions dealing with the vote stand. After all, almost all elections were local. Only one of the newly created federal offices was subject to direct popular vote. Neither senators nor the President were elected by the general population. Only members of the House of Representatives stood before the people for election. The Constitution in effect integrated whatever the states might say about the right to vote into the new federal system. Each state was required to have a republican form of government, but no more than that.

In the time that has passed since our founding document was adopted, nothing has been more sharply disputed than our voting rights. Not taxation policy. Not government regulation. Not our safety net—Social Security, Medicare, welfare. Not railroads. Not the Internet. Not freedom of speech. Not health care. Nothing rivals the intensity of, the importance of, or the blood spilled over our nation's debate on the right to vote—a subject that was so ambiguously and elliptically avoided in the Constitution.

Today, in the wake of a civil war that left more than 600,000 dead, eight constitutional amendments, two monumental social protest movements, the youth quake of the 1960s, the transformative lawmaking of Congress in 1965, and the convulsions of the 2000 presidential election, most Americans feel reasonably confident that they have something approaching a right to vote.[1] Or maybe it's just a privilege.

To a degree, the easiest way to think about our voting rights system is as a sedimentary rock formation, its layers laid down and intermingled over centuries with federal and state constitutional provisions, laws, and regulations evolving over the course of our

---

[1] They have doubts, to be sure, about how votes are counted, how elections are administered, and how responsive our government is, as will be discussed in later chapters.

history. But the foundational layer—the right to vote—has never been laid.

Since there is no overarching federal "right to vote" in our Constitution, on a national level, the right to vote might best be understood in the negative. The United States has universal suffrage, almost. The vote cannot be denied to a citizen on the basis of race, gender, age (once the voter is above age eighteen), nor ability to read or to pay a poll tax. But some categories of people can still indisputably have their right to vote denied: felons or non-citizens, for example. An individual's vote cannot be diluted, made to count less than another person's. However, as simple as it might be to formulate the principle "one man, one vote," implementation is not nearly so straightforward. And the right to vote, to the extent there is one, must be equally protected. Though like "one man, one vote," implementing equal protection is not clear-cut.

Beyond that, whether one has a *right* to vote is largely a matter of state law. So citizens of Missouri have the right to vote written into their 1945 constitution. "No power, civil or military, shall at any time interfere to prevent the free exercise of the right of suffrage." Citizens of Indiana, whose constitution was written in 1851, do not.

The right to vote in the most practical sense—the way people cast their votes and have them counted—can be restricted and made difficult in numerous ways. And whether efforts to restrict the ability to vote go too far is determined by a blend of state and federal law.

As the U.S. Supreme Court said in 1974 in *Storer v. Brown*, determining whether a law infringes on voting rights is "very much a matter of 'considering the facts and circumstances behind the law, the interests which the State claims to be protecting, and the interests of those who are disadvantaged by the classification.' What the result of this process will be in any specific case may be very difficult to predict with great assurance." In other words, who knows?

If there was any doubt, in December 2000, the U.S. Supreme Court made it abundantly clear in relation to presidential elections in *Bush v. Gore*. "The individual citizen has no federal constitutional right to vote for electors for the President of the United States unless and until the state legislature chooses a statewide election as the means to implement its power to appoint members of the Electoral College."[2] And lest anyone drew comfort from the fact that presidential electors are currently selected by popular vote, the Supreme Court hastened to add that "the State legislature's power to select the manner for appointing electors is plenary," in other words absolute.

The bottom line: voters in the United States simply have no constitutional right to vote for President. The fact that Americans can vote for the electors who then vote for the President is a generous gift given by state legislatures. They are free to take it back whenever they want.

In the wake of the 2000 election and *Bush v. Gore*, a blue ribbon commission headed by two former presidents, Jimmy Carter and Gerald Ford, was appointed to help sort through the mess. When the commission issued its report, it casually noted: "The U.S. Constitution does not provide a right to vote." They elaborated, "It provides that state governments shall determine who is eligible to vote in either state or federal elections, though subsequent (constitutional) amendments offer guards against discrimination in the grant or denial of the franchise."

A TALE OF TWO STATES

Eight years after the *Bush v. Gore* decision, a group of would-be Indiana voters represented by the state's Democratic Party pled their

---

[2] Chapter 4 discusses the Electoral College and the way we elect presidents in further, and less lawyerly, detail.

case before the U.S. Supreme Court. The issue wasn't presidential elections in particular. It was about how all Indiana elections would be conducted. And their case, coupled with a parallel case brought in Missouri at around the same time, more than anything else, illustrates the complex, contradictory interweaving of federal and state law surrounding the way we vote.

On a warm January day in 2008, the Yale-educated lawyer Paul Smith stood before the Supreme Court and began, "Mr. Chief Justice, and may it please the Court: This case involves a law that directly burdens our most fundamental right, the right to vote."

The case had begun in 2005, when Indiana enacted a new law requiring that all voters present government-issued photo identification when they attempted to vote in person at polling places. Indiana's goal in implementing the requirement seemed to be relatively simple: prevent someone from coming into the polls claiming to be someone he or she was not and then casting a fraudulent vote. If everyone has to present photo identification, the state reasoned, the risk of voter impersonation would be nil.

Since a substantial number of Indiana residents did not have government-issued photo identification, opponents of the law were profoundly worried that the requirement would suppress the vote, particularly of the poor and elderly. A lawsuit challenging the law was brought almost immediately after the law was passed, and every court considering the matter prior to the Supreme Court upheld the constitutional validity of the identification law. The case came before the Supreme Court on an almost theoretical basis. Indiana's voter identification laws had not been widely implemented. So, the question before the Court was whether the law—and the burden it imposed on voters—was on its face an unconstitutional impediment to voting.

Smith managed to speak for about fifty seconds before members of the Court began peppering him with questions. And what they were curious about, more than anything, was whether and how people were actually going to be affected by this law—which had not even been widely implemented when the case was brought. Smith told them that it was hard to say exactly how many people would be substantially burdened by the requirement.

On the low end of the estimates, one percent of the voting-age Indiana population—about 43,000 people—lacked government-issued photo identification.[3] At the high end, as much as 10 percent of the population, more than 400,000 people, did not have such identification.[4] But why not just go get the identification, the Justices wondered. Both the conservative Justice Samuel Alito and the more liberal Justice David Souter were curious. How much of a burden could that be? Since a photo identification required a certified birth certificate, which costs money, and time off work to go to the Bureau of Motor Vehicles, it was a significant burden, Smith argued. He pointed out to the Court: "The record shows . . . that 60 percent of the time, when people go in and ask for one, they get sent home."

With his thirty minutes to speak to the Supreme Court drawing to a close, Smith spoke to Justice John Paul Stevens, widely regarded as one of the swing votes in the case. "What there is in the record, Your Honor, is the testimony from the Lafayette Urban Ministry, which helps the needy in Lafayette, Indiana. They had 150 people come to them and say: We want your help to get IDs. A year later,

---

[3] This number was derived by subtracting the number of people who had Indiana-issued photo identification from the population of Indiana. The number was considered low since the number of photo identifications is inflated by the presence of people who have moved or who have died. Nevertheless, it can reliably be considered the minimum number of people affected by the state's requirement.
[4] This number was derived by surveying a representative sample of Indiana residents.

less than 75 had succeeded because they found themselves caught in this Catch-22, where they went to get a birth certificate, they didn't have a driver's license, they didn't have the other kinds of very narrowly specified IDs they needed, and so they were basically in this bureaucratic maze and they couldn't get out of it."

With that Smith sat down. He was followed by the two lawyers defending Indiana's statute: Paul Clement, the Solicitor General of the United States, which was backing Indiana's position, and Indiana's Solicitor General, Thomas Fisher.

Almost four months later, the Court handed down its six-to-three decision in *Crawford v. Marion County Board of Elections*. The Indiana law was constitutional.

There was one fact no one disputed. The Indiana law was aimed at preventing in-person voter impersonation. But "the record contains no evidence of any such fraud actually occurring in Indiana at any time in its history," the Court conceded.

The Court assessed the nature of Indiana's interests in imposing the law. There was, of course, its overall interest in election integrity and preventing fraud. True, there was no evidence of the particular type of fraud that the statute sought to prevent, but there had been other types of fraud before. So the Court created a transitive property of fraud. And there was the fact that the state's voter rolls were a mess, full of registered voters who had died or were otherwise not eligible to vote. It did not seem to concern the Court that the new law did nothing to clean up those rolls. That was already being done in other ways. Finally, of course, public confidence in the integrity of the system is important. No matter that, as regards in-person voter impersonation, there was absolutely no reason for the public to doubt the integrity of the system, which imposes up to a five-year prison sentence for this type of fraud.

Weighing in against these generic and unquantified concerns was the substantial chance that anywhere between 43,000 and 400,000 people would find voting more difficult if not impossible due to the new law. But the Court breezily dismissed these burdens.

The Court conceded that the law probably imposed special burdens on elderly people born out of state, poor people, people who find it hard to find their birth certificate (a prerequisite for government-issued photo identification), homeless people, and people with religious objections to being photographed—more than the "usual burdens" on voting that the Court would normally tolerate. But not to worry, the state had it all figured out: have them cast a provisional ballot on election day. Then by noon on the second Monday after the election, the would-be voter would have to show up at the local circuit court and sign an affidavit that he or she was indigent and could not obtain the identification or produce photo identification and sign an affidavit that he or she cast the provisional ballot. Easy, right?

The dissenting justices, Stephen Breyer, Ruth Bader Ginsburg, and David Souter would have none of it. They remembered the days not too long ago when states imposed poll taxes on people trying to vote.[5] And to them Indiana's photo identification requirement crossed the line:

> The State's requirement here, that people without cars travel to a motor vehicle registry and that the poor who fail to do that get to their county seats within 10 days of every election, likewise translate into unjustified economic burdens uncomfortably close to the outright $1.50 fee we struck down 42 years ago. Like that fee, the onus of the Indiana law is illegitimate just because it correlates with no state interest so well as it does with the object of deterring poorer residents from exercising the franchise.

---

[5] The history of the poll tax and its elimination is discussed in Chapter 2.

Meanwhile, in 2006, Missouri's state legislature had passed a law requiring voters to present government-issued photo identification when showing up at the polls. The requirement was signed into law in mid-June. Four months later, Missouri's Supreme Court struck down the law under Missouri's constitution. Six of the seven members of the state Court had no doubts about Missouri's position in the voting rights pecking order: "Due to the more expansive and concrete protections of the right to vote under the Missouri Constitution, voting rights are an area where our state constitution provides greater protection than its federal counterpart."

From a legal standpoint, this meant that the Missouri Supreme Court evaluated the law using a tougher standard than the U.S. Supreme Court used for Indiana's law. While the U.S. Supreme Court uses a "flexible" standard to evaluate laws that impact people's ability to vote, Missouri courts apply strict scrutiny: "any limitation on a fundamental right must serve compelling state interests and must be narrowly tailored to meet those interests." As in Indiana, there was no evidence that in-person voter impersonation had ever occurred during Missouri elections. But unlike Indiana, the identification requirement passed by the Missouri state legislature in the summer of 2006 could not meet the strict scrutiny of the state Supreme Court.

Safe behind the walls of the state's explicit, actual "right to vote," Missouri's three million voters[6] went to the polls in 2006, 2008, and 2010.[7] In 2008, almost 68 percent of that state's voting-eligible

---

[6] Missouri has a voter-eligible population of 4.3 million. In the 2008 presidential election, 2.9 million Missourians voted.

[7] Missouri does have an identification requirement today, but a variety of documents like bank statements or utility bills satisfy the law.

population cast ballots. In Indiana, 59 percent of its voting-eligible population voted.

On a national level, where laws affecting the right to vote are judged on a "flexible" basis, things stand differently. According to the U.S. Supreme Court, states are free to erect bureaucratic edifices—deadlines, requirements, regulations—almost to their heart's content. These byzantine systems are not meant to encourage voting or ease its burdens. The Supreme Court almost delights in this intricacy and in the quest for order over sloppy democracy: "As a practical matter, there must be a substantial regulation of elections if they are to be fair and honest and if some sort of order, rather than chaos, is to accompany the democratic processes. . . . The States have evolved comprehensive, and in many respects complex, election codes regulating in most substantial ways, with respect to both federal and state elections, the time, place, and manner of holding primary and general elections, the registration and qualifications of voters, and the selection and qualification of candidates." The need for tidiness is elevated to a first-order principle.

The absence of a federal right to vote coupled with the Supreme Court's inclination to value procedure over real world voter behavior has dramatic consequences for America's elections. Each state is free to set its own policies and procedures in its quest for orderly elections. There are few standards or overarching goals. With each election district free to pursue its own goals, confusion and contradictions abound. Voter registration requirements are convoluted. Voter rolls are purged chaotically. Ballot design is unregulated and amateurish. Polling hours are haphazard. Voting equipment ranges from the high-tech to derelict. Vote counting and recounting systems are unsystematic. (Election administration will be explored in more detail in Chapter 5).

In 1964, the Supreme Court proclaimed that "no right is more precious in a free country than that of having a voice in the election of those who make the laws under which, as good citizens, we must live." But under the Court's decisions, voters might be forgiven sometimes for feeling more like mice in a maze than like citizens of the world's greatest democracy.

INEZ MILLHOLLAND LEADS A PARADE FOR WOMEN'S VOTING RIGHTS IN WASHINGTON, D.C., *on March 3, 1913, the day before Woodrow Wilson was to be inaugurated as President. Several thousand women participated, including Helen Keller. More than half a million people, in town for the inauguration, watched the suffrage parade. After the women marched a few blocks, the crowd surged into the street harassing and assaulting them.* **Photo Credit:** *Library of Congress*

CHAPTER 2

THE EPIC BATTLE FOR THE VOTE

Who Gets to Vote in America and the
Quest for Universal Suffrage

"DEMOCRAT, n. One who adheres to a government by the people, or favors the extension of the right of suffrage to all classes of men."

Daniel Webster, Webster's American Dictionary of the English Language, *1828*

VOTING IN THE UNITED STATES has never been an easy matter. The who, what, when, where, and why of voting have always been debated and fought over. A contemporary American transported to the Philadelphia of July 1787 would be bewildered and likely outraged by some of our Founders' disdainful thoughts about "the people" and democracy. By the same token, many of their concerns would sound startlingly familiar.

ONE HOT SUMMER IN PHILADELPHIA

Coming as they did from states and cities where overall less than 60 percent of the white male population was entitled to vote, the Founders did not seriously contemplate imposing universal suffrage and voting rights in the Constitution. The language of pure democracy did not yet dominate American politics. But it was coming, very soon, and the Founders knew it.

By the time the 4,500-word document was finished, the constitutional structure created in Philadelphia contained numerous democracy-restraining features. But these republican[8] elements are notable only for their presence in a document that had a sharp tilt toward democracy, especially when compared with either the Articles of Confederation or prevailing state constitutions of the time. It is worth exploring some of the democratic and republican structural elements of the Constitution because they offer insight into the Founders' overall attitudes about the impact of voters on government. In 1787, the Constitution's drafters were more concerned with institutions and structures than with the role of the individual in government, which is one reason why the document is so silent about voters themselves. Individual liberties were, of course, addressed in rapid order in the Bill of Rights adopted by Congress in 1789 and ratified in 1791. But even the Bill of Rights did not address individual voting rights.

The new federal government crafted in 1787 contained one unmistakably democratic feature. The House of Representatives was overtly, aggressively democratic. Its members were subject to direct vote by the people. The number of representatives was proportional to each state's population. The House was a significant democratic step, a sharp departure from the Congress created in the original Articles of Confederation, which was unicameral, not proportional to population, and not subject to direct popular vote.

The new Senate, however, served to restrain the House's populist impulses. Created by the Connecticut Compromise at the

---

[8] Throughout this book, "republican" and "democratic" are used distinctly from "Republican" and "Democratic." The Republican and Democratic political parties were not established until the early decades of the nineteenth century.

Convention, the Senate was an unabashedly quasi-democratic institution, a bulwark against popular sentiment. Appointed by state legislatures rather than by popular election and serving six-year terms, senators were positioned to protect states, not democracy per se.[9] As Virginia's James Madison wrote, "The House of Representatives will derive its powers from the people of America. . . . The Senate, on the other hand, will derive its powers from the States, as political and co-equal societies; and these will be represented on the principle of equality in the Senate." Even today, the majority does not rule in the Senate. The majority of states, not people, governs. Twenty-six states representing only slightly more than one-sixth of the population of the United States can block any legislation from passing. (In fact, given the Senate's filibuster rules, twenty-one states, with slightly more than 10 percent of the population, can stop all laws.) Senate voting patterns today are not, of course, strictly small state versus large state. But North-South and East-West regional voting blocs have developed, and even in the modern era, small states still gain substantial advantages in the Senate due to their equal voting power.

Like the Senate, the office of President also was only quasi-democratic. Though one of the men who crafted the sections of the Constitution dealing with the presidency proclaimed that "he should be in a strict sense of th[e] expression, *The Man of the People,*" the

---

[9] Senators were elected by state legislatures until 1913, when the Seventeenth Amendment was adopted providing for direct popular election of senators. In the late nineteenth century, Senate elections were plagued by mismanagement, bribery, intimidation, and corruption. Nine bribery cases involving the selection of senators were brought before the Senate between 1866 and 1906. Twenty state legislatures deadlocked forty-five times in picking their senators between 1891 and 1905, resulting in numerous delays in seating senators. In 1899, Delaware's problems were so intractable that the state legislature did not send a Senator to Washington for four years. By 1913, the people seemed better guarantors of liberty than the wise men of their state legislatures.

President nevertheless was selected by an elite group of electors, not by direct popular vote.

Moreover, the Constitution imposed several supermajority requirements, inhibiting democratic action by simple majority. The President—one man (and it would of course be a man in the Founders' world)—had the right to veto legislation. That veto could be overridden only by a vote of two-thirds of both the Senate and the House. In order to amend the Constitution, a two-thirds majority had to be reached in the Senate and House, and then three-quarters of the states had to ratify the amendment. As a final check on majority rule, the judicial system was created to review the constitutional validity of laws.[10]

The Constitution contained one more anti-democratic provision, a monumental transgression against the spirit of the revolution: the three-fifths clause. Without ever using the word "slavery," the document institutionalized slavery and imbedded it deeply in the innermost workings of our democracy. Though Congress was given the power to bar the slave trade—in 1808, after eleven years had passed—it was not given the power to bar slavery itself among the original colonies. The Constitution ensured that, were a slave to escape and flee to a non-slave state, he or she would have to be returned to his or her owner. And most troubling for a nascent democracy, the number of seats allocated to a state in the House of Representatives was based on a population count that included what the Founders hazily called "other Persons." "Representatives . . . shall be apportioned among the several States . . . according to their respective Numbers, which shall be determined by adding to the whole

---

[10] The judiciary's power to rule on the constitutionality of statutes was firmly established by the Supreme Court in *Marbury v. Madison* in 1803. The scope and nature of this review and its "anti-democratic" impact have never ceased being a matter of debate.

Number of free Persons . . . three fifths of all other Persons," the Constitution read.

Not many people were fooled. The "other Persons" were slaves. Pennsylvania's delegate Gouverneur Morris exclaimed: "The inhabitant of Georgia and S.C. who goes to the Coast of Africa, and in defiance of the most sacred laws of humanity tears away his fellow creatures from their dearest connections and damns them to the most cruel bondages, shall have more votes in a Govt. instituted for the rights of mankind, than the Citizen of Pa. or N. Jersey, who views with a laudable horror so nefarious a practice." The Founders knew what they were doing, and most of them approved the three-fifths clause as yet another compromise necessary to bring the Convention to a successful conclusion. New York Convention delegate Alexander Hamilton noted that without the three-fifths clause, "no union could have possibly been formed."

All of the quasi- and anti-democratic elements of the nation's new civic structure were perfectly sound, indeed necessary mechanics to the Founders. Many, though not all, Founders had deep-seated doubts about the good judgment of the people. "I have ever observed that a choice by the people themselves is not generally distinguished for its wisdom," wrote Thomas Jefferson, who learned of the Convention's debates from letters written to him by friends while he was in Paris serving as the Minister to France. John Adams, serving as Minister to Great Britain in London during the Convention, was blunter: "If by *the people* is meant the whole body of a great nation, it should never be forgotten, that they can never act, consult, or reason together. . . . The proposition, that they are the best keepers of their own liberties, is not true. They are the worst conceivable; they are no keepers at all."

Morris, so offended by the three-fifths compromise, however, was not so sure about broad suffrage rights. "Give the votes to people who have no property and they will sell them to the rich," he warned. Morris proposed that the Constitution restrict the right to vote to property holders. His proposal was sent to a committee for consideration. While the committee worked, George Washington went fishing. Like so many fishermen before and after him, he had limited success: "Friday. In company . . . I went up to Trenton on another Fishing party. . . . In the Evening fished, not very success-fully. . . . Saturday. In the morning, and between breakfast and din-ner, fished again with more success (for perch) than yesterday."

When Washington returned and debate resumed, Morris's pro-posal was roundly rejected. Benjamin Franklin's witty dig at prop-erty requirements held sway:

> Today a man owns a jackass worth 50 dollars and he is en-titled to vote; but before the next election the jackass dies. The man in the mean time has become more experienced, his knowledge of the principles of government, and his ac-quaintance with mankind, are more extensive, and he is therefore better qualified to make a proper selection of rul-ers—but the jackass is dead and the man cannot vote. Now gentlemen, pray inform me, in whom is the right of suf-frage? In the man or in the jackass?

Still, no one at the Constitutional Convention proposed universal suffrage or sought a right to vote. A creative, ambiguous silence hung over the matter that summer in Philadelphia. The Founders struck a balance by staying quiet on the matter and leaving the ques-tion of voting rights and suffrage requirements to the states.

The republican and quasi-democratic sentiments and structures of that time are often used as a justification today to proceed with caution before implementing more purely democratic reforms. But it would be a profound mistake to view the Founders as dogged re-publicans, hostile to pure democracy. There were committed demo-crats at the Convention. And the writing was on the wall, plain to see, for those who were not. The spirit of the age was democratic, and the Founders knew it. They may have fussed over its implications, feared what Hamilton called "the amazing violence & turbulence of the democratic spirit," but they knew what was coming as the first generation of Founders gave way to the next.

The Constitution they drafted had a pronounced tilt toward democracy. It "positioned itself on the democratic frontier," as the constitutional scholar Akhil Amar has written. Even the ratification process itself leaned into the democratic winds. The *Federalist Papers*, used and sometimes abused by people debating our history, the great advocacy pieces for the Constitution, were written for the masses, published in newspapers and broadsheets. Though not directly adopted by public referenda, the state-based ratification process was the most democratic system ever used worldwide at that time. The Founders quite explicitly sent the Constitution to the "the People" for ratification. Most states created special conventions to consider the Constitution's ratification, except in Rhode Island where the document was sent to the state's town meetings for consideration and rejected 2,708 to 237. The delegates to each of those conventions were elected by the people of the state. In eight of those states, traditionally restrictive suffrage rules were relaxed, and even men without property were allowed a voice in the process used to create the new government.

More dramatically, every federal office—Representative, Senator, President—was open to men regardless of wealth, in sharp contrast to most state constitutions of the day, where property requirements were typically imposed. A man could serve as a member of the House of Representatives even if he could not vote for himself in his own state and even if he could not serve in his own state's government. The only limitations on holding federal office were age, citizenship, and residence.

The Constitution was a bold democratic gesture, even if it did not contain a right to vote, a phrase that would not make its appearance in the document until 1868. In the years between 1787 and 1868, however, more changed as the democratic trends of the eighteenth century gained momentum in the nineteenth century.

In 1776, during the second Continental Congress, Adams debated voter qualifications with a friendly correspondent. He warned against the slippery slope that comes from tinkering with the question of who can vote: "It is dangerous to open so fruitful a source of controversy and altercation as would be opened by attempting to alter the qualifications of voters; there will be no end of it. New claims will arise; women will demand a vote; lads from twelve to twenty-one will think their rights not enough attended to; and every man who has not a farthing, will demand an equal voice with any other, in all acts of state." Adams was right. There was no end of it.

When the Constitution was written, less than 60 percent of the white male population in the original thirteen states was allowed to vote.[11] Women could not vote, except in New Jersey, where a few rich widows were given the franchise, a privilege that was taken away soon enough. Catholics were barred from voting in five states, Jews in four. Native Americans were often able to vote, technically. Free blacks were allowed to vote (tacitly) in many states. Paupers and felons were almost uniformly disenfranchised.

By 1825, every state but Rhode Island, Virginia, and Louisiana had instituted universal suffrage for white men. By 1855 almost every economic requirement for the free exercise of the franchise by white men was eliminated. As a delegate to Louisiana's 1845

---

[11] There was, of course, considerable variation among the states and even within the states on a municipal level. All students of the history of voting in America owe an enormous amount to the historian Alexander Keyssar whose book *The Right to Vote: The Contested History of Democracy in the United States* is the foundation for much of this chapter.

Constitutional Convention noted: "If a man can *think* without property, he can *vote* without property."

The steady expansion of voting rights to men regardless of property or wealth requirements was not, however, completely predicated on starry-eyed idealism and principled devotion to the mystical value of the vote. From the outset, politicians knew that votes led to power, and so political power was brought to bear on voting. As the historian Alexander Keyssar has written, "Parties were always alert to the potential advantage (or disadvantage) of enfranchising new voters and potential supporters."

Political parties as we know them today did not exist when the Constitution was written. Factionalism and its progeny, political parties, were feared greatly by the Founders, who were concerned that the spirit of the revolution would devolve into bitter fights for power and advantage. Less than two decades after the Constitution's ratification, political parties were being established. A host of political parties emerged, including the dominant Whigs and Democrats, sometimes also called the Democratic-Republican Party. The Republican Party developed later in large part as the successor to the fading Whig Party. And as the Founders dreaded, members of the parties squared off against each other for power. After the parties arose, their ideologies fluctuated over time with their adherence to democratic or republican principles often flipping back and forth. Sometimes Democrats aggressively suppressed the vote while Republicans espoused broad suffrage—at no time more apparent than during the Civil War and its aftermath when Republicans were the stalwart defenders of the black vote while Democrats violently tried to suppress it. Late twentieth and early twenty-first century notions of liberal and conservative ideologies do not have much bearing on how we should understand nineteenth-century political parties.

By the early nineteenth century, partisan fights over voting laws were common. Whigs sought to limit the franchise or to institute registration requirements. Democrats opposed the efforts. In 1836, when the Whig-dominated Pennsylvania legislature passed a law creating its first voter registry, the requirement was imposed only in Philadelphia, home to a large concentration of Democratic voters. Democratic delegates cried foul. They objected that the system would disenfranchise poor voters, who would not be home when the assessors came to their houses to register them. (In contrast to current registration systems, early registries were often lists created by government officials who went door to door and registered people.) The requirement was imposed anyway. One year later, when the Democrats sought to impose the same registration condition throughout the state, taking the fight into Whig strongholds, their proposal was rejected. What was good for the goose, as it turned out, was not good for the gander.

But the course of true love never did run smooth. Even as property and economic requirements for voting were fading, a bevy of new restrictions and voting barriers emerged. The few women in America who could vote were among the first on the chopping block. In 1807, New Jersey eliminated the "defect" in its constitution that granted women the right to vote. Though five states in New England granted blacks the right to vote, every state entering the union after 1819 restricted the franchise to whites.

The matter of immigrant voting was even more complex. In most states, citizenship was a requirement for voting. States with large immigrant populations instituted complex voter registration systems to confirm citizenship or long residency requirements to bar them from voting once they were citizens. In contrast, many Midwest states, eager to attract immigrant farmers, explicitly offered non-citizen immigrants the right to vote. However, one group of immigrants was barred from citizenship and consequently the ability to vote: non-white immigrants. The United States passed its first naturalization law in 1790. To become a citizen, an immigrant had to have resided in the United States for two years, have "good moral character," and be white.

Later naturalization laws altered the length of residency and modified the character requirements, but the limitation on naturalized citizenship to whites persisted well into the twentieth century. The American-born children of non-white immigrants could become citizens following the passage of the Fourteenth Amendment, which established citizenship for all people born in the United States. In 1870, Congress also amended the naturalization laws to allow citizenship for people of African ancestry. But for other immigrants, there was considerable litigation over what it was to be "white," with at least fifty cases brought in federal courts by immigrants asserting that they should be counted as white under the statute. In 1887 in the case *In re Ah Yup,* a Chinese immigrant of Mongolian descent argued he was white. The court denied his argument. In the 1920s, Japanese and Indian immigrants also sought naturalization by asserting they were white. Both lost their cases. The race-based limitation on naturalization was finally lifted in 1952, when Congress passed a new comprehensive immigration statute.

For blacks, though, the path to citizenship and then voting rights would be bloodier. By 1861, America's cataclysmic confrontation with the question of slavery and the legacy of the three-fifths clause—the Civil War—was under way.

THE RIGHT TO VOTE MAKES ITS APPEARANCE IN THE CONSTITUTION

"When the fight is over, the hand that drops the musket cannot be denied the ballot," Union General William Tecumseh Sherman predicted. Almost 2 percent of the population of the United States died during the course of the Civil War. Three million enslaved people were emancipated. The former Confederate states were ejected from Congress and denied representation in the government that ruled them.

The matter of the black vote was front and center. Astonishingly few seemed to want to grant blacks the vote. Throughout the North, efforts to give the franchise to blacks repeatedly failed. Between 1863 and 1870, fifteen northern states and territories rejected granting blacks the right to vote.

Even the Fourteenth Amendment to the Constitution didn't necessarily help. By June 1866, congressional Republicans passed the Fourteenth Amendment. It was ratified in 1868. Not a single southern state voted for it. The phrase "right to vote" appeared for the first time in the Constitution.[12] But not so fast. The Fourteenth Amendment did not create a right to vote. Perversely, it simply contemplated the possibility that the "right to vote," whatever that was, would be abridged and then created a mechanism for dealing with its

---

[12] Most people know the Fourteenth Amendment for its first section: "Section 1. All persons born or naturalized in the United States, and subject to the jurisdiction thereof, are citizens of the United States and of the State wherein they reside. No State shall make or enforce any law which shall abridge the privileges or immunities of citizens of the United States; nor shall any State deprive any person of life, liberty, or property, without due process of law; nor deny to any person within its jurisdiction the equal protection of the laws." Section 2 dealt with voting rights. In the mid-twentieth century, the Fourteenth Amendment's equal protection clause from Section 1 would come to be applied to voting matters. But even then, the failure to enshrine the right to vote on a foundational basis has had a curious effect on how the right to vote is equally protected. As the Supreme Court noted in *Bush v. Gore*, "having once granted the right to vote on equal terms, the State may not, by later arbitrary and disparate treatment, value one person's vote over that of another. See, e.g., *Harper v. Virginia Bd. of Elections*, 383 U.S. 663, 665 (1966) ('Once the franchise is granted to the electorate, lines may not be drawn which are inconsistent with the Equal Protection Clause of the Fourteenth Amendment')." The first step in analyzing voting laws under the first section of the Fourteenth Amendment, then, turns upon the state's often unrestricted decision on whether and how to "grant the right on equal terms."

suppression. "But when the right to vote . . . is denied to any male inhabitants of such State . . . or in any way abridged . . . the basis of representation therein shall be reduced in the proportion which the number of such male citizens shall bear to the whole number of male citizens twenty-one years of age in such State," it read. Was this post–Civil War Congress really saying what it seemed to be saying? Go ahead and abridge the right to vote, but the state that does so will just have fewer representatives in the House? It was. In 1866, this was about as far as Republicans could press the matter. And even then the amendment's provisions specifically relating to voting were never enforced. Indeed, they never have been, even to this day.

However, buoyed by a string of election victories in late 1866 and determined to win a voter base in the South, congressional Republicans began to push for a more meaningful national "right to vote" available regardless of race. They began with the requirement, imposed in the Reconstruction Act of 1867, that all former Confederate states permit blacks to vote. A surge in black voting in the South helped send General Ulysses S. Grant to the White House in 1868. But Republican control of Congress was imperiled as Democrats gained in that election. Ironically, blacks were still largely disenfranchised in the North and Midwest. Continued Republican control of Congress turned on the party's ability to attract the black vote. In their quest for black votes to maintain power, congressional Republicans began crafting the Fifteenth Amendment to the Constitution.

Debate on the Fifteenth Amendment began in January 1869. The nation at last began to directly address the black vote. Congress settled on an admirably brief formulation:

> Section. 1. The right of citizens of the United States to vote shall not be denied or abridged by the United States or by any State on account of race, color, or previous condition of servitude.

Section. 2. The Congress shall have power to enforce this
article by appropriate legislation.

But there's a lot more to it than that. First and foremost, the right
to vote was not affirmatively established. The right to vote just cannot be denied on account of race. But doesn't that mean that it can
be abridged on any number of other bases? Sex? Yes. Women had no
right to vote. Class? Yes. States still were free to impose economic
requirements or other restrictions on the right to vote. Indeed, an
earlier version of the Fifteenth Amendment had anticipated these
problems and sought to bar efforts to restrict voting "on account of
race, color, nativity, property, education or creed." But after weeks
of debate and political intrigue, only the narrower proposal centered
on race and slavery was accepted and sent to the states for ratification. Republican-dominated state legislatures throughout the nation
rapidly ratified the amendment, eager to reap their reward, a grateful black constituency, in time for the 1870 elections. The vote, as
ever, was tied to power.

In the wake of the Fourteenth and Fifteenth Amendments' ratification, more than one million black men entered the voter rolls. The
first black member of Congress was elected in 1870. He was from
South Carolina.

But it did not last. The broadly crafted but rejected version of
the Fifteenth Amendment anticipated future developments in electoral manipulation. The congressmen who drafted that broad version of the amendment were category experts in elections. They
knew, more than anyone, how voting could and would be manipu-
lated by parties and people in search of power. The broader version of the amendment could have helped to block some of the
anticipated vote suppression techniques. But when Congress failed
to pass the broad version of the amendment and settled for a more
limited construction, the legal groundwork was laid to undo its
positive effects. The signal accomplishments of the post–Civil War

Congress in giving black men the franchise began unraveling very quickly. By 1877, Reconstruction was over. By 1890, the Jim Crow era had dawned.

Mississippi showed the South, and ultimately the nation, how to do it. In 1868, Mississippi had been forced to write another state constitution, one that gave blacks the vote. In 1890, the state decided to write another constitution. While the Fifteenth Amendment clearly blocked the Mississippi Constitutional Convention's delegation from explicitly disenfranchising black voters, it did not hamper their creativity in finding powerful alternatives. A two-dollar poll tax was instituted. Voters were required to be current on all other tax obligations. Literacy tests were imposed. Felon disenfranchisement—explicitly implemented to affect blacks—was expanded. Residency requirements were extended. The 1890 constitution was adopted though it was never sent to the people of Mississippi for ratification.

Throughout the South, states followed Mississippi's example. "What is it we want to do?" asked John B. Knox, President of the Alabama convention of 1901. "Why, it is within the limits imposed by the Federal Constitution, to establish white supremacy in this State."

It worked. Turnout dropped precipitously. In the aftermath of the Civil War amendments and Reconstruction, turnout in the South had once reached 85 to 90 percent. In the wake of Jim Crow, it fell into the teens. Mississippi turnout in 1876 had reached 80 percent. In 1900, it was 17 percent. The pattern repeated itself throughout the South.

Blacks were not the only victims of these laws. Poor whites throughout the South also lost their ability to vote. And the South was not alone or unique in restricting access to the ballot box. Throughout the rest of the nation, similar, though less draconian laws were implemented, aimed at recent immigrants: the Irish, German, and Italian in the East and Mexicans in the West.

A new pattern in the right to vote had been set. The right was narrowly protected by law and the Constitution: it could not be voided or abridged in a relatively limited set of circumstances, on the basis of race or color. But if legislators could find another way to restrict the vote—even better if they could be certain that the restriction would fall most heavily on blacks, immigrants, or other disfavored classes of people—then the "right to vote" would simply be a dead letter. In Louisiana, 130,000 blacks had been registered to vote in 1896. In 1904, they numbered a mere 1,342. Voter turnout for presidential elections dropped in states that instituted literacy tests and poll taxes. (See Table 1.) Throughout the South, very little changed for the next sixty years.

"REMEMBER THE LADIES"

The year 1890, as Mississippi neared perfection in its efforts to disenfranchise blacks, was significant for quite another reason. That year, Wyoming became the forty-fourth state to apply for admission to the union. Wyoming's system of government had one distinct feature: women could vote. The U.S. Congress didn't like it one bit and attempted to have the state repeal its women's suffrage provision as a condition for admission to the union. Wyoming's legislature refused. It sent a telegram to Washington: "We will remain out of the Union one hundred years rather than come in without the women." Wyoming was admitted to the United States in the summer of 1890, with its women voters. Six years later, Utah joined the nation and became the second state to grant women the right to vote.

But 1890 was just a midpoint in the effort by women to obtain the right to vote. In 1776 Adams, who had warned there would be no end of efforts by people to obtain the vote, had a taste of what would come in a letter from his wife Abigail: ". . . and by the way in the

TABLE 1. RELATIONSHIP OF POLL TAX AND LITERACY TEST LAWS TO PRESIDENTIAL TURNOUT IN SOUTHERN STATES, 1892–1916

	Absence of Literacy Test	Presence of Literacy Test
Absence of poll tax	72%	57%
Presence of poll tax	40%	24%

Source: Frances Fox Piven and Richard A. Cloward, Why Americans Still Don't Vote, 2000.

new code of laws I suppose it will be necessary for you to make, I desire you would remember the ladies. . . . If particular care and attention is not paid to the ladies we are determined to foment a revolution, and will not hold ourselves bound by any laws in which we have no voice or representation." Adams put his wife off affectionately. "Your letter was the first intimation that another tribe more numerous and powerful than all the rest were grown discontented. This is rather too coarse a compliment but you are so saucy. . . ." But he was clear with her. "Depend on it, we know better than to repeal our masculine systems."

The revolution Abigail Adams threatened began in earnest in 1848 at Seneca Falls, New York. At a convention attended by almost three hundred people, Lucretia Mott and Elizabeth Cady Stanton rallied attendees to support women's suffrage. One hundred of the convention's attendees signed a resolution calling on the government to grant women "their sacred right to the elective franchise." The effort begun in 1848 was slow to gain adherents. In the years preceding the Civil War, women's suffrage advocates won few battles. Then with the advent of the war and Reconstruction, women's suffrage took a back seat to civil rights for black Americans. Given the rhetoric of the era, many women's vote advocates had thought the time was ripe to grab the golden ring. They were mistaken. "One question at a time. This hour belongs to the Negro," the powerful Massachusetts abolitionist Wendell Phillips pronounced.

Women's vote advocates suffered an immediate setback in their quest with the passage of the Fourteenth Amendment. When the Fourteenth Amendment was drafted, its Republican authors explicitly—and contrary to constitutional precedent—put the word "male" in its text. Recall that the Fourteenth Amendment provided a mechanism for reducing representation in the U.S. Congress as a penalty for denying black men the right to vote: deprive men the right to vote and the state would have its representation in the House reduced by the portion that the number of suppressed votes bore to the number of "male" inhabitants of the state. If a state suppressed 20 percent of its male vote, then its House delegation would drop by 20 percent. In the 1787 constitutional provision dealing with the matter, representatives were apportioned according to population, male and female. But not in 1866. In 1866, representation was to be gauged under the Fourteenth Amendment according to the number of "male citizens."

The Constitution's three-fifths clause had been nullified following the Civil War. A new zero-fifths clause for women was inserted into the Fourteenth Amendment. Unlike the three-fifths compromise, which aimed to address a North-South imbalance, the Fourteenth Amendment's provision addressed an East-West imbalance. Women made up almost 50 percent of the population throughout the East but typically took up a far smaller portion of the population in the West. Doing the math, the Fourteenth Amendment's drafters realized that were women included in its formulation, eastern states would come out ahead. In other words, were women included in the population base, when eastern states disenfranchised blacks, as contemplated by the flawed amendment, their penalty would be relatively lower than similar moves would incur in the West.[13] And so, women's right even to be counted in the population was jettisoned as part of a regional power play. As legal scholar Akhil Amar has written, "Indeed, it was in no small measure the woman issue that ultimately dictated the precise shape of the Fourteenth Amendment's eventual solution to the urgent question of black suffrage." And three years later, when the Fifteenth Amendment was ratified, it implicitly approved discrimination based on sex. It was a bitter defeat to women's suffrage advocates, who had also fought so long and hard for the black vote.

Outraged, in November 1872, a leading women's rights activist Susan B. Anthony went to her Rochester, New York, polling station and cast a ballot for President after winning a fierce debate with the local poll workers over her right to do so. She was arrested two weeks later for illegally voting. Anthony took the arrest in stride and milked it for every bit of publicity she could. Six months later, after a trial, a judge found her guilty. Before she was sentenced, Anthony addressed that judge, objecting that she had been denied a trial by jury.

The judge rebutted her: "The Court must insist the prisoner has been tried according to the established forms of law." Anthony shot back at him, reminding him that there was a time not long past when

---

[13] Once again, a group of constitutional drafters demonstrated that their math skills were better than their sense of justice. If men and women were included in the population count, then when a western or eastern state disenfranchised blacks, representation in the House would drop for both equally. In contrast, if women were omitted from the formula, then the math would play out to the western state's advantage. Say California and Massachusetts had a population of 1 million men and women and disenfranchised 100,000 men. Their House delegations would both be reduced by 10 percent. If women were subtracted from the population base, then California's male population would stand at 700,000 and Massachusetts's would be 500,000. The western state's House delegation would be reduced by one-seventh, but Massachusetts would incur a higher one-fifth penalty.

slavery was the law and that she meant to fight for her right to vote with all the moral certainty that had been brought to bear in the fight against slavery:

> Yes, your honor, but by forms of law all made by men, interpreted by men, administered by men, in favor of men, and against women; and hence, your honor's ordered verdict of guilty; against a United States citizen for the exercise of 'that citizen's right to vote,' simply because that citizen was a woman and not a man. But, yesterday, the same man-made forms of law, declared it a crime punishable with $1,000 fine and six months imprisonment, for you, or me, or any of us, to give a cup of cold water, a crust of bread, or a night's shelter to a panting fugitive as he was tracking his way to Canada. And every man or woman in whose veins coursed a drop of human sympathy violated that wicked law, reckless of consequences, and was justified in so doing. As then, the slaves who got their freedom must take it over, or under, or through the unjust forms of law, precisely so, now, must women, to get their right to a voice in this government, take it; and I have taken mine, and mean to take it at every possible opportunity.

The judge then told Anthony to sit down. "The Court orders the prisoner to sit down. It will not allow another word." But she kept speaking. When the judge finally got her to stop talking, and it took him a while, he sentenced her to a $100 fine. She told him in court that she would never pay it. And she never did.

Women's advocates feared that the Civil War amendments were a setback to their cause. They were correct. In the following half-century, women's vote advocates pursued a variety of strategies in their restless quest for the franchise. In 1887, they sought the franchise on a national basis and lost a vote for a constitutional amendment 34 to 16 in the Senate, with twenty-six abstentions, crushingly short of the fifty votes needed to send the amendment to the states for ratification. Sometimes, though, they fought for half a loaf and won, getting the right to vote in local elections for boards of education or other political offices. Women in the West, particularly in Wyoming and Utah, made more headway than women in the South.

No argument was too lofty or too low. Voting was a natural right of all citizens who took part in society. Why should women pay taxes if they had no representation? Women were a better, purer group of prospective voters, less corrupt, better for society. Movement leader Stanton made cause with white supremacists and anti-immigrant forces, advocating literacy tests. Working women joined the fight. Upper-middle-class educated women in their pristine white dresses and extravagant hats marched in parades.

On March 3, 1913, one day before Democrat Woodrow Wilson's inauguration as President, 5,000 supporters of women's suffrage paraded in the streets of Washington, D.C. Their procession featured nine bands, four mounted brigades, three heralds, and about twenty-four floats. They were led by the Brooklyn-born, twenty-nine-year-old lawyer Inez Millholland, astride a white horse, wearing a white cape. Millholland, single at the time, married in London later that year after proposing herself to the Dutch-born coffee importer and international playboy Eugen Boissevain.[14]

A crowd of almost half a million was in town for Wilson's inauguration. Soon, the women's parade was surrounded by men, impeding its progress, grabbing and shoving the marchers. One hundred women were sent to the hospital that day. Federal cavalry troops were called in to help control the crowds. Nevertheless, many women completed the march. The *New York Times* called it "one of

---

[14] She did not live to see the vote granted to women, dying three years later of pernicious anemia. In 1923 Boissevain remarried to the poet Edna St. Vincent Millay.

the most impressively beautiful spectacles ever staged in this country." Two years later, the *Times* took another view and editorialized, "The grant of suffrage to women is repugnant to instincts that strike their roots deep in the order of nature. It runs counter to human reason, it flouts the teachings of experience and the admonitions of common sense."

Throughout most of the fight, the women's suffrage movement stayed remarkably nonpartisan. But in 1914 and 1916, the movement made efforts to mobilize women in the states where they could vote to cast their ballots against Democrats. Their effort had no appreciable impact. Democrat Woodrow Wilson was reelected in 1916. In the winter of 1917, suffragettes began picketing the White House as the movement took a more militant stance. Arrests and hunger strikes followed. So did success. Six midwestern states gave women the right to vote. New York followed suit. In the midst of World War I, the momentum was unstoppable. President Wilson spoke in favor of women's suffrage "as a war measure." In the summer of 1919, a constitutional amendment granting women the right to vote was sent to the states for ratification. Tennessee became the thirty-sixth state to ratify it in 1920, and a week after that state's vote, the Nineteenth Amendment to the Constitution became law.

The phrase "right to vote" made its third appearance in the Constitution. Following the precedent of the Fifteenth Amendment, however, women were not so much granted the "right to vote" directly as states were barred from denying them the vote on the basis of sex. But in stark contrast to the Civil War amendments, the passage of the Nineteenth Amendment had virtually no impact on the power dynamics of the early twentieth century. Indeed, unlike almost all other controversies surrounding voting in America, women gained the vote because their impact on political power was understood to be neutral. "The victories of the suffrage drive," noted Keyssar, "were built in part on the ever-widening perception among men that the enfranchisement of women would not significantly transform politics or policy." The voting gender gap that we know today was not a worry in the early twentieth century.

A BRIDGE IN SELMA, ALABAMA

No such thing could be said about the potential impact of the African American vote in the South. As the civil rights movement of the 1950s and 1960s gained momentum, the equation was simple. Votes equal power. And southern white supremacists knew that the African American vote would go a long way toward depriving them of power. They did everything they could to keep African Americans away from the polls.

African Americans, lacking money and the vote, used the only thing left to them: their bodies. In sit-ins. In marches. On buses. In prison cells. At lunch counters. In churches. They were fire-bombed, attacked by dogs, fire-hosed, beaten, lynched, shot. All so they could vote.[15] "When an individual is protesting society's refusal to acknowledge his dignity as a human being, his very act of protest confers dignity on him," the March on Washington's organizer Bayard Rustin wrote.

The turbulent 1950s and 1960s redrew America's relationship with voting rights. By the end of the 1960s, the final major layer of voting rights had been laid.

Voting activists had long tried to have poll taxes repealed in the states or declared unconstitutional. In 1937, deep into the Depression and the New Deal, they lost their gambit before the Supreme Court. "[The] privilege of voting is not derived from the United States, but is conferred by the state and, save as restrained by the Fifteenth

---

[15] The civil rights movement, to be sure, was fought over much more than the right to vote.

and Nineteenth Amendments and other provisions of the Federal Constitution, the state may condition suffrage as it deems appropriate," the Court stated in *Breedlove v. Suttles.*

Poll tax opponents did not stop and looked to Congress to make poll taxes illegal. But they lost skirmish after skirmish in Congress, consistently blocked by southern congressmen and senators. In the early 1960s, with the backing of President John F. Kennedy and a maverick southern Senator, Florida's Spessard Holland,[16] a constitutional amendment to bar the poll tax was passed by Congress. The Twenty-fourth Amendment was ratified in early 1964. Two years later, the U.S. Supreme Court finally held that poll taxes were unconstitutional in all elections—in state, county, and municipal elections, not just federal ones. Applying the Fourteenth Amendment's equal protection clause, in *Harper v. Virginia Board of Elections,* the Court reversed its earlier decision upholding poll taxes.[17] Black voter registration surged in the South, quadrupling from 10 to 40 percent in some districts.

But the poll tax was just the opening salvo in the fight for voting rights in the 1960s. Civil rights activists had more than the poll tax in mind. They wanted the federal government to step in and aggressively dismantle Jim Crow. The main front was fought over how extensive and forceful the federal government would be in protecting

---

[16] Today, visitors to Cape Canaveral can play golf at the nearby Spessard Holland golf course, designed by Arnold Palmer.

[17] Most state restrictions on paupers also fell at this time. From the founding of the nation until the 1960s, it was common for states to deny the franchise to recipients of public assistance. By the time the *Harper* decision came down, a majority of states had already eliminated their pauper restrictions, and the few that had restrictions on their books rarely enforced them. Still, as late as 1972, Massachusetts held a public referendum to strip the pauper exclusion clause from its statute. The clause was deleted. Twenty percent of the voters on the referendum, however, supported its maintenance.

TABLE 2. VOTER REGISTRATION RATES IN SOUTHERN STATES, MARCH 1965

State	African-American Registration Rate	White Registration Rate
Alabama	19%	69%
Georgia	27%	63%
Louisiana	32%	81%
Mississippi	7%	70%
North Carolina	47%	97%
South Carolina	37%	76%
Virginia	38%	61%

Source: Bernard Grofman, Lisa Handley, and Richard G. Niemi, Minority Representation and the Quest for Voting Equality, 1992.

voting rights writ large. The battles culminated in the drafting and passage of the Voting Rights Act of 1965, which reshaped America's conception of voting rights and the role of government in protecting them.

African American registration in the South had been steadily increasing since 1940, spurred by a civil rights movement determined to overcome barriers. (See Table 2.) In 1940, region wide, African American registration stood at 4.5 percent, then 12.5 percent in 1947, 20.7 percent in 1952, 29.1 percent in 1960, and finally 35.5 percent in 1965. In 1964 and 1965, the question was how to dismantle the final barriers.

But first voting rights advocates had to put their bodies on the line one more time. In the late winter of 1965, a group of about 600 peaceful civil rights protesters set off on a march from Selma, Alabama, to the state's capital, Montgomery. Their route lay across the Edmund

Pettus Bridge, named for a Confederate Civil War general. On that Sunday, March 7, as they crossed the bridge, they were assaulted by state troopers and local police with billy clubs and tear gas. Two days later, 2,000 peaceful marchers crossed the bridge, and held a brief prayer service. Three white ministers who joined in that march were beaten that night. One of them, the Boston minister James Reeb, died from his beating two days later. On March 16, Martin Luther King Jr. started with 8,000 people on the road from Selma to Montgomery. Their route took them along Jefferson Davis Highway, where they were guarded along the way by thousands of Army soldiers and FBI agents. Their route took them through one county where the population was almost 20 percent African American, but where not a single African American was registered to vote.

When they reached Montgomery on March 24, thousands more joined them. The next day, 25,000 people marched to the state capitol building. King addressed them:

> Our whole campaign in Alabama has been centered around the right to vote. . . .
>
> Today I want to tell the city of Selma, today I want to say to the state of Alabama, today I want to say to the people of America and the nations of the world, that we are not about to turn around. We are on the move now. . . .
>
> Let us march on ballot boxes, march on ballot boxes until race-baiters disappear from the political arena.
>
> Let us march on ballot boxes until the salient misdeeds of bloodthirsty mobs will be transformed into the calculated good deeds of orderly citizens . . . .
>
> Let us march on ballot boxes until we send to our city councils, state legislatures, and the United States Congress, men who will not fear to do justly, love mercy, and walk humbly with thy God.
>
> Let us march on ballot boxes until brotherhood becomes more than a meaningless word in an opening prayer, but the order of the day on every legislative agenda.

Let us march on ballot boxes until all over Alabama
God's children will be able to walk the earth in decency
and honor.

That night a woman who had been driving protesters from Selma
to Montgomery to participate was killed by the Ku Klux Klan. The
day after King started the third march from Selma, on March 17,
President Lyndon B. Johnson sent a draft of the Voting Rights Act to
Congress for its consideration.

The Voting Rights Act of 1965 took a sledgehammer to Jim
Crow. The legislation began with a basic reiteration of the Fifteenth
Amendment: "No voting qualification or prerequisite to voting, or
standard, practice, or procedure shall be imposed or applied by any
State or political subdivision to deny or abridge the right of any citizen of the United States to vote on account of race or color." Ninety-
five years after the Fifteenth Amendment was enacted and 177 years
after the Constitution was ratified, the federal government was finally going to tackle the right to vote with real resources and consistent attention.

This time, they meant it.

The act immediately suspended literacy tests and other vote suppression devices such as "good character" requirements for registration in all states and counties where voter turnout was less than 50
percent in the 1964 election.[18] It sent federal examiners into the
South to affirmatively enroll voters. And it created a preventive
medicine regimen for those states and local districts that had historically suppressed the black vote. This "pre-clearance" mechanism
of the act required that any change to "voting qualification or prerequisite to voting, or standard, practice, or procedure with respect

---

[18] When the Voting Rights Act of 1965 was renewed in 1970, literacy tests were
barred nationwide. Eighteen states were still using them at the time. In 1975,
they were permanently barred.

to voting" be submitted to the Department of Justice for review and approval.

By the end of 1965, 250,000 new African American voters had registered, one-third of them brought onto the rolls by federal examiners. In Mississippi, African American voter registration surged from 10 percent in 1964 to 60 percent in 1968. In Alabama, it jumped from 24 percent to 57 percent. Within a few years, a million new voters were registered.

The year before, in 1964, the U.S. Supreme Court had announced a new standard for judging the apportionment of representation: "one man, one vote." The Fourteenth Amendment, largely moribund as it related to voting rights, came to life, only this time via its equal protection clause. In *Reynolds v. Sims*, a group of Alabama voters challenged yet another way Jim Crow had found to disenfranchise African Americans. The voter suppression technique at issue in the case was applied on a mass level. No need to directly attack individual voters. So much easier to gerrymander or to finagle proportional representation as a way to deny African American representation. Alabama drew its state Senate and House districts according to population. But it had not redrawn the districts since the 1900 census. As a result of population growth and shifts since 1900, counties like Jefferson, with a population of more than 600,000, and Lowndes, population 15,417, each had one state Senator. The Court found "25.1% of the State's total population resided in districts represented by a majority of the members of the Senate, and only 25.7% lived in counties which could elect a majority of the members of the House of Representatives." In other words, one-quarter of the population had political control over the remaining three-quarters.

Chief Justice Earl Warren had their number: "One must be ever aware that the Constitution forbids 'sophisticated, as well as simple-minded, modes of discrimination.'" He would not hear assertions that the matter was too complex or political for the Court to deal with: "We are cautioned about the dangers of entering into political thickets and mathematical quagmires. Our answer is this: a denial of constitutionally protected rights demands judicial protection; our oath and our office require no less of us."

As the 1960s gave way to the 1970s, America had one more door to open. In 1970, President Richard Nixon had signed a law requiring that states reduce their voting age to eighteen. Oregon and Texas challenged the law, and the Supreme Court struck it down at the end of 1970. Less than three months later, the U.S. Senate voted to send a constitutional amendment lowering the voting age to the states by a vote of 94 to 0. The House followed less than two weeks later, voting 401 to 19. Four months later, the amendment was ratified by the states. On July 7, 1971, the Twenty-sixth Amendment became a part of the Constitution. It was the fastest any constitutional amendment had ever been proposed and adopted in America's history.

Proposals to lower the voting age had emerged in the midst of every major war fought by the United States. The logic was hard to refute. If someone was old enough to be drafted and to die for his or her country, he or she was certainly old enough to vote. Still the voting age remained at twenty-one throughout the nation, defended by people who distinguished between the attributes necessary for good soldiering and smart voting. The Vietnam War and the youthquake of the 1960s swept away these objections. By 1970, no credible politician could vote to support the war in Vietnam while denying eighteen-year-olds the right to vote.

As with all other voting-rights amendments, this one followed the Fifteenth Amendment's formulation. The Twenty-sixth Amendment read:

Section 1. The right of citizens of the United States, who are eighteen years of age or older, to vote shall not be

denied or abridged by the United States or by any State on
account of age.

Section 2. The Congress shall have the power to enforce
this article by appropriate legislation.

The epochal voting rights movement of the 1960s and 1970s
closed. So did America's last major effort to ask itself what the "right
to vote" means. In 2006, the Voting Rights Act was reauthorized
for the fifth time by Congress. Forty-one years after the act passed,
seven states—including Arizona, Mississippi, South Carolina, and
Texas—and parts of nine others were still subject to "pre-clearance,"
the act's preventive medicine requiring states to seek approval of
changes to their voting systems. The House voted for the act by 390
to 33. In the Senate the vote was 98 to 0. President George W. Bush
signed the act into law. It expires in 2031.[19]

Looking back on the history of voting rights in America from the
vantage point of the twenty-first century, it is easy to think that
the major battles have been won, that the right to vote is settled.
But inveterate mountain hiker and Supreme Court Justice William
O. Douglas warned in 1962: "So far as voting rights are concerned,
there are large gaps in the Constitution." With the exception of the
Twenty-sixth Amendment setting the voting age at eighteen, we live
under the same Constitution that Douglas described. We still do not
have an affirmative right to vote.

It is hard to imagine that today's voters and would-be voters could
ever muster the anger, courage, and determination it took to march
across the Pettus Bridge in Alabama or in the streets of Washington

---

[19] The Voting Rights Act is not uncontroversial. Its extension until 2031 does
not guarantee its ongoing vitality, as funding for its enforcement can be limited
and other modifications made. And recently, two states, Texas and Florida, have
challenged its constitutionality. These cases were pending as of mid-2012.

the day before a presidential inauguration. The battle over voting rights has shifted from whether a person can vote generally to more specific questions: How will I vote? Where and when will I vote? What documents do I need to vote? Messy, petty bureaucracy now stands in people's way, sometimes with quite devastating effect. Voting lines are often interminable. Votes are lost or not counted. Registration and voting requirements confuse, frighten, and inhibit people from voting. Vote suppression groups lurk around polls, challenging people, or send pamphlets out with grievous misinformation. Without an affirmative right to vote, cutting through the barriers is nearly impossible. There is no bridge to cross now, just miles and miles of bureaucratic red tape.

A VOTER MOBILIZATION POSTER BY THE CONGRESS OF INDUSTRIAL ORGANIZATIONS (CIO) FROM THE 1940S. One of the best predictors of whether a person will vote is whether that person's parents voted. Voting is an ingrained habit formed early in life. **Photo Credit:** *Smithsonian Institution from a CIO Political Action Committee poster*

CHAPTER 3

★ ★ ★

TO VOTE OR NOT TO VOTE

Who Votes and Why

"In his reflective moments even the most experienced politician
senses a nagging curiosity about why people vote as they do.
His power and his position depend upon the outcome of the
mysterious rites we perform as opposing candidates harangue
the multitudes who finally march to the polls to prolong the
rule of their champion, to thrust him, ungratefully, back into
the void of private life, or to raise to eminence a new tribune of
the people."

V.O. Key, The Responsible Electorate, *1966*

WE'RE ACCUSTOMED TO AND MAYBE a bit sick of the idea of answering pollsters' questions about political contests. But on
election day November 3, 2008, 163 voters in Ann Arbor, Michigan,
and Durham, North Carolina, took part in one of the odder voting
experiments in recent memory. On that Tuesday, as millions of their
fellow Americans were going about their daily lives, and also voting for President, they came to a medical lab and chewed gum to
give researchers a sample of their saliva. Later that night, as soon as
they learned that Barack Obama had been declared President, they
popped another piece of sugar-free Trident into their mouths and

chewed for science. They chewed gum again twenty minutes later and then again forty minutes later. The next day they handed the gum over to the scientists for examination.

When the scientists at Duke University and the University of Michigan finished analyzing the spit they had collected, their research proved something many had long suspected: when American males vote, they are putting their manhood on the line. The men in the study who supported Obama had higher levels of testosterone after learning he had won. And the men supporting Senator John McCain experienced a notable drop in their testosterone levels after they learned he had lost the presidential election. Their testosterone drops were similar to the declines experienced by men who had just lost a one-on-one contest for dominance (e.g., a fist fight). The losing McCain voters were not happy. "Those who voted for a losing candidate felt significantly more controlled, submissive, unhappy, and unpleasant at the moment of the outcome than did those who voted for the winning candidate," the researchers wrote. And, as for those Obama supporters, one researcher suggested there might be an Obama baby boom.

Voting, it seems, has its risks as well as its rewards.

The vote is almost mystically revered among Americans. It is the very bedrock of our democracy. Politicians wax rhapsodic about voting and democracy. Voting is a sacred duty taught in civics classes. And representative democracy is touted as the only form of legitimate government and the ultimate guarantor of liberty. America cannot, would not, and should not exist without the consent of the governed. Every man, woman, and child in this nation knows the rallying cry of the American Revolution: "No taxation without representation."

Thomas Jefferson put it more elegantly: "Governments are instituted among Men, deriving their just powers from the consent of the governed." This was radical thinking at the time and today forms the moral bedrock of our democracy. People are not objects to be ruled but are individuals with dignity and agency over their lives. As James Madison, the Constitutional Convention's preeminent philosopher, said, "It seems indispensable that the mass of citizens should not be without a voice in making the laws which they are to obey."

When it comes to testing that consent, voting is our way of answering the two most fundamental questions facing a democratic society: who takes part in the decisions and deliberations of our government and how do they do it. Americans do it by showing up at polling stations and voting for President every four years, for representatives every two years, for senators every six years, and myriad other times for mayors, governors, city councilors, sheriffs, Board of Education commissioners, judges, coroners, bond proposals, referenda items, and the list goes on.

In a nation that esteems voting and that ties it to its core values, the failure of a large group of Americans to vote is baffling. Every member of the political thinking class—from pollsters to journalists, economists to anthropologists—has spilled gallons of ink and gathered terabytes of data trying to figure out why some people vote and some people don't. Many of them are trying to find a magic formula that will increase voter participation. Most of them, though not all as we will see, believe in the vital importance of voting.

True, more than 130 million people voted in the last presidential election, but what can we say about the more than 80 million eligible voters who did not? And how do we absorb the fact that in nonpresidential elections, often less than 20 percent of potential voters cast ballots? We should find those facts troubling because voting is a critical way of achieving our democratic ideals, and when major portions of the body politic withdraw, it threatens the profoundly important American experiment in self-governance. So the unfinished quest to understand what makes people voters is imperative.

THE VOTING PARADOX

To some voting is a duty. To some it's a form of ecstatic participation. To some it's a calculated act aimed at protecting self-interest. To some it is a battle. To some it is a chore. To some it is a sport.

But to serious economic analysts, voting is a paradox. Or worse, it is nonsensical, because no rational person should vote. Every model of voting demonstrates that voting is simply a waste of energy and time. After all, one vote really cannot affect the outcome of an election; so it's just not logically worth spending any effort on voting. The odds that one person's vote will actually change the outcome of any election are about the same as being hit by lightning (actually, they are probably lower).

As the great battles over voting rights for African Americans were gaining momentum in the 1950s, academics were beginning to use new, more sophisticated survey techniques and economic models to understand this perplexing human act: voting. In 1957, the then twenty-seven-year-old economist Anthony Downs published a book that no serious voting analyst has been able to get away from since. In *An Economic Theory of Democracy*, Downs systematically stripped all sentiment from voting. "Every rational man decides to vote just as he makes all other decisions: if the returns outweigh the costs, he votes; if not, he abstains."

Voting rewards can be easily calculated, according to Downs and a host of his followers. First, determine the odds that your vote will make a difference, then multiply it by the benefits of having your preferred candidate win. After all, voting is simply a way of expressing our preferences about how we will be governed, and our preferences should be determined by a rational evaluation of the benefits we will derive from one candidate winning over the other. However, even if we conclude that there are dramatic differences among candidates and that the outcome will have a significant impact on our personal well-being, the odds that our vote will actually matter are infinitesimal. And so as one economist has put it: "The fact that people vote is a longstanding puzzle to economists. Since instrumental benefits are close to zero, but not so the costs from going to the polls, a rational individual should abstain from voting."

But it turns out what is rational to an economist is not necessarily logical to living, breathing participants in society. We do vote. Indeed, far more people vote than the economic models would suggest is rational. Yet, on the other hand, almost every election every year brings a fresh howl of despair about low American voter turnout.

Voter participation hit its all-time peak in the United States in the late nineteenth century, when political party machines were at their height and the election system was least regulated. Turnout for presidential elections often hit 80 percent, and during non-presidential years it hovered between 60 and 70 percent. But with the advent of Jim Crow and the introduction of the modern election mechanism at the turn of the twentieth century, voter turnout began a long epoch of decline. By the 1920s, less than 50 percent of the eligible population voted for President. Turnout began rebounding shortly thereafter. (See Figure 1.)

In the 1960 presidential election, forty-two-year-old John F. Kennedy was the underdog. His Republican opponent Richard M. Nixon was leading in the polls coming out of the late summer party conventions. In late September and through October of that year, Nixon and Kennedy held four televised debates. Seventy million people watched, more than 60 percent of the population. When the election was held less than three weeks later, voter turnout hit a high for the twentieth century: 64 percent. The election was one of the closest in American history with only 112,000 votes nationwide separating Kennedy from Nixon.

After that banner year, turnout began declining again, dropping to below 52 percent in 1996. In the 2008 presidential election,

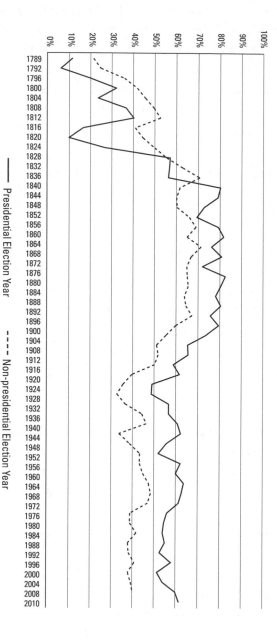

FIGURE 1. VOTER TURNOUT IN THE UNITED STATES: 1789–2010

(as a percentage of the eligible voting population)

——— Presidential Election Year   - - - - Non-presidential Election Year

Source: Michael P. McDonald, United States Election Project, May 2012.

Note: Many states appointed presidential electors in the early decades of the nineteenth century so voter turnout in presidential elections was structurally depressed.

American voters made a run at the record set in 1960 but fell short when only 62 percent of the eligible population turned out.

When it comes to non-presidential-year federal elections, voter turnout drops even lower, to less than 50 percent of the eligible population. In fact, in the non-presidential federal election year that followed the Obama election, 2010, turnout was 41 percent. And if the election does not involve any of the major federal offices—Representative, Senator, or President—the numbers are even smaller.

In 2011, ten cities with populations greater than half a million held mayoral elections.[20] Collectively more than 12 million people live in those cities—ranging from the Midwest's Chicago to the Southwest's Phoenix to Charlotte in the South. Almost every one of the cities was facing financial difficulty, struggling to find the money to pay for police and to maintain basic city services.

Former San Francisco City Supervisor Matt Gonzalez didn't mince words about the 2011 mayoral race in that city. He wasn't running for Mayor. Sixteen other people were, including the incumbent Mayor, Ed Lee, who had assumed the role after the previous Mayor was elected to another job. But Gonzalez had some experience with elections, having campaigned as Ralph Nader's running mate in 2008. So, shortly before the fall elections, he took to the Internet with a video: "What's at stake? No less than the future of San Francisco."

San Francisco's voters dutifully went to the polls, only the turnout for their fiercely contested mayoral election was the lowest in the city's history: about 42 percent of registered voters or 28 percent of the voting-age population in the City by the Bay. Apparently not even a majority of San Franciscans were concerned with "the future" of their city.

---

[20] The ten cities with population greater than half a million that held mayoral elections in 2011 were Baltimore, Charlotte, Chicago, Columbus, Houston, Indianapolis, Philadelphia, Phoenix, San Francisco, and Tucson.

Still, San Francisco surpassed every other major American city in its mayoral election turnout in 2011. The average turnout of the registered voters in the other major cities was 27 percent, while the average turnout of their voting-age population was 20 percent.[21] Houston and Baltimore tied for the lowest turnout, with only 13 percent of their registered voters showing up to vote for Mayor. In Indianapolis, the candidates ran the most expensive mayoral campaign in the city's history, raising almost $6 million. Only 30 percent of the city's registered voters voted. The candidates ended up spending almost $33 per vote cast.

There is another way of looking at the presidential turnout numbers, one that paints an even grimmer picture. Calculating turnout rates is not as straightforward as it would seem. Turnout calculations divide the number of people who vote in a particular election by the number of potential voters overall. But both the top number (the numerator) and the bottom number (the denominator) in the equation are subject to dispute. For example, we do not actually know with certainty how many people voted for President in 2008, though we're pretty close.

But determining how many people are potential voters (the denominator part of the equation) can be even more difficult. The number of potential voters can be assessed by looking at the voting-age population, the voting-eligible population, or the number of registered voters. Voting-age population is the number of residents older than eighteen. Voting-eligible population subtracts non-citizen and other disenfranchised people (e.g., ex-felons) from that number. (It is the method used in the preceding discussion of presidential election turnout.) Registered voters is conceptually straightforward, but

---

[21] Voting-age population was used for assessing mayoral race turnout because the necessary data for calculating voting-eligible population in these jurisdictions were not available.

in practice the number tends to be inaccurate, as will be discussed in Chapter 5.

It's important, though, to consider voting-age population because, after all, these are the people who are governed. Many of them might be non-citizen immigrants or ex-felons, but they are all indisputably people who are subject to the law, the people Madison and Jefferson were concerned about. In 2010, almost 18.6 million people were over age eighteen but ineligible to vote. So when one looks at turnout rates of the voting-age population, the turnout numbers look worse. In the 2008 presidential election, turnout was 57 percent by that measure, and in 2010 it was 38 percent (versus 62 and 42 percent using voting-eligible population as the denominator).

This is not a small matter. Democracies "of the people, by the people and for the people" make assumptions about who "the people" are. In 1787, the people of the United States were just beginning to embrace the notion that they belonged to a distinct nation of people bound together by a shared vision of a civil and economic society. Yet at the time large categories of people were barred from voting— from blacks, to women, to Native Americans, to people without property. The settled belief of 1787 that the relevant "people" were white, property-owning men would not hold for long. And achieving consensus about "the people" was never again as easy as it was in 1787. From 1861 to 1865, deciding who "the people" were was determined at the end of a rifle by a civil war. In the twentieth century, during the civil rights movement, it was determined again via protest and blood. As the political scientist Robert Dahl has noted, "while the exclusions are invariably said to be justified on the ground that the demos includes everyone *qualified* to participate in ruling, the hidden assumption dispatched to the shadow theory of democracy is that only some people are competent to rule [via voting]."

As a smaller and smaller portion of the governed actually vote, the value or validity of the consent to be governed might be said to decline.

And as it happens, the United States, the world's oldest continuous democracy, has the lowest voter turnout among the world's established democracies. Although voter turnout has been declining in almost all established democracies worldwide, the United States ranks 139th out of 172 countries based on average voter turnout since 1945.[22]

Not everyone thinks that low turnout is a bad sign. Some argue that it is evidence of happiness and satisfaction with our political system and that it helps maintain a sort of calm and normalcy. Around the time Congress was passing a law to ease voter registration requirements in the late 1990s, the conservative columnist George Will wrote that "non-voting may be passive consent, reflecting contentment." Today, the argument does not quite ring true in an era where most people are either enraged by current American politics or in despair about the economic future of the nation. Under this thinking, then, turnout should be nearing 100 percent. And the argument does not really explain why America's poor and underprivileged are so content and happy that they vote at significantly lower rates than the rich and older, who vote at significantly higher rates.

But perhaps when it comes to voting, it's really quality not quantity that counts. Survey after survey shows that American voters are woefully unaware of or ignorant about key policy issues or basic facts about government. The majority of Americans do not know who the Chief Justice of the Supreme Court is and cannot find Pakistan or Iraq on a map. According to political journalist Alexander Burns, "'fickle' is a nice way of describing the voters of 2012, who appear to be wandering, confused and Forrest Gump–like, through the expe-

---

[22] Scholars debate why American turnout is so low compared with that of other countries. The analysis is made difficult by the enormous variation among countries in their history, laws, and social structures. Nevertheless, it is indisputable that the United States, which takes so much pride in its role as the world's preeminent democracy, has lower turnout than most other democracies.

rience of a presidential campaign. It isn't just unclear which party's vision they'd rather embrace; it's entirely questionable whether the great mass of voters has even the most basic grasp of the details— or for that matter, the most elementary factual components—of the national political debate."

Despite rising education levels in the nation, this lack of knowledge about specific facts and aspects of our government is a persistent problem, stretching back at least fifty years when researchers began consistently measuring it. In fact, it's likely been a problem since 1787. Nevertheless, one essayist wrote: "The last thing America needs is more voters—particularly badly educated and alienated ones—with a passion for politics." When underinformed people vote, as the Georgetown philosophy scholar Jason Brennan argued in 2011, "they *pollute* democracy with their votes and make it more likely that we will have to suffer from bad governance."

It's easy to dismiss these arguments as elitist. They certainly sound elitist, though their authors would hasten to say that they are merely stating facts about the level of voter education. Their arguments are coupled with a conviction that only well-educated voters can deliver the best outcome. They are convinced that what a democracy needs is a class of deeply informed voters flush with civic pride and imbued with an unselfish commitment to the common good who can decide what's really best without interference from the less informed. Some contemporary commentators are quite forthright about this. "All kinds of voters hope to make society better off, but the well educated are more likely to get the job done," writes the economist Bryan Caplan. Or as a libertarian think tank scholar puts it, "when turnout drops, it tends to leave the pool of remaining voters with an improved average level of political knowledge and policy know-how."

This perspective is not new. It is as old as our nation's history. The prominent Revolutionary-era New England clergyman and historian Jeremy Belknap put it this way: "Let it stand as a principle that government originates from the people but let the people be taught . . . that they are not able to govern themselves."

Whether these arguments and their supporters are insulting or just misguided, what they assume about the fundamental goals of democratic government says a lot. They think that there is an objective common good, though they are plagued by doubts about whether it can or should be achieved by aggregating millions of votes reflecting millions of voter preferences. At heart, they believe that there is only one criterion by which we judge the success of a democracy: whether it yields rational and efficient government decisions, as judged by an economist. Almost anything that helps achieve that goal is acceptable, except, of course, a dictatorship.

But what voting and democracy do best is produce decisions that let our society move forward. Democracy resolves conflict, even if it does not necessarily produce perfect agreement. As the political scientist Amy Gutmann puts it, "the basic problem of democratic politics [is] . . . how to make legitimate decisions for the society as a whole in the face of fundamental disagreement."

THE MEANS JUSTIFY THE ENDS

The idea that uninformed voters make bad laws while good, well-educated voters make smart laws is belied by our past. American political history is full of all types of laws: visionary and self-destructive, clever and inane, tyrannical and uplifting. Every era in our history has produced good laws and bad laws, by our own standards as well as the standards of the time.

One of the best-educated Congresses passed the Alien and Sedition Acts in 1798. The Sedition Act, among other things, criminalized "false, scandalous, and malicious writing" against the government, Congress, or the President. It made it illegal to attempt "to excite . . . against them the hatred of the good people of the United

States. . . ."[23] The law was flagrantly unconstitutional, an abuse of the First Amendment.

It was signed by one of the best-educated presidents in American history, John Adams. Twenty-five political opponents of Adams including a member of Congress and Benjamin Franklin's grandson were arrested under the laws.[24] Well within living memory of the idealism of the revolution and sent to power by the most select, best-educated (for the time) voters in American history, the Adams presidency descended into what the writer Ron Chernow described as "a time of political savagery with few parallels in American history."

Adams's chief rival, Thomas Jefferson, was then Vice President and consequently set to preside over the Senate as it deliberated passage of the acts. Jefferson found the proposals "detestable." He left the Senate for four months and took refuge in Monticello rather than preside over the Senate during consideration of the measures. But at some level he was sanguine about the laws because he understood that the people would see reason. He wrote to a fellow Virginian, "A little patience and we shall see the reign of witches pass over, their spells dissolved, and the people, recovering their true sight, restoring their government to its true principles."[25]

In 1971, facing inflation rates as high as 6 percent, an intolerably high rate at the time, a Republican President, Richard M. Nixon,

---

[23] Most contemporary cable news hosts likely would be in prison if the law were in effect today.

[24] Franklin's grandson was arrested under earlier libel laws and, after the passage of the Alien and Sedition laws, was also prosecuted under them.

[25] Jefferson was not entirely passive in his opposition to the Alien and Sedition Acts, and indeed his efforts to oppose the laws on a state level laid the philosophical groundwork for the southern secessionist movement that culminated in the Civil War. The acts expired in the midst of Jefferson's presidency and were not renewed. The Supreme Court never ruled on their constitutionality.

instituted a ninety-day freeze on wages and prices, now widely regarded as one of the more hare-brained ways a government can attempt to control inflation.

And yet our democracy has also produced extraordinary laws.

Consider the 1957 Civil Rights Act. That year, the nation was gripped by efforts to desegregate public schools in Little Rock, Arkansas. In early September, nine African American students were blocked from entering their high school by armed soldiers from the state's National Guard. The students were surrounded by screaming crowds threatening to lynch them. By the end of that month, Republican President Dwight D. Eisenhower had sent in the U.S. Army to escort them into their schoolhouse. Earlier, in that same month, the U.S. Senate overcame a filibuster by South Carolina Senator Strom Thurmond and passed the first civil rights act in more than eighty years. The law, which among other things established the Civil Rights Division in the U.S. Department of Justice, was deeply flawed. It was the quintessential "half a loaf," but it marked a major turning point in the history of the civil rights movement. For the first time in living memory, Congress was able to act in support of civil rights.

Or consider deregulation efforts. A mere seven years after Nixon imposed wage and price controls, a Democratic President, Jimmy Carter, oversaw deregulation of the airline industry. From 1937 well into the 1970s, the federal government had regulated interstate airline travel, setting prices, routes, and schedules. Deregulation unleashed an era of unprecedented growth and innovation in airline travel.

Did the intelligence of American voters about economic issues change so dramatically between 1971 and 1978? Were the members of Congress who passed the Civil Rights Act of 1957 elected by voters who were more devoted to liberty and freedom than the ones who elected the Congress that passed the Alien and Sedition Acts in

1798? Probably not. A functioning democracy produces both good and bad results.

Today, federal government spending constitutes almost 25 percent of our gross domestic product.[26] More than 200,000 members of the million-member armed forces are deployed across 150 nations and on every continent. Our governments—operating on the national, state, local, city, county, and school district levels—perform tasks ranging from picking up the garbage to launching a Mars space probe, from determining local utility rates to providing health care insurance to more than 47 million people over age sixty-five via Medicare, from providing free public education to almost 56 million children ages three to eighteen to determining the safety and efficacy of new drugs on the market.

Is any voter really smart enough to know all that needs to be known about our government and then to rank their policy priorities for all aspects of government and then to evaluate candidates against those priorities and vote accordingly?

What goes through our heads when we vote, in that moment before the lever is pulled, the circle is filled in, the screen is tapped, the card is punched? That moment is the culmination of years of habituation, of exposure to politics and society and to our family and friends as we talk about the issues of the day. Social scientists believe that what makes a voter can best be described as a funnel of factors, with each factor gaining in intensity and significance as it reaches the tip of the funnel and then finally makes someone a voter.

Our socioeconomic background—for example, race, religion, education, class, and parents' background—starts us off down the funnel. All of these impact our party identification—most people

---

[26] In the years preceding the economic crisis that began in 2008, the percentage was closer to 21 percent.

tend to affiliate with the same political party as their parents—which is next in the funnel. Travelling further down the funnel, the party we associate with strongly affects our evaluation of candidates and issues. As an election draws near, episodes and events from the campaigns creep into the funnel. And near the end, our immediate social surroundings—family and friends—enter the equation. The cumulative weight of these factors takes us through the funnel. And at the tip is our vote.

The funnel doesn't say precisely how we'll vote or whether we'll vote wisely. And it doesn't say how we'll behave when a host of barriers, from a voter identification requirement to a long line at the polls to a bad cold or a boss who wants us at work early, stand in our way. In fact, the need to predict whether we'll vote and then whether we will vote Republican, Democrat, or Independent (or for that matter Libertarian, Constitutionalist, Green, Tea Party, or Socialist) propels a multibillion dollar political industrial complex employing countless pollsters, media consultants, and grass-roots activists. Some of them are the people who bring us the news that seeing a flag right before one votes increases the chances that one will vote Republican. They tell us that "able looking" people win elections, and then provide helpful clues on what is "able looking"—short hair that comes to a slight widow's peak and is parted on the side, for one.

Most voters know they have limited information, but they engage in a number of fast and furious efforts to make up for it and use short cuts to navigate the complexities of voting and deciding. They ask trusted friends and family members what they think. They have a set of standing principles and guiding visions about government. When they vote, they determine how closely candidates and parties come to align with those principles. People can be capricious or illogical about particular politicians and issues, to be sure. But at bottom, they primarily tend to base their decisions on the few key areas where their opinions are fixed, well informed, and guided by their principles—even as they give vent to some of their more anarchic passions.

We are social animals who live in association with one another. We need one another to survive and thrive. And when we live with one another, we must inevitably make and then obey collective decisions. Over time the social human mind has developed to judge and respond to situations and rules according to a series of instinctive guideposts.

We have deep-seated reactions to each other's behavior—was it fair or not fair, sacred or profane, loyal or disloyal, compliant or subversive? These guideposts help us evaluate whether our associations (and governments and laws) meet base-level requirements for our continued participation in the group. And as the psychologist Jonathan Haidt says: "If you put individuals together in the right way, such that some individuals can use their reasoning power to disconfirm the claims of others, and all individuals feel some common bond or shared fate that allows them to interact civilly, you can create a group that ends up producing good reasoning as an emergent property of the social system."

The Harvard political economist V.O. Key put it more succinctly: "Voters are not fools."

"Ambition Must Be Made to Counteract Ambition"

Still, a very large portion of the American population is disengaged from, or worse, hates the political process. Political disengagement is not, contrary to some thinking, a good thing. But is it bad?

Low turnout is driven by a host of institutional, social, and attitudinal factors. Scientists have explored many of them. Good or bad weather affects turnout. Whether one's neighbors also vote has an impact. Close elections lead to high turnout. Divided government drives turnout down. Winner-take-all elections lessen turnout.

Limited polling hours inhibit turnout. In short, voting is prompted by a complex brew of factors. (See Table 3.)

But create a breed of Americans who think that candidates cannot be trusted, that interest groups control government, that there is no difference among the parties, and that politics is hard to understand, and you will create a host of people who do not vote.

And American frustration with government and politics is running near an all-time high.[27] In 1958, 74 percent of the public said it trusted the national government to do the right thing most of the time. In 2011, only 19 percent felt that way. Despair, disgust, and anger are common threads in our political dialogue. Abuse and mockery often greet politicians and fellow voters.

Today, one out of three voters believes a group of people randomly selected from the phone book would do a better job than Congress. Forty-three percent of voters believe that most members of Congress are corrupt, and another 30 percent are not sure. More than half of likely voters believe that members of Congress get reelected because the rules are rigged. A mere 17 percent believe they get reelected because they do a good job.

Modern disengagement with politics and political parties began in the 1960s. The percentage of Independents (including independent Democrats and Republicans) jumped from about 18 percent then to approximately 40 percent today. Attachment to and interaction with political parties began declining in that same period. Meanwhile, the geographic partitioning of American voters on ideological lines increased. In 1976, 27 percent of Americans lived in "partisan counties," or counties where a single political party consistently domi-

---

[27] At least for the modern political era and as measured by polls. Americans had a similar level of distrust for politics at the height of the Watergate scandals. Moreover, the level of distrust for politics is closely tied to the state of the economy, so we cannot be sure that these opinions will persist.

nated election results. In 2008, 48 percent of the population lived in a partisan county.[28]

The recent decline in voter turnout coincides with all of these developments, though social scientists vigorously debate exactly how much these changes in party loyalty and attitudes toward politics have impacted turnout.

Low turnout is not spread uniformly across all categories of Americans. When one starts looking at voter turnout in detail, troubling patterns emerge. Overall turnout may have been 62 percent in 2008, but some groups of Americans had even lower turnout rates: Asian Americans, Latinos, people between the ages of eighteen and twenty-four, poor people, single people. All vote at rates 20 percent below average. Meanwhile, older people and the wealthy vote at far higher rates. In 2008, 72 percent of people ages sixty-five to seventy-four voted. Only 48 percent of eighteen-to-twenty-four-year-olds voted. When the 2010 elections rolled around, only 21 percent of eighteen-to-twenty-four-year-olds voted. And a staggering 92 percent of people who made more than $100,000 per year voted. Although African Americans vote at a lower rate than white Americans, the gap is not as great as it is for other ethnic groups.

We can look at it another way and measure a participation gap—or how many more people from one group of prospective voters would have turned up at the polls had their turnout rate equaled that of the general population. By that measure, another 2.7 million Latino voters would have gone to the polls in 2008. More than 9 million people with a high school degree or less would have gone to the polls. Another 3.9 million eighteen- to twenty-four-year-olds would have voted. (Young Latinos have one of the lowest participation rates among all groups.)

---

[28] This is not to say that Americans are consciously moving into cities or counties because there are more like-minded Republicans or Democrats there.

TABLE 3. WHAT FACTORS MAKE SOMEONE A VOTER?

Demographics	Social and Economic Factors
age	interpersonal communications
gender	social identity
race	group consciousness
marital status	socialization
education	status of neighbors
income	political disagreement
occupation	social capital
home ownership	geographic mobility
religion	habituation
	unemployment rate

Institutional Factors	Attitudes and Behavior
polling locations	interest in politics
barriers to registration	access to information
frequency of elections	general political knowledge
early and absentee voting rules	level of partisanship
weekday vs. weekend voting	sense of civic duty
multiple elections/voter fatigue	sense of political efficacy
type of election (federal, state, local)	trust in political institutions
good or bad weather	religious service attendance
plurality systems	personal skill acquisition
divided government	humanitarianism
closeness of election	altruism
party mobilization efforts	patience
campaign activities	self-esteem
amount spent on political advertising	

One often-cited strand of research from the early 1980s holds that there is not much difference between voters and non-voters when it comes to issues. But more recent research that analyzes a broader array of opinions demonstrates that there is a marked difference between the two groups. In general, non-voters tend to be Independents and Democrats, not Republicans. They are more likely to support government spending on health and education and are more in favor of aggressive government support for jobs. But one should not jump to the conclusion that non-voters are just a bunch of liberals.

Non-voters are substantially more likely to support the use of school vouchers than are voters. In a 2007 analysis, non-voters were substantially more in favor of keeping troops in Iraq than withdrawing them. And when it comes to abortion politics, non-voters are resolute moderates. In contrast, voters tend to cluster on the extreme poles when it comes to abortion issues.

Social scientists look at these numbers and start trying to calculate whether any election outcomes would change and whether elected representatives would alter their behavior if everyone who doesn't vote suddenly did. Some election outcomes would probably change, possibly even the 2000 and 2004 presidential elections. But even if election outcomes were not radically altered, individual elected leaders would alter their behavior if their base of voters was broadened, as they would attempt to come closer to the center.

Political partisans look at these numbers and attitudes and make cunning decisions based on them. One group of partisans aggressively tries to increase turnout. Another group tries to suppress turnout. Meanwhile, average voters don't concern themselves too much with non-voters. Many Americans shrug their shoulders: if people who can't be bothered to vote have their preferences ignored by government, then they are hurting only themselves and have only themselves to blame.

Low turnout shouldn't concern us because it does or does not sweep particular parties into power. It should concern us because when the majority of Americans are disengaged from elections and our government, democracy as a whole suffers.

The Founders believed that the full engagement of the electorate was necessary to prevent government from being captured and used by factions. Our fourth President, James Madison, as astute an observer of fickle and dangerous human behavior as there ever was, put it this way in the *Federalist Papers*:

> Ambition must be made to counteract ambition. . . . Different interests necessarily exist in different classes of citizens. If a majority be united by a common interest, the rights of the minority will be insecure. There are but two methods of providing against this evil: the one by creating a will in the community independent of the majority—that is, of the society itself; the other, by comprehending in the society so many separate descriptions of citizens as will render an unjust combination of a majority of the whole very improbable, if not impracticable.
>
> It is no less certain than it is important, notwithstanding the contrary opinions which have been entertained, that the larger the society, provided it lie within a practical sphere, the more duly capable it will be of self-government.

From a practical standpoint, Madison believed democracy relies upon the full participation of all its members, if only to prevent one faction from abusing or misruling another. Moreover, broad participation increases the likelihood that even the people who disagree with government rules nevertheless will abide by them. In a democracy, the majority rules most of the time,[29] but it must justify the imposition of the majority opinion on the minority. When everyone has actually had his or her say and when the process is felt to have been fair, people buy in to the results. When fewer and fewer citizens participate, their conviction that the government is legitimate begins to dissolve.

Inclusive political institutions that distribute power broadly and equally are critical to our overall economic well-being. History

---

[29] Sometimes a "supermajority" rules, and often majority action is restricted by constitutional rights. But in general, it's fair to say that "the majority rules."

shows that it is often very hard for those who hold power to release it and to bring more and more people into the fold. But every time they do, society surges forward, generating a virtuous circle of political and economic rewards for everyone.

We cannot and should not be passive in the face of low voter turnout, particularly low turnout among particular groups of people: the young, the poor, Asian Americans, and Latinos. It should profoundly worry us, because in the end America needs their engagement and participation for the nation to thrive.

We know quite a bit about who does vote. They are engaged in politics and campaigns. They have strong opinions about the candidates. They feel they are effective participants whose voice counts. And they have a sense of political duty.

We know less about the people who don't vote, or rather we know less about how to turn them into voters. There is no little blue pill that can make them interested in politics or feel a sense of civic duty strong enough to go to the polls. Though oddly enough, if geneticists have their way, we might one day.

In 2008, a group of geneticists led by James Fowler decided to take a look at a large group of twins—one set of identical twins and another of non-identical twins—and then check whether they voted. By looking at the difference in their voting behavior, the researchers could judge to what extent voting was impacted by genetics. Because parental voting behavior is one of the strongest indicators of whether a person will vote, it stands to reason that there might be a voting gene. Fowler and his team found that genetic makeup strongly predicted whether a person would vote at all—up to 60 percent of the time. When they looked more closely at the genes involved, they found two likely, though not exclusive, culprits: a pair of genes that critically influence our brain's serotonin system, our body's chemical scheme for processing fear, trust, and social interaction.

Serotonin is one of those crucial hormones that shapes the human experience. It plays a vital role in the transmission of nerve impulses. It is a key part of the system that regulates learning, mood, sleep, and blood flow. Female mice that have been genetically engineered not to produce serotonin lose their maternal instinct and sink into despair. Monkeys with impaired serotonin systems are more impulsive and aggressive than usual. They also drink too much alcohol, though it's a bit unclear why scientists think it's wise to give monkeys alcohol. Lobsters injected with serotonin try to get into fights with other lobsters. People with impaired serotonin systems are antisocial and may be more susceptible to anxiety and depression. Fowler determined that people with two genetic variations that make their serotonin systems efficient and that are tied to emotional resilience and sociability are more likely to vote.

So maybe one day there will be a pill to help increase turnout.

Still, biology is not destiny. And no one is saying we should wait on the pharmaceutical industry to solve democracy's problems. Voting is our way of determining our nation's future, and consequently our own. It shouldn't be taken lightly. Every prospective voter has to make the decision whether to vote or not. And voting certainly can be a hassle. But democracy is a self-fulfilling prophecy that relies on ordinary people making an effort. When the economist Anthony Downs tried to figure out why so many more people voted than his model predicted, the dispassionate rationalist remarkably turned into an idealist: when we vote we invest in democracy. And in our fraught times, we need every investment we can get.

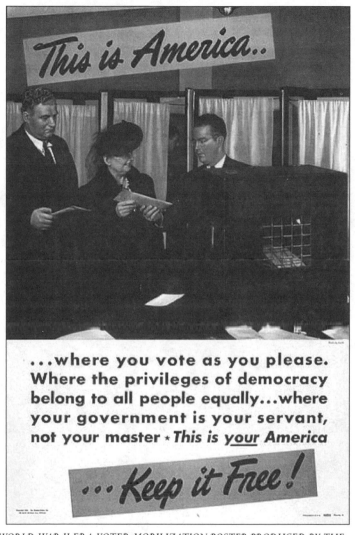

*A WORLD WAR II ERA VOTER MOBILIZATION POSTER PRODUCED BY THE FEDERAL GOVERNMENT. Faced with the widespread overseas deployment of American soldiers and increased mobility brought on by World War II, the government responded with aggressive efforts to register people and to increase turnout. That effort, coupled with patriotic fervor, had the effect of increasing turnout in many elections. Indeed, the presidential election of 1944 had the highest voter turnout in almost twenty years as wartime voters came to the polls in droves. Turnout began declining again after the war. **Photo Credit:** National Archives*

THE WHITE HOUSE—THE ULTIMATE PRIZE FOR WINNING THE ELECTORAL COLLEGE VOTE. *This photograph was taken on December 7, 1941. Late into the night, the White House was ablaze with lights, and people gathered in front of it, still stunned by the Japanese attack on Pearl Harbor. The next day President Franklin Delano Roosevelt addressed Congress. He asked for and received a declaration of war on Japan. America entered World War II. It was the last time America formally declared war on another nation.* **Photo Credit:** *The Associated Press*

CHAPTER 4

★ ★ ★

THE MYSTIC AGENCY OF THE ELECTORAL COLLEGE

The Bewildering Way America Elects Its Presidents

"The fundamental maxim of republican government . . .
requires that the sense of the majority should prevail."

Alexander Hamilton,
"Federalist, No. 22," December 14, 1787

The Electoral College "installs a mystic agency between the
electorate and the President. It systematically distorts the
popular vote. It is impossible to explain to foreigners. Even
Americans don't understand it."

Arthur M. Schlesinger Jr.,
The Cycles of American History, *1999*

CONGRESS WROTE THE LAW TELLING them what day they would meet: every four years on the Monday following the second Wednesday in December. So on that day in 2008, in state capitals across the United States, 538 men and women gathered to cast their votes and to elect the President. On December 15, 2008, Barack H. Obama was elected President of the United States.

On that unseasonably warm and drizzly day in Indiana, eleven Hoosiers, Jeffrey L. Chidester, Butch Morgan, Michelle Boxell,

Charlotte Martin, Jerry J. Lux, Connie Southworth, Alan P. Hogan, Myrna E. Brown, Clarence Benjamin Leatherbury, Daniel J. Parker, and Cordelia Lewis Burks, waited to be called forward to cast their votes for President. They gathered in the state's grand neoclassical capitol building. Standing in a line at the rear of the capitol's House chamber, they were summoned to their seats by the Secretary of State. A military color guard escorted them in and held the American and Indiana flags high as the national anthem was sung. They solemnly walked in and voted.

The youngest voter there, nineteen-year-old Ben Leatherbury, was excited. It was his first presidential election. And in stark contrast to virtually every other presidential voter in Indiana, his vote really counted.

It was the first time since 1964 that any Indiana Democrat had been allowed to vote for President. And the eleven men and women who sat in the Indiana House chamber that day were all Democrats who not very surprisingly voted unanimously for Obama to be President and for Joe Biden to be Vice President.

The 1,374,039 Hoosiers and 69,456,897 Americans who voted for Obama on November 4, 2008, might be forgiven for thinking that that Tuesday was election day and that they were the ones who voted for President. But they would be wrong. Obama became President by a 365 to 173 vote in the Electoral College, more than a month later. And although he won 53 percent of the popular vote, because of the Electoral College, he actually became President by a 68 percent to 32 percent margin.

HOW THE ELECTORAL COLLEGE WORKS TODAY

Americans don't vote for President. They vote for electors who vote for President.

Modern gatherings of these rare people, these members of the Electoral College who actually get to vote for President, reflect the changes and modifications made to our electoral system over the course of the last two centuries. But despite the march of time, the catalogue of controversial and sometimes botched presidential elections, and the modernization of the American democratic system, the college still functions in all its arcane glory—mind-bending to anyone accustomed to the idea that the way to decide an election democratically is to count the number of votes and declare the winner based on who gets the most votes.

After all, in a democracy, the majority rules. But the Electoral College works differently.

In step one, each state and the District of Columbia is allocated a number of electors equal to the number of members it sends to the House of Representatives plus another two for its senators, totaling 538 since 1964. The allocation is based upon the population of the state and thus potentially changes every ten years as a result of the census. In 2012, Ohio and New York both lost two electoral votes while Nevada gained one and Texas gained four. (See Table 4.) And then each state is given an additional two electors as the Connecticut Compromise of 1787 continues to wend its way into modern federal elections.

Theoretically, then, the popular vote is reflected and given substantial weight in dictating the presidential election outcome via the number of electors assigned based on population, while small states get a thumb on the scale via the two votes they are each given regardless of population size.

In step two, the state selects its electors. Under the Constitution, each state is allowed to appoint its electors in any manner it chooses. Unlikely as it is, Indiana, indeed any state, could pass a law to appoint its electors using a basketball tournament, scratch-off lottery cards, or at the sole discretion of the Governor.

In the first presidential election in 1788, New York couldn't decide how to appoint electors so did not cast any electoral votes at

TABLE 4. APPORTIONMENT POPULATION AND NUMBER OF REPRESENTATIVES, BY STATE: 2012

State	Apportion-ment population	Number of apportioned represen-tatives	Electoral votes	Population per electoral vote	Change in apportion-ment since 2000
Alabama	4,802,982	7	9	533,665	0
Alaska	721,523	1	3	240,508	0
Arizona	6,412,700	9	11	582,973	+1
Arkansas	2,926,229	4	6	487,705	0
California	37,341,989	53	55	678,945	0
Colorado	5,044,930	7	9	560,548	0
Connecticut	3,581,628	5	7	511,661	0
Delaware	900,877	1	3	300,292	0
D.C.	617,996	0	3	205,999	0
Florida	18,900,773	27	29	651,751	+2
Georgia	9,727,566	14	16	607,973	+1
Hawaii	1,366,862	2	4	341,716	0
Idaho	1,573,499	2	4	393,375	0
Illinois	12,864,380	18	20	643,219	−1
Indiana	6,501,582	9	11	591,053	0
Iowa	3,053,787	4	6	508,965	−1
Kansas	2,863,813	4	6	477,302	0
Kentucky	4,350,606	6	8	543,826	0
Louisiana	4,553,962	6	8	569,245	−1
Maine	1,333,074	2	4	333,269	0
Maryland	5,789,929	8	10	578,993	0
Massachusetts	6,559,644	9	11	596,331	−1
Michigan	9,911,626	14	16	619,477	−1
Minnesota	5,314,879	8	10	531,488	0
Mississippi	2,978,240	4	6	496,373	0
Missouri	6,011,478	8	10	601,148	−1
Montana	994,416	1	3	331,472	0
Nebraska	1,831,825	3	5	366,365	0

State	Apportion-ment population	Number of apportioned represen-tatives	Electoral votes	Population per electoral vote	Change in apportion-ment since 2000
Nevada	2,709,432	4	6	451,572	+1
New Hampshire	1,321,445	2	4	330,361	0
New Jersey	8,807,501	12	14	629,107	−1
New Mexico	2,067,273	3	5	413,455	0
New York	19,421,055	27	29	669,692	−2
North Carolina	9,565,781	13	15	637,719	0
North Dakota	675,905	1	3	225,302	0
Ohio	11,568,495	16	18	642,694	−2
Oklahoma	3,764,882	5	7	537,840	0
Oregon	3,848,606	5	7	549,801	0
Pennsylvania	12,734,905	18	20	636,745	−1
Rhode Island	1,055,247	2	4	263,812	0
South Carolina	4,645,975	7	9	516,219	+1
South Dakota	819,761	1	3	273,254	0
Tennessee	6,375,431	9	11	579,585	0
Texas	25,268,418	36	38	664,958	+4
Utah	2,770,765	4	6	461,794	+1
Vermont	630,337	1	3	210,112	0
Virginia	8,037,736	11	13	618,287	0
Washington	6,753,369	10	12	562,781	+1
West Virginia	1,859,815	3	5	371,963	0
Wisconsin	5,698,230	8	10	569,823	0
Wyoming	568,300	1	3	189,433	0
TOTAL	309,801,459	438	538		

Source: U.S. Census Bureau. Apportionment population includes the resident population for the 50 states, as ascertained by the 2010 Census. Apportionment population includes overseas U.S. military and federal civilian employees (and their dependents living with them) allocated to their home state, as reported by the employing federal agencies.

all. The electors who did manage to get appointed in 1787 cast their votes in their respective states sometime in the thirty-four-day window before the first Wednesday in December of that year. (It seems no matter what the century, the method for determining the college's meeting times is positively druidic.) In that first presidential election at least, and despite New York's breakdown, everything was comfortably resolved. George Washington was elected unanimously.

During the first few presidential elections, electors were selected in a variety of ways. A majority of the original thirteen American states appointed their electors through their legislatures. But by 1832, every state except South Carolina selected electors by popular vote.

But that doesn't tell the whole story. Even today, although popularly elected themselves, electors do not campaign for votes. In fact it's unlikely that individual voters even know the names of the electors they are voting for since most modern ballots dispense with the formalities and simply give voters the choice of presidential candidates. Electors stay in the background. They never get posters or pollsters. Hardly anyone knows their names, except for the political parties in each state that appoint the electors. Ben Leatherbury got to be an elector in Indiana because his father, a Democratic Party activist, got a call from the head of the state's Democratic Party asking him to be an elector. Leatherbury's father wasn't interested in doing it in 2008, and he suggested his nineteen-year-old son for the job. So in yet another odd Electoral College twist, the citizens of every state vote democratically for their Electoral College representatives, yet those very representatives are selected to stand for office by political party insiders.

Which brings us to step three: How does the state allocate its electoral votes? California may have fifty-five Electoral College votes to Alaska's three, but both states cast them in a winner-take-all system. In 2008, John McCain won the popular vote in Missouri by 3,903 votes or 0.1 percent of the votes cast. Yet he received all nine of that state's votes.

Forty-eight states and the District of Columbia cast their electoral votes using the winner-take-all approach. Only Maine and Nebraska buck the trend. Those two maverick states award their two guaranteed non-population-based votes to the overall state winner and then allocate their population-based votes to the winner in each of their congressional districts.

The winner-take-all system has a certain appeal. It has dominated the way states cast their electoral votes since the mid-nineteenth century. By awarding their electoral votes in a bloc, states improve their appeal to national presidential candidates. States with large collections of electoral votes become juicy plums, rewards for the concentrated attention of the candidates. This is particularly so if the state is a so-called swing state where competition between Democratic and Republican presidential candidates is so intense and the vote so close that the winner-take-all reward is credibly dangling in front of both of them. And so candidates are forced to take the state's concerns and needs seriously if they want to capture a large bloc of votes.

Swing states are loath to abandon their attention-getting bloc of votes. And states that are solidly in one or another political camp would never give away electoral votes to the enemy voluntarily.

However, since each state is allowed to appoint its electors at its sole discretion, it could allocate its votes in a variety of ways. Even though it seems self-evident that at a minimum the bulk of a state's electoral votes should go to the candidate who gets the most popular votes, not all current proposals to substitute a different allocation scheme for the dominant winner-take-all approach adhere to this principle. In 2011, legislators in Harrisburg, Pennsylvania, proposed a new and improved way to allocate the state's twenty electoral votes. As with Maine and Nebraska, the two set electoral votes would go to the statewide popular vote winner. The remaining eighteen votes would be allocated by each congressional district according to who won the popular vote in that particular district.

But the Pennsylvania proposal demonstrates that Electoral College politics are sometimes more about facility with Excel spreadsheets and partisan game theory than with fundamental democratic fairness. Because of the way Pennsylvania has drawn its congressional district boundaries, it is possible for a candidate to win the statewide popular vote by winning the popular vote in only six of Pennsylvania's eighteen districts.[30] And so under the proposal, the statewide vote winner would get eight of twenty Electoral College votes. The loser would win.

In one final Electoral College twist, despite the winner-take-all system, not all electors are bound to cast their votes for the winner of the state's popular vote. Only about half the states have laws requiring their electors to vote for the popular vote winner. In the early days of the nation, electors were expected to exercise independent judgment, though they certainly weren't encouraged to disregard popular opinion or the partisan preference of the legislature that had appointed them. In practice, few electors have ever cast a heretical vote contrary to the popular will of their state. In the fifty-six presidential elections held since 1787, only 11 of the 22,453 electoral votes cast for President have been faithless.[31] And only Pennsylvanian

---

[30] Pennsylvania's Democratic vote tends to be concentrated in five urban districts located near Philadelphia and one in Pittsburgh. Obama won the statewide vote in Pennsylvania in 2008 but won majorities in only six of that state's eighteen congressional districts. The large margins Democratic presidential candidates historically tend to win in those six districts enable them to make up their losses in the remaining twelve districts.

[31] In 1872, New York's Horace Greeley running as a Democrat and Liberal Republican died before the Electoral College met, and sixty-three of the electors pledged to him accordingly changed their votes. These votes are often counted as "faithless" but have not been included in this book.

Samuel Miles's faithless vote in 1796—for Thomas Jefferson—could have conceivably altered the outcome of the election.[32]

In 2000, elector Barbara Lett-Simmons's name entered the roll book of faithless electors when she abstained from voting to protest the lack of voting rights for the District of Columbia. The Washington, D.C., Democrat had been a member of that city's Board of Education and pledged to vote for Al Gore. But when the moment came to cast her vote on December 18, 2000, she wrote instead, "This blank ballot is cast for all the colonists of the District of Columbia." A few moments later, standing before a bank of television cameras and reporters eager to cover this rare event, she proclaimed: "Taxation without representation is tyranny." Lett-Simmons faced a storm of criticism and ostracism from voters, the press, and her fellow Democratic Party members, though she faced no legal consequences for what she did. Her abstention had no practical impact on the election.

Despite the rarity of faithless electors, efforts to encourage faithlessness spring up in every close election. In 1976, when the race between Jimmy Carter and Gerald Ford potentially turned on fewer than ten thousand votes in Ohio and Hawaii, the Ford campaign prepared a faithless elector strategy. "We were shopping—not shopping, excuse me—looking around for electors," Senator Bob Dole, Ford's running mate, told the Senate Judiciary Committee. "It just seems to me that the temptation is there for [electors] in a very tight race to really negotiate quite a bunch."

---

[32] Electors also cast separate ballots for Vice President. There have been considerably more "faithless" Electoral College votes for Vice President. In 1836, the Democratic nominee for Vice President, Richard Mentor Johnson of Kentucky, was rejected by the twenty-three electors from Virginia. The Virginians refused to vote for him because he had lived with and fathered children with a black woman. As a result of their refusal to vote for him, the election was thrown to Congress, which elected Johnson to the vice presidency.

Some basic math shows more ways the Electoral College system can go off the rails very quickly. Not only is a tie possible, but it is also possible to garner a majority of Electoral College votes without winning the popular vote. In other words, it is entirely possible that in a democracy, the loser wins.

Armed with that knowledge, every four years, the presidential candidates fill their war chests, hire their pollsters and strategists, film their commercials, write their speeches, print their leaflets, and send out waves of volunteers and paid staff to states to launch get-out-the-vote efforts. And every single one of them allocates their attention and resources according to an Electoral College strategy.

Candidates count the Electoral College votes they are virtually guaranteed from states that are single-party dominated. And then they battle for the remaining swing state votes needed to take them across the magical 270 threshold. Winning the popular vote would be nice, but it is certainly not necessary as far as presidential campaigns are concerned.

While it might seem surprising that anyone would consider taking the presidential oath of office having failed to win the popular vote, recent history shows that the American public has been copacetic with presidents who lack the backing of the majority. In 2000, George W. Bush took office despite losing the popular vote. And in 1992, Bill Clinton took office with less than 50 percent of the popular vote. Both won the Electoral College vote outright. There was no rioting in the streets. There were no sustained or serious efforts to reform or abolish the Electoral College.

The strategists who run presidential elections long ago learned a basic math lesson—craft an Electoral College victory and hope a democratic majority comes with it. No political party is immune to pursuing an Electoral College strategy. In late 2004, Bush's campaign strategist told a reporter that the campaign had not taken a national poll in two years. It had only conducted polls in eighteen swing states. "If people don't like it, they can move from a safe state to a swing state," President Bush's press secretary Ari Fleischer said. More recently, President Obama's chief strategist David Axelrod pointed out: "There are a lot of ways for us to get to 270." Indeed, that is the only number that really matters in a presidential race.

However, with 538 votes in the college, it should come as no surprise that there can be a tie. Or in the event of a strong third-party challenger, that none of the candidates would gain a majority. Pondering an Electoral College tie is a favorite parlor game among some lawyers and political observers. Many of them went into excited overdrive in the early fall of 2008 when they brooded over what would happen if Obama won every state that went for Al Gore in 2000 plus Colorado, or if Obama won every state that John Kerry won in 2004 plus Iowa, New Mexico, and Nevada but lost New Hampshire. Both of those scenarios would have given Obama 269 Electoral College votes and McCain 269 Electoral College votes.

During the chaotic and bitterly close campaign of 1800, the math came home to roost when, for the first and only time in American history, the Electoral College tied. Thomas Jefferson and his running mate Aaron Burr both got 73 votes.[33] John Adams,

---

[33] One can only imagine Jefferson's reaction when he learned that his own running mate had ended up with the same number of votes as him. The tie was due to the complex procedure initially envisioned in the Constitution. Electors in the Constitution as drafted in 1787 each cast votes for two people for President. At least one of those people had to be from a different state than the elector. This process was put in place in order to force electors to look outside their own state or region for qualified presidential candidates. Vice presidents were not voted on specifically. The Vice President would simply be the man who came in second. The Founders fully anticipated that the Electoral College might not reach a majority decision and that elections might often be sent to the House of Representatives for resolution. After the election of 1800, the Constitution was amended to give electors only one vote for President and one vote for Vice President.

Jefferson's opponent for the presidency, fell short by eight votes. The election was then thrown to the House of Representatives to decide. In another variation on the winner-take-all system, the Constitution dictates that votes in the House of Representatives be cast by states rather than individual members of Congress. In 1800, Virginia got one vote and Rhode Island got one vote. Jefferson eventually won the election by courting the lone congressman from Delaware and winning that state's vote. But not before the House deadlocked over the course of five frustrating days as its members cast thirty-five inconclusive votes. Jefferson became President by a vote of ten to four.

Moreover, from the time of the 1800 presidential election through today, the Electoral College has given more weight and power to the voters of smaller states, challenging the idea that all votes should count equally. In 2012, Wyoming will get one electoral vote for every 189,433 of its citizens. California will get one for every 678,945. A Wyoming resident's vote has three and a half times more weight in the presidential election than a Californian's. (See Table 4.)

But from a practical standpoint, the Electoral College has usually worked. Crudely speaking, the candidate with the most votes wins (most of the time), so why bother with the mathematical indignities or statistical worst-case scenarios?

Still, since World War II, a majority of Americans have consistently favored the abolition of the Electoral College. Indeed, proposals to abolish the Electoral College and institute direct popular election of the President surfaced almost as soon as the Constitutional Convention ended, starting in 1814. Andrew Jackson—the college's first casualty—called for its abolition every year during his presidency in the mid-nineteenth century. More recently, in 1968, the House of Representatives overwhelmingly passed a constitutional amendment for its abolition only to see the measure founder in the

Senate more than a year later. In the last few years, a state-by-state effort to allocate electoral votes to guarantee that the person who wins the popular vote wins has gained momentum.

But from the day the Constitution was ratified to this day, the Electoral College has remained firmly in place, its members wending their way to their state capitals and meeting regularly every four years to elect the President.

It probably seems like a quaint, ceremonial institution, a quirk of constitutional history that has no practical effect on who becomes President of the United States. Except when it does.

Four U.S. presidents have been elected and served in office even though they lost the popular vote. Four times the wrong guy won.

HISTORY OF THE COLLEGE

A President's election and the office's powers were a matter of intense debate in Philadelphia in 1787. Had the Constitutional Convention's debates turned out differently, we might have had a three-person presidency serving for seven years with no possibility of re-election, for no pay, and appointed by a group of Congressmen selected by lottery.

The mechanism for selecting a President was one of the most contentious issues at the Convention. Debate over the election process prolonged the Convention by weeks, with delegates voting at least sixty times on how presidents were to be selected, rejecting versions of the Electoral College several times. In short, they were against it before they were for it.

By late August 1787, almost three months into the Convention, its members had twice rejected popular election of the President. During one nine-day period in July they voted to have the President selected by Congress, then voted to have him (and it certainly would have been a him) selected by electors determined by state

legislatures, then reversed course and turned to congressional selection again, then rejected that idea a day later, then readopted it.

Finally, oppressed by the late summer heat, weary of each other's
company, and under pressure to finish their work, they created the
aptly named Committee of Postponed Matters and took a break. At
the time the committee was created, most delegates assumed that
assessing the popular will in electing a President was a dead letter
and would be rejected by the committee. They had after all voted
against direct election twice. Most of the delegates were firmly of
the opinion that popular election was a bad idea. Virginia's George
Mason declared, "It would be as unnatural to refer the choice of a
proper character for chief Magistrate to the people, as it would to
refer a trial of colours to a blind man."

The delegates had two fundamental worries about popular election: regionalism and an uninformed, inflamed electorate. Many,
though not all, came to the Convention skeptical about widespread
suffrage, profoundly distrustful of the seething mass of voters.
Alexander Hamilton fretted that summer, "The people are turbulent
and changing; they seldom judge or determine right. Give therefore
to the first class a distinct permanent share in the government . . . .
Can a democratic assembly who annually revolve in the mass of the
people be supposed steadily to pursue the public good?"

There were to be sure many delegates to the Convention who favored broad suffrage and participatory democracy. Pennsylvania's
James Wilson proposed direct popular election of the President at
the Convention only to see it voted down emphatically on the first
day of debate on the presidency. He persisted in his dedication to the
people's sovereignty. During his state's winter 1787 debate whether
to ratify the Constitution, he proclaimed, "For the truth is, that the
supreme, absolute and uncontrollable authority, *remains* with the
people. . . . I consider the people of the United States as forming
one great community. . . . The people, therefore, have a right, whilst

enjoying the undeniable powers of society, to form either a general government, or state governments, in what manner they please; or to accommodate them to one another, and by this means preserve them all."

In the summer of 1787, as the Founders debated popularly electing a President, their fears were not specifically about an uncontrollable mass of wild voters as much as they were a realistic and practical concern about the feasibility of conducting educated and reasoned nationwide elections. They did not doubt voters could be intelligent. Rather, given eighteenth-century communication patterns, they doubted that the voters could practically obtain the knowledge needed to make a well-informed judgment about who would be a good President.

Wilson, of course, had no such fears. "Continental characters will multiply as we more and more coalesce." He was proven right. But in 1787, it was not so clear. Only George Washington, the man all the delegates rightly assumed would be the first President, had a national reputation. He was known throughout the thirteen colonies. But he had spent seven years leading an army, marching up and down the eastern seaboard earning his status. Few other men could claim such a national reputation or even realistically aspire to one given the condition of the roads in colonial America.

Most delegates believed that in the absence of adequate information, voters would either select poor candidates or would turn to regional or state favorites. Either outcome was unsupportable. So they ultimately turned to the Electoral College as a solution. The proposal satisfied men like Wilson and Delaware's John Dickinson, who helped draft the provision. It incorporated a mechanism for measuring popular will and held out the promise of more over time. But to men like George Mason and Massachusetts's Roger Sherman, it guaranteed that the popular will would be channeled and guided via a body of wise men who would exercise their best judgment in

selecting the President. Those wise men—members of the elite—
would tend to already know the candidates. If not, their good
opinion could be sought and won by candidates more easily than ap-
pealing to hundreds of thousands of potential voters.

The Electoral College's impact on presidential elections was felt
almost immediately and nowhere more profoundly than in the way
it buttressed and amplified the power of the slave states. Throughout
most of America's history, and long after the abolition of slavery, the
Electoral College bolstered the South's electoral power. It skewed
and warped our nation's best and worst efforts to deal with slavery
and later with the vicious suppression of the black vote.

By rejecting a direct popular vote and allocating Electoral College
votes based upon representation in the House of Representatives,
the college ingested the grim consequences of the three-fifths compromise. In 1787, with almost 700,000 slaves living in the South,
from Maryland to Georgia, the three-fifths compromise gave the
South at least a dozen additional congressional seats and, as a result, a dozen slave-based electoral votes. Those twelve slave-based
electoral votes almost certainly lifted Thomas Jefferson, who won
seventy-three Electoral College votes to Adams's sixty-five, to ultimate victory in 1800. For fifty of the nation's first sixty-two years, a
white slaveholder occupied the presidency.

The abolition of slavery and adoption of the Fourteenth and
Fifteenth Amendments did not end the Electoral College's disrup-
tive effect. During the Jim Crow era, extending from 1890 to the
1960s, the segregationist South enjoyed the benefits of what one
commentator has called the five-fifths clause. Black citizens were
counted for apportionment and Electoral College allocation purposes, but white supremacists faced no real risk that they would
actually vote.

To Americans voting after the passage of the monumental Voting
Rights Act of 1965, this sad legacy of the Electoral College is a mat-

ter of history. More troubling perhaps to contemporary eyes, the college system has let the loser win in four presidential elections.

WINNERS, LOSERS, AND CLOSE CALLS

James Wilson's prediction that nationally known candidates would soon emerge was proven in 1824 when Andrew Jackson, the hero of the War of 1812, ran for President. In a four-way election, Old Hickory was pitted against Georgia's William H. Crawford, Kentucky's Henry Clay, and Massachusetts's John Quincy Adams. Despite Jackson's national renown, the regionalism feared by the Constitution's drafters dominated the election. Jackson won approximately 41 percent of the popular vote and carried twelve states.[34] But Adams swept seven states in the Northeast. Clay carried his own state plus Ohio and Missouri, and Crawford took parts of the South. Jackson was left with a plurality of the Electoral College, not the majority needed to avoid sending the election to the House of Representatives. Once in the House, presidential candidate and sitting Speaker of the House Clay took advantage of the opportunity to play kingmaker. Striking what Jackson's supporters branded as the "corrupt bargain," Clay shifted his support to Adams, who was duly elected President despite running a distant second in the popular vote. Clay was appointed Secretary of State.

"The people have been cheated," Jackson declared. He returned to Tennessee and prepared his next move. Four years later, Jackson was elected President, the first to live west of the Appalachian Mountains. The 1828 presidential campaign was the most expensive in American history up to that time. It was the first, though most

---

[34] In 1824, six of twenty-four states still appointed their electors in the legislature, so a popular vote count from those states does not exist.

definitely not the last, time that more than $1 million was spent on an election.

The debacle of 1824 set the stage for the theft of the century—the election of 1876. By December 1876, Democratic candidate Samuel Tilden seemed confident of victory. He held a popular vote lead in excess of 250,000 votes. And with 184 electoral votes in hand, he was one vote short of an Electoral College victory. Indeed, he was poised to capture 200 electoral votes. Faced with the loss of the presidency and the final collapse of the Reconstruction agenda, Republican Party insiders swung into overdrive.

Republican Party members controlled the election canvassing boards in three critical southern states: Florida, Louisiana, and South Carolina. In all three states, the election had been characterized by widespread corruption and intimidation, with the Democrats ruthlessly and violently keeping blacks from the polls. The Republicans certified the election results for Tilden's opponent, Ohio's Rutherford B. Hayes. Not to be outdone, the Democratic governors of the three states in contention prepared rival slates of electors pledged to Tilden.

As the winter wore on, the Senate and House were paralyzed, unable to decide between the rival slates of electors from the southern states. Finally, Congress appointed a special fifteen-member commission to decide the matter, scrupulously appointing seven Republicans, seven Democrats, and one independent to the commission. Then the Democrat-controlled Illinois State Senate appointed the independent commissioner to be its U.S. Senator, hoping he would feel grateful to the party. He expressed his gratitude by resigning from the commission and was replaced by a Republican.

With a Republican majority on the fifteen-person commission, the selection of the teetotaling Hayes seemed a foregone conclusion. But House Democrats threatened to filibuster the final vote. With the clock ticking down on sitting President Ulysses S. Grant's time in office, the nation faced the distinct possibility that it would not have a President in office when Grant's term expired. In late February, a small group of Republicans and southern Democrats met in Washington's Wormley House Hotel to cut a deal. Under the Compromise of 1877, federal troops were withdrawn from the South. Reconstruction and federal oversight of the South came to an end. Hayes, who had lost the popular vote, became President. He was sworn in in secret. Two days later he went through the ritual of a public inauguration. And so two months into 1877, the nation finally had a President, the Gilded Age of America's robber barons had dawned, and the groundwork was laid for Jim Crow.[35] Hayes and the Republican Party, at least, did not deliver on one part of their Wormley House deal. When their agreement to subsidize construction of a railroad line in return for putting Hayes in office was made in public, congressional support for the subsidy evaporated.

Eleven years later, the Electoral College sent the wrong man to the White House again. The 1888 election pitted sitting-President Grover Cleveland against Indiana's Benjamin Harrison. America's only bachelor President, Cleveland swept the South, losing his own home state of New York's electoral votes likely due to the influence of the Tammany Hall machine. Harrison, the Republican grandson of American's ninth President, William Henry Harrison, won the Northeast and the Midwest. Neither candidate won a majority of votes, with several third parties, from Prohibitionists to Unionists,

---

[35] The Compromise of 1877 did not, strictly speaking, lead to Jim Crow. It simply eliminated any federal government oversight of the South's practices. Jim Crow began emerging after the compromise and was precipitated by a number of factors including the unprecedented alliances being forged between blacks and poor whites in the South. As that alliance grew stronger, southern Democratic politicians at last felt real threats to their power. Jim Crow was devised to break the alliance and to disenfranchise blacks.

capturing a small portion of the vote. Allegations of corruption and voter fraud were widespread. But Cleveland indisputably led the popular vote by 95,000 votes. He lost. The Electoral College voted 233 to 168 for Benjamin Harrison.

Four years later, Cleveland unquestionably won election to the presidency. He entered the White House for a second term, this time a married man, having wed twenty-one-year-old Frances Folsom in 1886 during his first term in office. Cleveland never seemed to like the comforts of the White House. "I must go to dinner," he wrote a friend, "but I wish it was to eat a pickled herring, a Swiss cheese and a chop at Louis's instead of the French stuff I shall find." He may not, after all, have minded the four-year interlude given him by the Electoral College.

With the passage of time, late into the twentieth century, Americans might have been forgiven for thinking that these Electoral College miscarriages belonged firmly to the past.

But on the evening of Tuesday, November 7, 2000, and the early morning of Wednesday, November 8, the inconceivable, peculiar workings of the Electoral College led to two of the testiest phone calls in the history of American politics.

Late that Tuesday night, Vice President Al Gore called Texas Governor George W. Bush and conceded the presidential election.

A few hours later, at three in the morning, he called back.

"Circumstances have changed," Gore said.

Bush was flabbergasted. "Let me make sure I understand. You're taking back your concession?"

"Well, you don't have to be snippety with me," Gore reportedly said.

"Well, Mr. Vice President, you got to do what you got to do," Bush replied.

Even on the Wednesday after the 2000 election, long before hanging chads and the Supreme Court argument, Gore led the popular vote by more than 500,000 votes. No matter how Florida turned out, he had won the popular vote. As it turned out, he did not win Florida's Electoral College votes.

The lessons of the 2000 election, to most Americans, are about vote counting, butterfly ballots, military ballots, and court decisions. But at the simplest, most straightforward level, in the 2000 election the man with the most votes lost. Gore accepted almost without question the way the Electoral College worked.

The elections of 1824, 1876, 1888, and 2000 are not the only ones to reveal the risks inherent in the Electoral College. In the twentieth century, a few thousand votes in the elections of 1916, 1948, 1960, 1968, 1976, and 2004 could have turned popular-vote losers into Electoral College winners.

Four thousand votes in California in 1916 would have sent Charles Evans Hughes to the White House instead of Woodrow Wilson, who led the popular vote by more than half a million votes. "Dewey beats Truman" almost came true in 1948—if 46,000 votes had shifted in Ohio and New Jersey. Slightly more than 8,000 votes in Illinois and South Carolina would have sent Nixon to the White House instead of John F. Kennedy in 1960. In 1968, Alabama's George Wallace led a third party to forty-six electoral votes drawn from the Deep South. A shift of 80,000 votes in Missouri and Illinois would then have made Hubert Humphrey President over Nixon that year. In 1976, 9,000 votes in Ohio and Hawaii would have given Carter a second term even though he had lost the popular vote by more than 1.5 million votes. And finally, four short years after the chaos of 2000, 59,000 more votes in Ohio would have elected John Kerry President, even though he lost the popular vote by more than three million votes.

With so many Electoral College dramas under his belt, it's no wonder Nixon advocated elimination of the institution. His effort in 1969 to eliminate the college passed the House of Representatives by a vote of 339 to 70. But it failed in the Senate, victim of a filibuster led by southern senators. As Alexander Keyssar has written, "The political landscape was . . . shifting, and after the Voting Rights Act of 1965 the Electoral College could never serve the white South as it had in the past. But in 1969 no one knew how it would all turn out, or how George Wallace might fare in 1972. Savvy old-timers . . . were preserving the familiar, protecting states' rights wherever they could, resisting further intrusions by the federal government. Direct elections were one more threat to the old order, and this was a battle that the South could—and did—win."

In the immediate aftermath of the 2000 election, some called for the abolition of the Electoral College. Indeed, Congress has considered more bills concerning the Electoral College—more than seven hundred—than on any other subject. But in 2001, the proposal was tepidly received and never gained momentum. Too many previous efforts had ended in futility. Though he led a special commission to examine the 2000 election and to propose election reform measures, former President Jimmy Carter was unenthusiastic about addressing the institution. "I think it is a waste of time to talk about changing the Electoral College," Carter said. "I would predict that 200 years from now, we will still have the Electoral College."

Carter himself had led the last major effort to eliminate the Electoral College in 1977. His reasoning then was straightforward. Presidential elections should "ensure that the candidate chosen by the voters actually becomes President." Carter was joined in his effort then by Richard Nixon, Gerald Ford, Hubert Humphrey, and Edward Kennedy. Organizations like the League of Women Voters, the AFL-CIO, and the Chamber of Commerce backed his initiative. But the constitutional amendment to abolish the Electoral College crashed in the Senate, well short of the two-thirds needed to send the proposal to the states.

In the years after the 2000 election, one attempt to correct the distorting effects of the Electoral College quietly gained momentum. Rejecting a constitutional amendment strategy, backers of the National Popular Vote effort pursued a state-by-state approach. Taking advantage of the Constitution's provision giving states the unfettered right to allocate their electoral votes, the National Popular Vote is an interstate compact whereby a bloc of states agree to commit their electoral votes to ensure that the popular vote winner gains a majority in the Electoral College. Once a group of states controlling 270 electoral votes join the compact, they will then be obliged to assign enough (or if need be all) of their electoral votes to the popular vote winner—regardless of how that candidate may have fared in their states. Under the effort, the winner would always win.

In 2011, California committed its votes to the cause, binding itself to cast its electoral votes to the popular vote winner. Two previous efforts by California to join the compact had been vetoed by the state's then-Governor, Republican Arnold Schwarzenegger. When Democratic Governor Jerry Brown signed the law reordering how the state would cast its electoral votes, he noted: "California should not be taken for granted in presidential elections, and it seems logical that the occupant of the White House should be the candidate who wins the most votes. That is basic, fair democracy." As of early 2012, the measure had been enacted in states with 132 electoral votes—49 percent of the 270 electoral votes needed to activate the legislation. Backers hope the compact will become binding by 2016.

THE PROBLEM OF THE ELECTORAL COLLEGE

In our modern democracy, few people defend the Electoral College as a pure democratic institution. It distorts the direct operation of the popular vote, as historian Arthur Schlesinger Jr. has pointed out. Under it, losers can and have won. And even in modern times we are at risk it could happen again. People's votes are not counted equally. The disproportionate influence of a small group of swing states in determining the outcome of a presidential contest distorts the election process and potentially drives state-specific policy decisions at odds with national best interests. Voter turnout in nonswing states is potentially depressed, since residents of the solidly "red" and "blue" states feel their vote does not matter. And at least some analysts think the Electoral College sustains two-party dominance and inhibits the emergence of a credible third party.

But the college has its defenders. Alarmed by the progress of the National Popular Vote effort, Senator Mitch McConnell called the initiative "the most important issue in America that nobody is talking about" and decried it as an "absurd and dangerous concept. . . . We need to kill it in the cradle before it grows up."

The college's adherents defend it as an accepted and legitimate way to elect presidents. Despite winning the popular vote but losing the Electoral College vote, Gore accepted the outcome because the college system is constitutional and legal. It was the system he agreed to run under, and so he acceded to the outcome it dictated.

In addition, by giving swing and rural states an advantage in presidential elections, it encourages and rewards their residents' participation in our democracy. Without the college, analysts worry that campaigns would focus on large cities and states where the candidates are guaranteed to rack up huge vote margins. Rural states would be ignored, they fear, and while swing states might still be fought over, attention to them would slip.

Finally, defenders of the college fear that its abolition would lead to the rise of third parties fueled by intense regional or ideological passions. Those third-party candidates would upend our two-party system and deprive future presidents of majority mandates. Indeed, in 1992, Texas's H. Ross Perot captured almost 19 percent of the vote, and Bill Clinton became President with only 43 percent of the vote. Perot did not receive a single Electoral College vote. In a world where the college did not exist, third-party candidates like Perot or 2000's Green Party candidate Ralph Nader could claim more rewards for their candidacies. And what would happen if, as a result of third-party candidates, no one gained more than 40 percent of the popular vote? Would America be prepared to support presidential runoffs?

Whatever the merit of their concerns, one thing is clear. Abolishing the college (or reworking it under the National Popular Vote effort) would disrupt settled expectations. Centuries of habit, ritual, and campaign strategy would fly out the window. And Ben Leatherbury's vote in 2008—his first ever for President—would have carried the same weight as every other nineteen-year-old's.

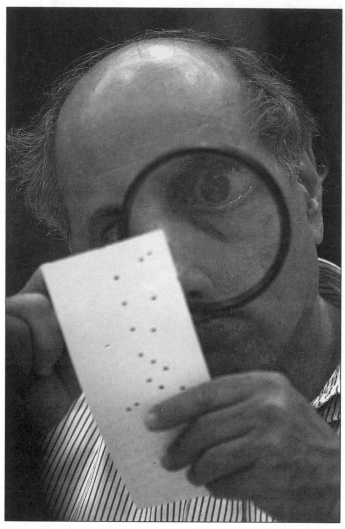

BROWARD COUNTY JUDGE ROBERT ROSENBERG INSPECTS A BALLOT DURING THE FLORIDA RECOUNT OF THE BALLOTS CAST IN THE 2000 PRESIDENTIAL CONTEST BETWEEN AL GORE AND GEORGE W. Bush. *Rosenberg, a Republican, was looking at the punch-card ballots for signs of the voter's intent and trying to determine if the voter had tried but failed to punch a hole through the ballot, leaving a "dimpled" chad. During the recount, tempers flared and at one point Broward officials called in sheriff's deputies to try to maintain order. Fewer than three weeks later, the U.S. Supreme Court halted Florida's recount.* **Photo Credit:** *The Associated Press*

CHAPTER 5

A RAMSHACKLE HOUSE

The Convoluted and Misunderstood Election System

"As the presidential election drama unfolded in Florida last November [2000], one thought was foremost in my mind: there but for the grace of God go I. Because the truth is, if the presidential margin had been razor thin in Georgia and if our election systems had undergone the same microscopic scrutiny that Florida endured, we would have fared no better. In many respects, we might have fared even worse."

Cathy Cox, chief election official of Georgia,
Testimony Before the National Commission
on Federal Election Reform, *2001*

One voter
14 constitutional provisions dealing with voting
50 individual state constitutions
13,000 election districts
110,000 polling places
220,000 full-time election officials
350,000+ voting machines

1,400,000 people working at polls on election day

133,000,000+ votes cast in 2008

186,000,000 million registered voters

$1,000,000,000+ spent annually on election
administration

* * *

A S AMERICANS WENT TO THE polls for the 2008 presidential election, many were gripped with a real fear that their votes would not be counted. They stood in long lines, deciphered poorly designed ballots, argued with poll workers when their names were missing from registration lists, contended with bewildering or malfunctioning machinery, and asked for help from harried and often poorly trained poll station volunteers. Maybe they voted early or got a provisional ballot or absentee ballot. Maybe it was counted. Many found it difficult to get a clear answer regarding where their polling station was. And too often it was impossible to know in advance what else was on the ballot, aside from the presidential candidates.

No wonder that in 2008, 30 percent of Americans doubted their own votes would be accurately counted. Even worse, 58 percent didn't think votes across the country were properly tallied. Mindful of the eroding confidence in our election system, the U.S. Department of Justice sent more than eight hundred election monitors to twenty-three states in 2008.

But if one were to ask the foremost international election monitoring group run from Atlanta's Carter Center to do the same and to send election monitors to the United States, the likely answer would be no. "Some basic international requirements for a fair election are missing," former President Jimmy Carter wrote in 2004, explaining in part why he would not monitor Florida elections, long after the 2000 debacle had spurred a nationwide voting reform movement. "The disturbing fact is that a repetition of the problems of 2000 now seems likely, even as many other nations are conducting elections that are internationally certified to be transparent, honest and fair."

A well-administered election system should be able to do two things efficiently and fairly: make sure all qualified voters who want to vote can vote and then count those votes accurately. But try as we might, America still cannot confidently say that it has a world-class election system. America's voting system is the product of myriad governmental entities, which may or may not coordinate with each other. Our system is almost entirely run on a state and local level with a modicum of federal oversight and money. We have more than thirteen thousand governmental entities in charge of voting in America. No one knows exactly how many. In general, most states have one person who oversees elections in that state— typically but not always the Secretary of State. The Secretary of State has some measure of authority, but often not much, over the counties and local governments that actually run elections in each of their areas. Our ramshackle system sprawls and twists, more often than not producing an accurate-enough result, but in the process angering and frustrating the people it is supposed to serve—voters.

LIZARD PEOPLE, THE FLYING SPAGHETTI MONSTER, DINKYTOWN, AND THE FIFTH PILE

If the presidential vote had been close in 2008, it could have been a disaster. And as it happened it was very, very close in Minnesota's Senate race. When Wednesday, November 5, 2008, dawned, Republican Senate candidate Norm Coleman led his opponent Al Franken by 726 votes, less than 0.01 percent of all the votes cast.

In the next two weeks, as is standard practice, administrators at Minnesota's voting precincts double-checked their results to announce the official results. During that time, Franken gained 191 votes after the town of Buhl remembered to call its results in. On election night itself, they forgot. "One person thought the other person was going to do it, so they both went home," said Paul Tynjala, director of elections for St. Louis County. The next morning they made the call. On November 18, after all 4,130 of Minnesota's voting precincts had diligently double-checked their counting, the official results were announced and Coleman's lead was cut to 215 votes. The margin was so close that under the state's law an automatic recount was required. And so Minnesota was launched on one of the most vitriolic, protracted, and expensive recounts in federal election history— a thirty-five-week, $10 million odyssey to figure out who exactly had won its Senate election. More ballots were recounted in Minnesota than ever before in any individual election in American history.[36]

The tightest election in Senate history pitted Republican Louis Wyman against Democrat John Durkin in New Hampshire in 1974. Initially, Wyman was declared the winner by 355 votes. But a recount pushed Durkin into the victory column by ten votes. Wyman demanded another recount, which he won by two votes.

---

[36] Prior to the Minnesota recount, Washington State had undertaken the largest hand recount in U.S. history when in 2004 it decided its Governor's race between Democrat Christine Gregoire and Republican Dino Rossi. In that election, two initial machine-based counts had given the victory to Rossi by margins of 261 and 42 votes, respectively. In the midst of the hand recount, election officials discovered several hundred absentee ballots that had been wrongly rejected. Other election officials discovered hundreds of ballots that had been hidden underneath mail trays. Gregoire was ultimately declared the victor by 129 votes. She won reelection in 2008 by a substantial margin against Rossi.

The Republican Governor of the state certified Wyman the winner. But Durkin petitioned the Democrat-controlled Senate to refuse to seat Wyman.[37] The full Senate convened a trial to determine which of the two should be seated. After looking at more than 3,500 questionable ballots shipped to Washington, D.C., from New Hampshire, the matter was debated by the full Senate, which after six votes was unable to resolve the dispute. Finally, confounded by the entire process, Durkin agreed to Wyman's proposal that they should hold a new election. New Hampshire voters turned out in record-breaking numbers for a September 1975 election. Durkin won by more than 27,000 votes. He was defeated in his next election in 1980.

In 2008, the contested Minnesota Senate election threatened to be just as tortuous. Between November 15 and December 5, every ballot was gathered and sent to one of more than one hundred tallying stations scattered throughout the state. For the election, Minnesota had uniformly used paper ballots that were fed into optical scanners to be tallied. At the hand count stations, in the presence of observers from the Coleman and Franken camps and a group of independent watchdogs, election officials inspected each and every one of the more than 2.9 million ballots cast in Minnesota that fall day in 2008. As each ballot was examined, representatives from the warring camps made challenges. Was the mark on the ballot clear? Did an "x" next to the candidate's name

---

[37] Both the Senate and the House of Representatives are the final judges of who is seated as a Senator or Representative and do not have to accept state-issued certificates declaring someone an election's victor. There have been about six hundred contested House seats requiring that body to determine if it will actually seat the putative Congressperson. Approximately two-thirds of the time, the candidate leading the vote count after the election has been seated in the House. Almost two hundred times, however, the seat has been vacated or the election result reversed.

mean that the voter was in favor of that candidate or was actually opposed? And what were they supposed to do with the voter who penned "Lizard People" on the ballot as a write-in candidate, but who also filled in the oval for Franken? Or what about the voter who wrote "Flying Spaghetti Monster" near Franken's name? (See Appendix C for examples.)

In the meantime, 133 ballots from the Dinkytown neighborhood in Minneapolis had disappeared. So the "Dinkytown ballots" entered the Minnesota political lexicon. Counted on election night, the ballots were in an envelope that was lost in the following days. Allegations flew that thirty-two ballots had been sitting in an election official's car for days and that thousands of absentee ballots had been wrongly disqualified. The Democratic Secretary of State was accused of partisan manipulation. Franken's legal team was accused by the Coleman team of using "Florida-style" tactics. Franken's team shot back, charging that Coleman was trying to "disenfranchise just enough voters that they can win."

By December 5, the first round of the recount was over. Almost 7,000 of the 2.9 million ballots inspected had been challenged by one or the other candidate. All of those ballots were bundled together and sent to the state capitol for review by the bipartisan State Canvassing Board. Over the course of the next few weeks, the five-person board set to work dealing with the challenged ballots. By December 19, they were done. The Dinkytown ballots were never found but still counted based on the election night tally. Franken led by forty-nine votes.

The Lizard People ballot was tossed out, deemed an "overvote," or to have voted for two people. Around that time Bemedji, Minnesota, resident Lucas Davenport stepped forward and identified himself as the "Lizard People" voter. "I don't know if you've heard the conspiracy theory about the Lizard Men," Davenport said. He explained that a race of shape-shifting reptiles who can appear human rule the world. Davenport did not seem to believe the Lizard Men conspiracy. Just in case, he was willing to give them a position on the Minnesota Soil and Water Conservation District. But not a Senate seat. He told reporters that he did indeed vote for Franken. Meanwhile, the "Flying Spaghetti Monster" voter did have his or her vote for Franken counted. The "Flying Spaghetti Monster" voter never came forward for an interview.

Even as the Canvassing Board was dealing with the contested ballots, its members were also debating how to handle a set of absentee ballots that had been rejected in the local precincts. More than 288,000 absentee votes had been cast during the election. Almost 12,000 were rejected by election officials for one reason or another—the signature on the ballot did not match that of the voter on file, the return address on the ballot did not match that of the voter, the ballot was sent to the wrong precinct, or the voter had already voted in person. The absentee ballots that were rejected but not for any of the four standard reasons made their way into the "fifth pile." Ultimately 933 rejected absentee ballots were sent on to the Canvassing Board to determine their eligibility to be counted. On January 2, 2009, the board took a look at them. After, Franken led Coleman by 225 votes.

Franken declared victory. Four days later, Coleman sued. Among other things, he asked that the court send inspectors to eighty-six precincts to investigate voting irregularities surrounding absentee ballots.

When the presidential inaugural festivities began in Washington, D.C., the week of January 20, Franken came to town. But he came as a tourist, in a heavy coat and a large Russian-style fur hat, and sat in the general audience to watch the President's swearing-in at a 200-yard distance. Person after person kept approaching him and asking why he wasn't sitting up front with the senators.

"Aren't you a Senator yet?" they kept asking. "In a few weeks," he answered.

It would be six months before the court cases were over and he was sworn in.[38] The former *Saturday Night Live* performer and writer never seemed to crack a smile the entire time. Two years later, Coleman joined a Washington, D.C., law firm as a lobbyist.

Between the two of them, the Coleman and Franken campaigns spent more than $10 million in legal fees on the recount. One of Franken's Seattle-based attorneys was such a regular at the Minneapolis Radisson that he eventually convinced the hotel restaurant to add a selection of Northwest wines to its menu and to buy a better grade of steak for his meals. The court cases continued long past Franken's swearing in, but for him at least it was over. Two months after Franken became a Senator, five Minnesota television stations filed a request in court to examine several hundred absentee ballots. That lawsuit ended in November 2011 when the Minnesota Supreme Court rejected the request.

In the midst of the drama, Coleman's lawyer warned, "This really is a clarion call that the system of election administration in this country is broken. And there is a great tendency to try and keep the genie in the bottle in these cases. . . . This problem is never going to get fixed in this country if places like Minnesota, which are the best in the country, sweep it under the rug instead of dealing with what really is a serious problem."

---

[38] Not every state deals with recounts the way Minnesota does. In some states, the putative victor is certified as the contingent victor even as the recount goes on. That victor pending the recount is then allowed to take his or her seat in the House or Senate. In Louisiana's contested Senate race of 1996, Democrat Mary Landrieu was seated as a Senator even though her rival, Republican Woody Jenkins, was still pursuing a recount and had asked the Senate itself to examine the validity of her election. The Senate did not end its investigation until October 1997.

It wasn't supposed to happen again. Not after Florida and the 2000 election. And in fact, as harrowing as Minnesota's experience was, in many ways it could not have happened in a better-prepared state.

Election administration is not and likely never will be a sexy topic. But for a brief period after the 2000 election, election administrators were subject to more scrutiny than they had ever wanted. Everything they did was laid bare for dissection. And the results were not pretty. Many, indeed most, of the administrators under the microscope after 2000 were dedicated public servants doing the best they could with limited resources and training. And they had to follow the law, often vague or conflicting and quite frequently mean-spirited. No one ever said setting up a system to fairly and efficiently funnel more than 133 million people to polls on one day in the fall was going to be easy. The result was a patchwork quilt of election law and election-day practices. Any system that involves that much money, power, and public attention was going to attract its share of the saintly and the foolish, the bored and the altruistic, the mercenary and the greedy, the partisan and the manipulative, the incompetent and the efficient.

They all showed up in Florida in 2000. At 4:30 A.M. the Wednesday after the presidential election, George W. Bush was leading Al Gore by 1,784 votes in that state. When the results were cross-checked, his lead dropped to around 900 votes. An automatic recount was triggered. That quick mechanical recount dropped Bush's lead to 327 and led to a manual recount in a few select counties. And the nation descended into its brief but intense obsession with hanging chads and butterfly ballots. The Florida meltdown pulled back the curtain on a system where local county election officials designed ballots that bewildered voters and then, when forced to examine the actual votes cast, looked like more like tarot card readers than dispassionate judges.

In Palm Beach County a well-meaning election official, concerned about the eyesight of the many senior citizens in her district, designed a large-print, punch-card ballot that showed the candidates for President on either side of punch holes for voting—the infamous "butterfly ballot." The names of the candidates and the punch holes did not line up well, and consequently many voters likely "voted" for the wrong person or in confusion voted twice and thereby invalidated their ballot. The butterfly ballot wasn't the only thing that confused people. The use of punch-card ballots at all in Florida in 2000 perplexed many. Most states had already abandoned the punch-card system—exasperated by breakdowns, miscounts, and voter confusion. Flint, Michigan, may have had the worst of it when a rainstorm drenched a batch of its punch-card ballots in 1970. The city was forced to bake the ballots before they could be counted, lest the counting machines shred the soggy punch cards. By 1974, Michigan had largely rejected the system. Iowa abandoned the system in 1984, and in 1988 a group of computer professionals called for punch-card voting to be banned. Yet in 2000 approximately one-third of the nation's polling places still used the technology.

When it came to the recounts in Florida, the scattershot quality of the ballots and machines used made people shake their heads. And then people began complaining about unfathomably long lines in predominantly African American districts and about voter intimidation throughout the state. Then the absentee ballots, including overseas military ballots, had to be counted.

Florida was just the tip of the iceberg. A study led by political scientists at CalTech and MIT concluded that poor ballot design and antiquated machines lost 1.5 million votes that year. In Chicago, almost one of every ten ballots for President was not tallied. The study noted that in 2000 the margin of victory for the presidential candidate was less than one-half of one percent in four states: Florida, Iowa, New Mexico, and Wisconsin. But on average that year, 2 to 3 percent of all ballots in presidential contests were spoiled and uncounted. The spoilage rate was even higher for Senate and Governor contests.

Another 1.5 to 3 million voters did not vote because of registration problems. These voters showed up at the poll only to find their names were not on the registration list. Or they tried to register but were stymied by paperwork requirements. Meanwhile, almost one million voters didn't vote because the lines at their polling stations were too long or the hours were too short.

In 2001, the University of Virginia took the reins and commissioned a group of political luminaries to look at our election system. The commission was chaired by former Presidents Carter and Ford. Even the men who helped negotiate Middle East peace treaties and who suffered through the Watergate investigation were "struck . . . by the bewildering variety of procedures, criteria, and deadlines found around the country." But the commission was not deterred. It boldly stated: "In a world of problems that often defy any solution, the weaknesses in election administration are, to a very great degree, problems that government actually can solve."

Mindful that an election administration system is supposed to accomplish two seemingly simple tasks—allow the right people to vote and then count those votes—the commission addressed some of the key components of that system. First, how we register people to vote. Second, the machines and standards we use to count the votes. Third, how we deal with problems on election day, particularly how we deal with people who want to vote but who face administrative problems.

The commission laid down some fundamental principles:

> The American people should expect all levels of government to provide a democratic process that:
> - Maintains an accurate list of citizens who are qualified to vote;
> - Encourages every eligible voter to participate effectively;

- Uses equipment that reliably clarifies and registers the voter's choices;
- Handles close elections in a foreseeable and fair way;
- Operates with equal effectiveness for every citizen and every community; and
- Reflects limited but responsible federal participation.

The most startling thing about the commission's recommendations was that they had to be stated at all. It took a soul-searing experience like the 2000 election to force so obvious a set of observations and to get Congress to act on them.

By late October 2002, Congress had responded to many of the commission's suggestions and passed the Help America Vote Act, the most extensive and costly federal involvement in voting since the Voting Rights Act of 1965. The legislation authorized the injection of $3.9 billion into the election administration system—a cash infusion meant to upgrade voting machines, registration systems, and election administration as a whole. And it instituted a host of new improvements to our voting system. Confounded by the continued use of obsolete voting machines like the punch-card system, the lawmakers required that states upgrade their voting equipment. Embarrassed by reports that millions did not vote due to registration errors, the commission tackled both ends of the problem: upgrade voter registration systems and when all else fails make sure people who make it to the polls can cast a provisional ballot. Finally, frustrated by the lack of reliable data about election-related spending, practices, and results, Congress created a bipartisan commission tasked with collecting data and pushing reform.

MAKING A LIST AND CHECKING IT TWICE

In the two-year period following the 2008 election, state election administrators faced a tidal wave of more than 45 million registration forms, which was probably a relief after dealing with the record-number 60 million forms they received between 2006 and 2008. Every one of the forms had to be reviewed and processed in a labor-intensive, largely paper-based system that threatens to overwhelm officials. And every data entry slip, lost document, or misread form jeopardizes voters. But the election officials did their job. They filed changes of address. They registered new voters, and more than four million times, they rejected the form either because it was invalid or a duplicate.

The United States is one of only a few industrialized democratic nations that places the entire burden of registration on voters themselves. Figure it out yourself, America says to its voters. Every state has its own system and requirements, and even within the state the system might vary on a county-by-county basis. America keeps company principally with the Bahamas, Belize, Burundi, and Mexico in how we manage voter registration.

Throughout the rest of the world—from Iraq to England, Indonesia to Sweden—election administrators affirmatively attempt to build comprehensive and accurate voter rolls. There is considerable variation from country to country. In Australia, individual voter registration is mandatory, but the government also gathers data from a variety of databases and sends registration material to citizens it thinks are unregistered. In Saskatchewan, Canada, officials go door-to-door registering eligible voters prior to each major election. Throughout Canada, voters the administrators miss are allowed to register at the polls on election day. In Great Britain, election administrators conduct an annual canvass, mailing registration forms to each household and going door-to-door.

The effort pays off. Countries that take proactive steps to get people to register have significantly higher registration rates than does the United States. In the wake of a notably corrupt election in 1988, Mexico scrapped its entire voter registration system and built a new one from the ground up. The nation invested more than $1 billion in the system. It began by conducting a nationwide, door-to-door registration effort. Voters were issued unique voter identification cards with their photo and fingerprint. Today in Mexico, new voters are required to register in person, but the government also deploys mobile registration units. Using a registration system constructed for modern times and not cobbled together from outdated legacy systems, 95 percent of the eligible population is registered. In France, 91 percent of eligible voters are registered. In Indonesia, the number stands at 94 percent.

The United States consistently ranks last or near the bottom of every industrialized democracy in its registration rate. The percentage of registered voters in the United States as a percentage of the eligible population hovers between 68 and 72, and in some states the registration rate is much lower. Experts pin the blame squarely on a complex, cumbersome registration system, designed for the nineteenth century.

The earliest voter registration scheme in the United States was adopted by Massachusetts in 1801. But the registration mandate picked up steam in the late 1830s, when in the midst of an Irish and German immigration surge more states and local governments began implementing registration requirements in order to inhibit those immigrants from voting. Proponents of registration said they were trying to prevent fraud. But many early registration requirements were imposed in cities with high Democratic-voting immigrant populations while exempting rival party rural strongholds. By the 1870s, registration systems were spreading throughout the nation.[39]

Today, one state spurns voter registration: North Dakota. North Dakota abolished its voter registration system in 1951. Given the

---

[39] As late as 1927, eleven states in the Midwest still imposed registration requirements in cities while exempting rural districts.

vast distances and small population of the state, the registration requirement was proving too restrictive. And in a small rural state
with small voting precincts, legislators reasoned, everyone should
know everyone. So registration was scrapped more than sixty years
ago. Today, voters who walk into polls and who are on a list as having voted before are allowed to cast a ballot. New voters to a precinct are allowed to vote if a qualified person at the poll knows the
new voter. Even a complete stranger can vote as long as he or she
signs a form swearing that he or she is qualified to vote.

Until the passage of the Voting Rights Act in 1965,[40] many registration schemes were shamelessly constructed to disqualify and discourage people from voting. Literacy tests imposed throughout the
nation kept blacks from voting in the South and immigrants from
voting in the North and West. Long residency requirements also
aimed to disenfranchise immigrants. After the Voting Rights Act
was amended in 1970, other barriers to registration were dropped.
Requirements like Tennessee's, mandating that a voter must have
lived in the state for a year and in the particular county for three
months, were scrapped. Similarly, people were henceforth allowed
to register for presidential elections up to thirty days before the
election.

---

[40] While much of the Voting Rights Act was enacted using the federal
government's power to enforce the Fourteenth and Fifteenth Amendments,
other parts of it were derived from the Constitution's "Elections Clause."
Article One, Section Four of the Constitution gives Congress the power
to regulate federal elections: "The Times, Places and Manner of holding
Elections for Senators and Representatives, shall be prescribed in each State
by the Legislature thereof; but Congress may at any time make or alter such
Regulations." However, it cannot directly tell states how to administer non-
federal elections. Practically, though, states are unlikely to set up dual election
systems, one for federal and one for state elections. Consequently, federal
election mandates tend to become systemwide, but not always. For example,
registration deadlines still are enormously variable.

While the Voting Rights Act and the Twenty-fourth Amendment eliminated some of the more overtly discriminatory registration requirements, they did not address the labyrinthine set of registration practices developed by state and local governments. Many of those systems seemed practical or neutral, but they all took a toll on voters and registration efforts. The location of registration centers was often hard to discover or inconvenient to access. The hours kept were restrictive and problematic for people who had to work. The documentation required to register could be intricate. Registration might need to be renewed every few years, and if the voter had not showed up at the polls after a certain number of elections had passed, he or she might be purged from the lists. There are still minimum residency requirements and various deadlines for registration prior to the election. Registration rolls were often kept on paper, making updates difficult and introducing numerous errors onto the rolls.

Even into the late twentieth century, the registration system was a bureaucratic obstacle course for all involved. (And many would say it remains so.) While voter registration had surged in the wake of the Voting Rights Act of 1965, the following years saw a steady decline in registration rates. The people most likely to fall down on the obstacle course were the poor, minorities, students, and the elderly.

In the late 1970s and early 1980s, Republican Party and Democratic Party activists entered the fray with concentrated voter registration efforts. They decided to bring the mountain to Mohammed. Democrats were motivated by a quick look at the demographics. Surveys indicated that almost half of the eligible unregistered population was Democratic, while only a third was Republican. Republicans decided they had to match Democrats' efforts. The Moral Majority took its registration drive to the churches, set up phone banks, and ultimately claimed to have registered four to eight million people in the mid-1980s. The number was probably more like two million. Democratic activists likely brought another two million voters into the system, and African American registration rates rose to their highest level since the 1960s.

The Democratic registration drives of the late 1980s concentrated on locations where lower-income and minority voters were likely to be: welfare and unemployment offices, mass transit hubs, food banks. But they were not always well-received by elections administrators. A Cincinnati, Ohio, volunteer was arrested at a welfare office where he was registering voters. He was taken to the local precinct and strip-searched. Robin Leeds, working for a registration drive in Boston, had to spend weeks negotiating with the local Democrat-dominated city administration to set up a registration table at a major subway stop serving an African American population. The local Democrats were predominantly white and feared the impact an influx of African American voters would have on their power. When she finally got permission and showed up on the appointed day, the necessary election officials arrived hours late and left hours early.

Over time, critics of the shabby voter registration systems used throughout the nation made headway, and many states began upgrading their systems. They started affirmatively offering voter registration forms at driver's license and welfare offices. They began to allow registration by mail. In Michigan, which adopted many of these reforms early, voter turnout increased by more than 10 percent. However, many states refused. Republicans were worried that easier registration would benefit Democrats. "They are using taxpayers' money to register predominantly Democrats. There are not a lot of Republicans in the welfare lines," the chairman of the Texas Republican Party in the mid-1980s said. But by the late 1980s, Democratic Party activists were determined to force recalcitrant state and local governments to make registration easier. In 1992, they succeeded in persuading Congress to pass the National Voter

Registration Act. During the Fourth of July weekend that year, President George H.W. Bush vetoed the bill. He warned that the legislation would "[create an] unacceptable risk of fraud and corruption without any reason to believe that it would increase electoral participation to any significant degree."

One year later, President Bill Clinton signed a similar measure requiring (for federal elections at least) that states support simultaneous applications for a driver's license and voter registration, registration by mail, and registration at public service agencies like unemployment offices. After the law was implemented, registration did surge. In fewer than two years, nine million new voters entered the rolls. They were, as feared by some, predominantly Democrats, although in the South there was a notable increase in Republican registration. Today, 60 percent of all voter registration-related activity occurs via one of the three means implemented by the National Voter Registration Act, popularly known as the Motor Voter Act.[41] Fewer than 15 percent of people register in person at a dedicated voter registration office.

By the time the Help America Vote Act passed in 2002, the United States had a crazy quilt voter registration system full of legacy systems and deeply entrenched bureaucratic habits. The combined effect of the National Voter Registration Act and the Help

---

[41] Implementation of the Motor Voter Act's provisions is still inconsistent. Some states have done a far better job complying with its spirit than others. In 2011, for example, the U.S. Department of Justice sued the state of Rhode Island, asserting that four of its social service agencies had failed to provide the necessary registration forms. After the lawsuit was settled, registration via those agencies skyrocketed. In the two years prior to the lawsuit, 457 people had registered via the four agencies. In the four months after the settlement, 4,171 registration forms were submitted from the agencies' offices.

One of the major provisions of the act dealt with how and when voters can be removed from registration lists. That matter will be discussed in Chapter 6.

America Vote Act has been to significantly improve America's voter registration system, though not to the point where we can claim to have a system on par with either Mexico or Great Britain.

In the twenty-first century, registration reform has focused on two goals: making sure that registering is easy and straightforward, and cleaning up rolls so that they are accurate. The two goals are often at odds in the political arena. When a man in Albuquerque registers his dog Buddy, people fear widespread voter registration fraud. They call for ever-stricter registration rules. In response, the state might require that people who register present a Social Security card, and in consequence registration becomes increasingly difficult. But the main barrier to achieving these goals has been the diffuse distribution of registration authority throughout the states coupled with a reluctance to implement or pay for modern upgrades. Most of the problems could in fact be solved with sophisticated systems built for the modern era, the way Mexico did.

In most states prior to 2002, voter registration was accomplished on a local basis. And each county or city staffed registration offices differently and kept roll books differently. Faced with such a system, the Help America Vote Act aimed small. Rather than scrapping the system and starting with a new, modern approach, the act basically tried to improve coordination. The act aimed to generate more of a top-down, statewide approach. With state-level registration rolls and systems in place, registration could theoretically become more systematic and resources would be better allocated. Local and county offices would still have a vital role to play. Not only are they the main point of contact for registering voters, but on election day itself, their precincts and election officials are the ones who check the voter registration rolls before giving people access to the ballot box.

By the time the 2008 election rolled around, progress had been haphazard. Many states had begun creating statewide voter registration systems. But three of the five largest states, California, Illinois, and New York, with more than 20 percent of the population, still used diffuse local systems (as they do to this day). Texas, the fourth of the five largest states, uses a mixed system where many counties still are not integrated into the overall structure. In 2012, a major research institute, the Pew Center on the States, evaluated the systems and found approximately 24 million—one of every eight—voter registrations in the United States were either invalid or significantly inaccurate. Large numbers of dead people—1.8 million—remain on voter rolls. Almost 3 million people had multiple registrations. The voter rolls, in short, are still a mess.

The disorder of voter registration lists is not due to massive fraud, concerted efforts to steal elections, or gross incompetence by election officials. It's due to the way Americans live: they move; they have messy handwriting; they have nicknames. When people die, their surviving relatives have many higher priorities than calling the voter registration office to take the name off the list. One in eight Americans moves every year. In fact, almost a quarter of all Americans between the ages of twenty-five and thirty-four moved in 2009. A substantial portion of all Americans mistakenly believe that the postal service or local election officials will automatically update their registration file when they move.[42] Yet, they do not know that they can update their registration file via their Department of Motor Vehicles office at the same time that they change the address on their driver's license. Meanwhile, when they do fill out voter registration forms, it is almost always handwritten. Perhaps their numeral seven looks like a one. And when they show up at the polls and give their address, they are rejected as unregistered because the information was incorrectly entered into the system.

---

[42] Some of them are right, as a few states have begun doing this.

Meanwhile, at least 51 million eligible voters are unregistered. Stories about dead people or pets on registration lists make good copy. But the mania for orderly registration rolls has had troubling implications. Every year, millions of people who want to register are deterred. To be sure, not all unregistered people want to register. But one recent study found that in 2008, 5.7 million people faced a registration-related problem that had to be resolved before they could vote. Another 3 million people didn't even try to vote that year because of registration-related problems.

Maricopa County, Arizona, which includes Phoenix, got a head start on most other election districts. In 2002, it shifted to online voter registration. Its error rate dropped. Voters could even go online to check out their registration status, find their polling station, and track the status of their absentee ballots. County costs dropped dramatically. In fact, the average cost of voter registration in Maricopa is $.03 per voter, more than 90 percent lower than the average throughout the United States. But while Maricopa is a beacon of modern, efficient voter registration, Arizona as a whole lags behind in cleaning up its voter rolls. Meanwhile in Oregon, taxpayers paid $8.8 million for voter registration, an average of $7 per transaction.[43]

But even Maricopa has its problems. Registration might be easy, but how easy is actually voting? In the fall of 2011, Phoenix voters were asked to select a new Mayor. Democratic candidate Greg Stanton made education one of the centerpieces of his campaign. Meanwhile, local school districts had proposed new bond initiatives, desperately seeking cash from the voters after their budgets had been cut. In the early part of the decade, Phoenix had one of the highest

---

[43] As of 2010, secure online voter registration was available in seven states and was under development in at least five more.

high school dropout rates in the nation. The schools had begun to improve, but the budget cuts threatened the progress. And so the voters set off to cast their ballots in November 2011. But they had to go to not one but two polling places. City elections—for Mayor and city council—were held in one set of locations. County elections, on school board and public financing measures, were held in another. For Phoenix resident James Eastwood that meant he first had to go to his local library to vote for Mayor and then to the Salvation Army more than a mile away to vote on the school-district proposal. "You have to be really committed to voting," one Phoenix voter said.

Why can't voter registration systems work better? When they do, voter turnout goes up, notably.[44] And modern technology offers ample opportunity to build efficient systems, ones that are coordinated with other private and government databases and that minimize error while making it easy for people to register. But we use horse-and-buggy voter registration systems in the information age. In consequence our systems "are plagued with errors and inefficiencies that waste taxpayer dollars, undermine voter confidence, and fuel partisan disputes over the integrity of our elections," as the Pew Center on the States said.

The Help America Vote Act sought to create at least one failsafe mechanism: the provisional ballot. If a would-be voter walked into the polling station and poll workers could not find his or her name on the registration list or faced any other insurmountable barrier to voting, the voter would be offered a provisional ballot to be counted if the mix-up could be resolved.[45] Prior to 2000, seventeen

---

[44] States with lower registration burdens have turnout levels 7 to 10 percent higher than states with high registration barriers.

[45] To have a provisional ballot counted, the voter must still have been registered prior to election day. A number of states do not use provisional ballots because they allow voters to register on election day.

states had begun using provisional ballots to deal with administrative errors on election day. Still, one post-2000 election study had shown that as many as 1.5 million votes could have been "saved" if provisional ballots had been in place, particularly in Florida where numerous voters' names had been improperly struck from registration lists.

It seemed like a fairly commonsense proposal. And in 2004, 1.9 million provisional ballots were cast, demonstrating explicitly the sheer volume of administrative mess-ups on election day. Almost two-thirds of those provisional ballots were ultimately counted. In the 2008 election, the number of provisional ballots shot up to 2.2 million. Again, almost two-thirds of them were ultimately counted. A large portion of the rejections were because the voter was not properly registered. But a substantial portion was rejected because the voter, though registered, filed the provisional ballot in the wrong precinct.

In 2004, registered Missouri voter Claude Hawkins went to four Kansas City polling sites, trying to vote. He first went to the polling station he had voted at in the previous election. He then went to a polling station near his house. Each time he was told he was in the wrong place. But no one could tell him where he should go. Board of Election phones went unanswered all day. Finally, when he reached his fourth polling location, Hawkins used a provisional ballot. A few days after the election, he got a postcard from the board of elections telling him where his official polling place was. But his provisional ballot was rejected because he had filed it in the wrong precinct. After the twenty-four-year-old sued, his vote was counted in time for the final election results.

In the 2010 Cincinnati, Ohio, election, voters went to the polls to select a new juvenile court judge. They were confronted with a choice between Republican John Williams and Democrat Tracie Hunter, hoping to be the first African American juvenile court judge in the city's history. Two weeks after the election, after the state counted all the absentee and provisional ballots, Williams was declared the winner by twenty-three votes. Hunter immediately went to work and filed a court case to keep Williams from being officially certified the election's winner. Hunter wanted a large number of rejected provisional ballots to be counted. As it turned out, at least 269 people had used provisional ballots that had been rejected because while they showed up at the right voting station they went to the wrong precinct desk within the room.

"Right church, wrong pew," Hunter's supporters called it. If those voters had walked about twenty-five feet across the room to a different desk, their votes would have counted. Most of the problems had been caused by poll-worker error. In some cases, poll workers failed to advise voters that they had to go to another precinct to cast their provisional ballot and have it counted. Another poll worker directed some voters to the wrong precinct because he confused "odd" and "even" numbers. Another just let anyone vote at his precinct even if he knew the voter was in the wrong precinct. (Statewide in Ohio in 2011, more than 11,000 provisional ballots, 16 percent of all provisional ballots cast, were rejected for the same reason.)

So in late November 2010, Hunter sued. A district court judge ruled in her favor and said the rejected ballots should be counted. The County Board of Elections prepared to do so. Then in early 2011, a new Republican Secretary of State took office, reversed the decision of his Democratic predecessor on ballot counting, and ordered the County Board of Elections, under his jurisdiction, to declare John Williams the winner. The board then appealed the district court's ruling. It lost. The case came back to the district court. The election board lost again. In early 2012 the Secretary of State directed the board to appeal the case again. More than fifteen months after the election, the judge's seat remained open as the dispute over 269 ballots went on. But in mid-2011, Ohio's

Republican Governor appointed Williams to fill another vacant seat on the court. If Hunter wins her case, the Cincinnati Board of Elections will be obliged to reimburse her for her legal fees, likely $1.4 million. Administering the entire 2010 election in Cincinnati cost about $1.6 million.

Voter confusion in Cincinnati about precincts and polling locations shouldn't surprise anyone, much less the professionals who run elections. Nationwide, in 2008, 2 percent of voters, or 2.6 million people, reported difficulty finding their polling station. Another 2.1 million said that one of the reasons they did not vote was because they did not know where their polling stations were. One voter assistance hotline project that took more than 200,000 calls on election day reported that the two most common questions were "Am I registered?" and "Where is my polling place?" When the hotline forwarded the callers to local boards of election, the calls went unanswered half the time. By 2010, forty-eight states had finally implemented online polling location lookup tools for all of their voters. California and Vermont are the holdouts, with only partial systems in place.

At a high level, the provisional ballot system is a model of success. In 2008, more than 1.3 million people's votes were saved by the system. But in some states the system is still creaky. One pattern seems to be emerging: those states that have embraced provisional ballots and make frequent use of them also count more of them. Other states are stingy—both in providing them and then in counting them. Three states accounted for almost 60 percent of all provisional ballots cast in 2008: California, New York, and Ohio. Both California and Ohio ultimately counted more than 80 percent of their provisional ballots. New York counted 60 percent. However, in Texas and Virginia, where less than 0.1 percent of all ballots were provisional, more than 70 percent of the provisional ballots were rejected.

Voters in ten states had the ultimate fail-safe: show up at the poll on election day and register then and there. (And, as previously

noted, in an eleventh state, North Dakota, no one needs to register.) Idaho, Iowa, Maine, Minnesota, Montana, New Hampshire,
North Carolina, Washington, D.C., Wisconsin, and Wyoming all
allow election-day voter registration.[46] Not surprisingly, many of
these states have among the highest voter turnout rates in the nation, 10 to 12 percent higher on average. (Idaho and Wyoming have
turnout rates that are about average.) Election-day registration is a
user-friendly system that works for a variety of voters, from women
who have to look after young children, to young mobile students, to
people with disabilities. And since the registration occurs in person
and in front of an official, the chance for mischief is low.

But in the summer of 2011, Maine's legislature repealed its thirty-
eight-year-old same-day registration provision, a system implemented in the midst of the Watergate scandals. Republican Party
activists led the charge, with the state's Republican Party Chairman
Charlie Webster compiling a list of 206 college student voters who
he said should be investigated for voter fraud. They paid out-of-state
tuition but voted in Maine. It was not clear that they had registered
on election day, but nevertheless Webster wanted the state to investigate whether the student voters should be charged with a crime.
If they had committed voter fraud, they could be sentenced to up to
five years in prison.

Webster also feared that people would drive in from Canada to
vote in Maine's elections. "Do we want people who live in a mo-
tel deciding who we send to the state legislature when they never

---

[46] Washington, D.C. is technically not a state. Alaska, Connecticut and Rhode
Island allow same-day voter registration for presidential elections. Most but
not all of the ten states allow registration at the polling place, but some require
that prospective voters go to a separate registration site first before going to the
polls. In several other states, early voting and registration days overlap, but they
are not considered election-day registration states.

vote again in Maine?" he asked. "Do we want people who are illegal aliens—illegal Americans—from Canada or another state?. . . Do we want them influencing our elections?"

In the wake of Webster's charges, Maine's Secretary of State Charlie Summers launched an investigation into student and illegal alien voting. Almost three months after the legislature had voted to undo same-day voter registration, he announced his findings. The students had not committed voter fraud. But Summers had sent letters to many of the students warning them that they were under investigation. He told them that if they wanted truly to be residents of the state eligible to vote, they would have to register their cars in Maine. He also found one non-citizen who had voted, an El Salvadoran who voted in Portland, Maine, in 2002. The man had since been deported.

Summers's findings tracked those of academics who have analyzed whether fraud occurs in states with election-day voter registration. One study analyzed 4,000 news reports relating to fraud from 1999 to 2005 and found exactly one verifiable incident of voter impersonation: a seventeen-year-old who shared the same name as his father and who voted in his name in the New Hampshire Republican presidential primaries.

On election day 2011, Maine's voters reinstated election-day registration by a wide margin, 60 to 40 percent. As he cast his ballot to restore same-day registration, Augusta, Maine, voter George Cemodanovs noted, "With all the hubbub that was raised, they didn't really find anything to speak of that was a problem."

From Kangaroo Voting to Residual Votes

Cemodanovs voted using a paper ballot. Everyone in Maine does today. But until 1831, most elections in Maine were conducted publicly. People voted by voice or by holding up their hands, as they did in most states. Early American and pre-revolutionary elections were

often raucous affairs with "barbequed oxen, kegs of rum and everybody roaring drunk." By the mid-nineteenth century, however,
most states had begun using paper ballots. But election officials did
not print standard ballots for use by voters. Voters either hand-wrote
their selections on scraps of paper or came in with pre-printed ballots. Political parties widely distributed these pre-printed ballots to
voters with only that party's candidates on the slip of paper. Voters
then folded them up and dropped them in the ballot box. Early versions of the pre-printed ballots gave voters room to scratch out candidates' names and write in alternates. But parties soon learned
from their mistakes and began printing ballots that were so tightly
packed that most voters simply voted the straight party line. Since
most of the pre-printed ballots were visually distinctive from one
another—different colors, different shapes—officials and observers
at polling places were easily able to see who voted for whom. The
system was remarkably vulnerable to intimidation and corruption.
Reform-minded individuals in the late nineteenth century decided
to take it on. (See Appendix C for examples.)

One of the first men to look at the rickety system for casting and
counting votes was America's greatest inventor, Thomas Alva Edison.
In 1869, at age twenty-two, the Ohio-born Edison made the fate-
ful decision to abandon his job as a telegraph operator and commit
himself to inventing full time. His first patent was issued on June 1,
1869: "Patent Number 90,646 for the Electrographic Vote Recorder."
Shortly after the patent was issued, an investor took the device to
Washington, D.C., to show to a member of Congress. He was rebuffed. "If there is any invention on earth that we don't want down
here, that is it," a Representative told him. Edison read the market and
quickly moved on from voting equipment. His next invention was an
improved stock market tickertape machine. He made a fortune on it.

Instead, America's first major revolution in voting technology
was imported from Australia. In 1856, Australia was the first nation

to begin using uniform ballots with all candidates' names printed on them at the government's expense. The Australian ballot significantly decreased the likelihood of voter intimidation by making voting a private act and, when coupled with voter registration systems, decreased the opportunity for ballot box stuffing. It was much harder to cram a ballot box full of party tickets where there were actual records of how many people voted in a precinct and when the number of preprinted ballots was closely controlled. Of course, the Australian ballot did not eliminate intimidation and ballot fraud. They shifted in form. Election fraud henceforth turned on how ballots were counted. And election officials created ever more clever ways to throw out ballots. Was an "x" a mark in favor or against the candidate? Did the voter leave extraneous marks on the ballot? There was still plenty of room to manipulate the vote.

The United States was slow to adopt the Australian ballot, derided as "kangaroo voting." Opponents worried that it was yet another literacy test. Since literacy was not widespread among some groups of voters in late nineteenth-century America, filling out a long, complex preprinted ballot could be daunting. Moreover, government-produced, pre-printed ballots thrust election officials into the process of candidate selection. New bureaucratic schemes and barriers unfurled to determine whose names and what parties would have access to the ballot. Nevertheless, in 1888 the Australian ballot was in use in parts of Kentucky. By 1896, it was in use in thirty-nine states. The *Encyclopedia Americana* noted in 1911, "This ballot was intended to encourage freedom of choice on the part of the voters, and while it seemingly makes it easy to split the ticket (or to cast an independent ticket) it ofttimes disfranchises the voter because of his mistake in marking it."

The lever voting machine followed on the heels of the Australian ballot. Lockport, New York, near the northern end of the Erie Canal, introduced the Myers Automatic Booth lever voting machine in 1892. Its manufacturer, Jacob Myers, bragged that it would "protect mechanically the voter from rascaldom, and make the process of casting the ballot perfectly plain, simple and secret." Myers viewed the machine as the perfect antidote to the problems of the Australian ballot. Counting votes was easy: read the vote tally mechanically recorded in the machine. It was not vulnerable to the subjective counting rules used on Australian ballots. And the machine could also be configured for easy use by illiterate voters. All the candidates from a particular party could be lined up in a row, allowing straight ticket voting.

In that first Lockport election, Myers's machine produced unexpected results. The Democrat-dominated city council had bought the machines. In 1892, Lockport voters used the new lever voting machines to toss them out of office. Lockport became a haven for reform-minded Republicans. Meanwhile, Myers's hometown of Rochester, New York, followed Lockport's example and in 1896 became the largest city to use the machines citywide. Seventy-three machines did all the counting. It was a disaster. Myers's machines had a manufacturing defect causing them to rapidly degrade and miscount votes. Myers was fired by his own company's board of directors. Dejected, Myers moved to the Yukon to pan for gold.

But other companies moved into the space and produced lever machines that did not break down. Despite its terrible experience in 1896, two years later, Rochester was still using lever voting machines. Almost every major city quickly followed suit, including New York City.[47] And New York City clung to its lever voting machines for more than one hundred years until it switched machines in 2010—but only after being sued by the U.S. Department of Justice for violating provisions of the Help America Vote Act.

---

[47] In general, lever voting machines tended to be concentrated in urban areas where the larger tax base could support the purchase of the half-ton machines. Suburban and rural districts tended to use paper ballots.

New York had the worst record in the nation for complying with that law's requirements.

The Help America Vote Act had at least one clear mission—and billions of dollars to help make its point—to eliminate punch-card and lever voting machines. Those systems were clearly, unquestionably outmoded. Lever machines made recounts virtually impossible. They produced no permanent record of individual voter intent. So while one could recheck the totals, vote-by-vote reinspections were impossible. Punch-card systems with their high error rates were anathema after Florida. The act required, for federal elections at least, that states use voting machines that let voters correct errors in their ballots before finalizing them, produce a paper record so a manual audit would be possible, are accessible to voters with disabilities or alternative language needs, and have "a uniform and nondiscriminatory definition of what constituted a vote." No more haggling over dimpled chads after the law passed. No more senior citizens who voted twice for President because the ballot design misled them.

In the four years after the Help America Vote Act passed, more than half of America's election districts installed new voting machines. Election officials chose between two competing systems: direct recording electronic voting machines and optical scan systems. The electronic voting machines are much like ATM machines: the voter taps on a screen to vote. Optical scan systems use paper ballots that often look like SAT tests, and people vote by filling in the oval. The ballots are then fed into an optical reader, which tallies the votes.

Voters resisted both new devices. Decades of experience with old machines made many people resistant to new systems. And election administrators fumbled about as they learned new systems.

One of the biggest beneficiaries of the act was New York State, which got a $221 million check from the federal government to implement its provisions. The state pledged to use the money to upgrade its registration systems by November 2004 and to replace its lever voting machines by then too. It didn't make the deadline, not by a mile. So the state asked for and got a hall pass from the federal government. But in March 2006, with no realistic end to New York's delays in sight, the U.S. Department of Justice sued. More than four years later, in late 2010, New York City finally rolled out its new voting machines—paper ballots, with optical scanners to do the counting.

That year, New York voters were selecting their new Governor in a race fought between the son of a former Governor, Andrew Cuomo, and a colorful upstate businessman, Carl Paladino. Many voters were predictably confused and uncomfortable with the new paper ballots and scanning machines. They missed their lever voting machines, which had both a nostalgic appeal and a reassuringly solid feel. Many worried that the privacy of their vote was violated when they had to insert the ballot face up into the scanner. (As it turned out, they could insert it in a way that prevented the poll worker from seeing their votes, but not all poll workers knew that the machines worked that way.)

Some voters got mysterious messages from the scanning machine when they fed their ballot in to be counted: "You have over-voted. Do you want to proceed and cast this ballot or start again?" Not surprisingly most voters had no idea what the machine meant. What it meant was that they had filled in the oval for two of the gubernatorial candidates and needed to fix the ballot (by selecting only one oval) so it would be counted. Many people did not understand the flashing message on the scanner, almost 20,000 people statewide. In two Bronx election districts in New York City, almost 40 percent of the votes were not counted because they were "over-votes."

The 2000 election and the Help America Vote Act forced election administrators to reexamine voting fundamentals, like what is a vote and how do we count them? Ideally, voting machines are supposed to do two things: clearly present voters with their choices and then count those selections. Overall, the whole system should be secure, accurate, and fast, with those two final goals in tension with one another on occasion.

Post-2000, election administrators began refining the metrics they use to determine if they were meeting those goals. The primary measurements they use are residual vote rates and recount discrepancies. A "residual vote" is essentially the gap between the number of people who showed up at a polling place to vote and the number of votes counted for a particular ballot option. Typically the residual vote rate for "top of the ballot" races is very low. Most people who vote during a presidential election do cast a ballot for President. They may skip voting on a bond issue or a state Senate race, but the headline race grabs their attention. The further down the ballot, the higher the residual vote rate. By gathering the data across all races, election officials can see patterns and deviations from the norm.

When ten thousand people show up at one polling place to vote, but the machine only counts eight thousand votes for President, something is wrong. The problem could be the machine. The problem could be the way the ballot was designed. Print too small, maybe? Ballot unbelievably confusing? Palm Beach County—with its butterfly ballots—had a 6.4 percent residual vote rate in 2000, four times the statewide average. In fact punch-card machines produce higher residual vote rates than all other voting machines. Had Florida been gathering data prior to 2000, it likely would have spotted the problem with punch-card voting and with the butterfly ballot design particularly. Post-2000 residual vote rate analysis provided a powerful new diagnostic for spotting problems.

When 40 percent of the votes in two Bronx districts were "residual," the New York City Board of Elections should have known it had a problem. After all, in the rest of the city the residual vote count was less than one percent. But the Board of Elections either did not know or did not care about the problem. Then an outside legal group,

New York University's Brennan Center for Justice, gathered the data and published the results. But even then not all the data were available. More than half of the precincts in the city could not provide a residual vote count. When the Board of Elections failed to act on the shocking data, a New York City newspaper, *The Daily News*, got in on the act. In a first, the paper managed to get access to the actual ballots that were rejected as "over-votes." It found that the same scanner misread 156 ballots out of 289. It said they were "over-votes," that is, two ovals filled in when only one should have been. But when reporters looked at the ballots, all of them were correctly filled in. The machine seemed to be defective. The Board of Elections didn't comment.

Meanwhile, after the Brennan Center sued the Board of Elections, it agreed to change the "over-vote" wording to something approaching normal English,[48] something like, "You filled in too many ovals" and "These votes will not count."

Up in northern New York state, not too far from Lockport and near Niagara Falls, the 2012 city council election turned on results from its Third Ward. After the November election, Republican Augustine Beyer was declared the winner over Democrat Richard Slisz by one vote out of 869 cast. But thirty-one ballots showed no vote at all. After Slisz went to court to open the ballots, an inspection found that one voter had circled the oval for Slisz rather than fully filling it in. The race was tied. Then they found a ballot that the machine just hadn't counted. It was for Slisz, who now was the victor by one vote.

In Florida, election officials, chastened by 2000, moved much more quickly than New York. Most Florida officials opted for touch screen e-voting machines, like ATMs. Of all the new voting devices adopted after 2000, electronic voting machines faced the stiffest re-

---

[48] Or its Spanish or other language equivalent.

sistance. The devices were not new and had been used in many voting districts prior to 2000. And many election administrators saw real benefits to using the e-voting machines. They could be programmed in multiple languages. They were particularly useful for voters with disabilities.

But their rapid adoption in a climate of distrust and fear over vote counting after the Florida fiasco led to heightened opposition. Many of the machines lacked any mechanism for producing paper to independently verify counts. Without any physical audit trail, voters and academics worried that machine breakdowns and problems could not be caught. Then one academic gamely proved that within one minute he could hack an e-voting machine and reprogram it.

So when the 2006 Florida results in its election for a new member of Congress in its 13th congressional district came in, residents of the Sunshine State were stunned to find that their system had broken down again. And in the ultimate irony, the House seat in play had been held by Katherine Harris, the polarizing Florida Secretary of State who had overseen the 2000 vote recount. The 2006 election for her seat in Congress set Republican Vern Buchanan against Democrat Christine Jennings. Buchanan won by 369 votes. The 13th congressional district, on the west coast of Florida, covers four counties including Sarasota and Manatee. But when the residual vote metric came in, Sarasota County had a problem. Fourteen percent of the ballots in the race were not counted. More than 18,000 votes were at stake in an election whose margin of victory was 369.

Cries of fraud, election theft, corruption, computer bugs, and hacking rang out. Some people argued that 14 percent of the voters just decided not to vote in that race, an assertion that was quickly rebutted by looking at the data in other counties. In the end, the problem likely stemmed from something far more prosaic: ballot design. In Sarasota, the House race had been listed on the same screen as the Governor's race. The Governor's race had been highlighted and occupied almost 75 percent of the screen. Voters probably just inadvertently skipped the House race. And in fact, in election after election, residual vote rates spike when two races are put on the same e-voting screen. But it was all speculation. Since the machines had no paper trail, there was no way to see whether 18,000 votes were cast but not counted because of a computer bug, whether 18,000 people had over-voted, or whether 18,000 people had simply not voted at all.

In the wake of the Sarasota election crisis, many states began requiring that their e-voting machines also generate a paper trail for each vote. Theoretically at least, the voter can then look at the paper ballot and confirm that all of his or her votes were properly recorded. Of course, few people actually do so.

Other states that had just spent millions to buy the touchscreen voting machines decided to scrap them and buy optical scan systems. Cuyahoga County, Ohio, which includes Cleveland, spent $21 million to buy e-voting machines shortly after 2004. November 2007's election in Cuyahoga was not pretty. It was a local, off-year election, so turnout was light. Only about 200,000 voters turned out. After they tapped their votes and the polls closed, workers took the machines' memory cards out and transported them to a secure, high-tech counting center. Then the computer there crashed. They rebooted. It crashed again. The election officials persevered and by the next day had their results. But 10 elections were so close that a recount was in order. When election officials went to the machines to collect the election-day paper ballots for a hand tally, 20 percent of the printouts were illegible. So all the paper ballots had to be reprinted.

That election was tame compared to Cuyahoga's experience the year before. That year more than one hundred machines broke down. Dozens more had paper jams or crashes. Hundreds of devices used to create the voter-cards, which voters insert into the machine to vote, were missing. Poll workers lost at least twelve memory cards holding the voting counts from some of the machines, though they were able later to replicate the results. And after the election, an audit of select machines disclosed that almost 75 percent of them had discrepancies between the memory-card vote count and the paper trail vote count.

After their troubles in 2007, Cuyahoga County had had enough. It decided to ditch the e-voting machines it had spent $21 million on and invest $12 million to switch to optical scanners. Still, in 2012, according to one elections watchdog group, almost 25 percent of registered voters in America will use e-voting machines that do not produce a paper trail. And as of 2009, sixteen states, including Florida, New Jersey, and Tennessee, do not submit their machines for testing and evaluation to either the federal Election Administration Commission or independent evaluators.

The other powerful new metric for measuring election administration used after 2000 was the recount discrepancy. Voters are accustomed to election night results. But the numbers announced on election night rarely stand. In the weeks following every election, election administrators check and double-check all the results and produce a final number. The discrepancy between that number and the initial number is almost never because of fraud or vote manipulation. It's because in the rush to satisfy the public's demand for quick results, mistakes are made. By keeping track of recount discrepancies, election administrators can find bad machines, poorly run precincts, and other problems. Ironically, given all the bitter accusations of the 2008 Franken-Coleman recount, Minnesota is one of the states that takes gathering the data most seriously. Every two years, Minnesota audits a random sample of 5 percent of its ballots to double-check its electronic counting system against the paper ballots.

Unfortunately, neither the residual vote nor the recount discrepancy metric is used on a widespread and consistent basis. Problems like the ones the Brennan Center found in the Bronx in New York are likely more common than we know. The Brennan Center is one of the most sophisticated, best-funded, and most persistent organizations dedicated to improving voting systems. If it took a lawsuit from the center and a crusade by a local newspaper to analyze a few hundred wrongly rejected ballots and to change the wording of a message on a voting machine, average voters could be forgiven for thinking they don't stand much of a chance. In fact, in the 2008 presidential election, thirteen Florida counties used the exact same machines and the exact same message as that used by the Bronx precincts that had such a high residual vote rate. More than 12,000 votes were rejected there as "over-votes."

Still, the rapid and widespread adoption of newer e-voting and optical scan systems since 2000 has significantly improved vote counting and administration. Overall, both types of machines have residual vote rates lower than their predecessors, the lever machine and punch-card ballots. And when the use of the machines is coupled with systematic efforts to gather good data on precinct-level residual voting and recount discrepancies, many election administrators have managed to drag their systems into the twenty-first century. Many of the early errors from using e-voting and optical scan machines slowly but surely have been fixed.

Some errors probably cannot ever be fully fixed. Optical scan systems get tripped up when the voter uses an "x" or a circle to vote rather than fully filling in the oval. E-voting machines can record wrong votes or flip people's votes when people grasp the side of the machine with their palms. All voting systems are subject to human error or to people with nefarious intent. Voters and election officials make mistakes. Sometimes they act maliciously.

Yet, in many jurisdictions politicians cry potential fraud, putting the worst possible spin on voters for being predictably human when the fault actually lies with the underfunded and poorly constructed registration and voting systems. They shake their fists at the voters, frustrated and angry at them for their failure to navigate an incredibly complex system. But election systems are not supposed to be for the convenience of politicians and bureaucrats. A good election system deals with things as they are and doesn't punish voters for behaving like people. It seeks new ways to be efficient, to use best practices, and to help people to vote, which after all is supposed to be the goal.

Many of these problems can be minimized with some common-sense data collection and a will to act. The solution is relatively straightforward, as the Brennan Center notes: collect and publish regular reports on residual votes and recount discrepancies; investigate and act on significant discrepancies; provide public access to ballots; and professionalize ballot design.

Nothing causes problems or blocks such straightforward solutions more than the fractured and underfunded systems we have put in place to run our elections. There are approximately thirteen thousand election districts in the United States. Half of them serve fewer than 1,400 voters. Two-thirds have fewer than ten thousand voters. Many of the districts are badly underfunded. The city or county council overseeing any election district and its budget faces a wide array of demands from voters: keep the parks maintained; pick up the trash; pave the streets; run health care clinics for the poor and uninsured. Election administrators don't have much of a chance against those requirements. On a local and state level, America probably spends something like $1 billion a year nationwide on running its elections. No one knows for sure because the data are not regularly collected. In 2007, state and local governments spent almost $23 billion on solid waste management and $37 billion on parks and recreation.

Meanwhile no election jurisdiction can rely any longer on help from the federal government to upgrade its systems. The forward momentum for election-system reform achieved as a result of the Help America Vote Act has slowed as federal budget cuts have slashed money available to states.

In large election districts, officials can potentially turn to a large tax base to support sophisticated management. However, a large budget in itself does not guarantee good election administration. But without a sufficient budget, officials are left to cobble together scarce resources and hope nothing goes wrong. California's Los Angeles County has the largest election budget in the state. But it's near the bottom in what it spends per registered voter. It has the scale and skill to make big investments that pay off. Meanwhile, Alpine County, California, nestled between Lake Tahoe and Yosemite Valley, has the lowest election budget in the state. It has 1,230 voters and spent $20,000 on elections in 2008—more per voter than any other California county. All of its elections are conducted by mail.

For years, New York City had difficulty finding people who would maintain and repair its lever voting machines. "You make more money servicing laundry machines," said New York City election commissioner Douglas Kellner. One former Washington State election administration employee told a newspaper that she quit her job to work at the local Sizzler as a waitress. "I really felt that nobody took me seriously," said Tamira Bradley, who worked in elections in Longview, Washington, for $1,800 a month. When she went to Sizzler, "I made more money."

New York City spent millions to buy optical scanners for vote counting. On election day, after the polls close, the scanner reports the final vote tally. It spits out a roll of paper with the numbers. Polling station workers cut the roll of paper into sections according to election district. Then, they tally all the district votes by hand and write the total onto a piece of paper. Those pieces of paper are handed to police officers who carry them to station houses where they can be finally entered into a computer. For all our voting machine sophistication, it all comes down to people and paper. The same practice is repeated in many election districts throughout the nation.

REGISTERING VOTERS IN VERSAILLES, INDIANA, 2008. *Republican party activist Dee Dee Benkie (right) signs up a new voter. She was one of thousands of activists from both parties registering voters one at a time in the run-up to the 2008 presidential election. That year, Indiana added more than 740,000 new voters to its rolls.* **Photo Credit:** *Trio Pictures*

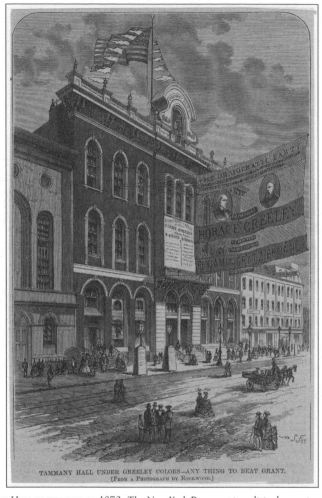

TAMMANY HALL UNDER GREELEY COLORS—ANY THING TO BEAT GRANT.
[From a Photograph by Rockwood.]

*TAMMANY HALL IN THE FALL OF 1872. The New York Democratic political organiza-
tion was backing the Liberal Republican presidential candidate Horace Greeley that
year. By 1872, Tammany's most famous boss—William Tweed—was losing power. He
had been arrested the year before, and by the end of the next year, 1873, he would be
convicted by a jury and imprisoned for corruption. Greeley resoundingly lost the 1872
election to Ulysses S. Grant. He died after the popular vote but before the Electoral
College vote. Almost all of his pledged electors gave their votes to other candidates.
That same election, Susan B. Anthony also tried to vote for President. She was arrested and convicted of illegal voting.* **Photo Credit:** *New York Public Library from*
Harper's Weekly

CHAPTER 6

THE GAMES WE PLAY

The Partisan Fight over Voting

The voter registration group Acorn "is now on the verge of maybe perpetrating one of the greatest frauds in voter history in this country, maybe destroying the fabric of democracy."

Senator John McCain, 2008

"I can't help thinking, since . . . we're supposed to be a country dedicated to liberty, that one of the most pervasive political movements going on outside Washington today is the disciplined, passionate, determined effort of Republican governors and legislators to keep most of you from voting next time. There has never been in my lifetime, since we got rid of the poll tax and all the other Jim Crow burdens on voting, the determined effort to limit the franchise that we see today."

Former President Bill Clinton, 2011

THE CITY OF CANTON LIES in the heart of Mississippi blues country. Until the late 1970s it was full of juke joints: New Club Desire, the Star Lite Café, Bessie's Hideaway, Club Delcce, and the Blue Garden, to name a few. The music used to spill out onto the streets from grocery stores and backyards. When B.B. King, Bobby Blue Bland, and Albert King played the blues circuit, they went to New Club Desire in Canton. The legendary blues singer and the king of the slide guitar Elmore James made his home there. More recently, the city produced Pittsburgh Steelers defensive left-end L.C. Greenwood, a starter on four Super Bowl-winning teams.

Canton is not far from the state capital of Jackson, but it's still a small town with slightly more than 13,000 residents. Today, its biggest employer is a Nissan automobile plant, though the hordes of tourists following the Mississippi Blues Trail probably also help the economy. The Hollywood movies filmed there recently—*O Brother, Where Art Thou?*, *A Time to Kill*, *Biker Zombies from Detroit*— have boosted civic pride and brought a little sex appeal to the city in the form of George Clooney and Matthew McConaughey. Still, more than 28 percent of the population lives below the poverty line. Almost 75 percent of the city's residents are African American. The city is a Democratic stronghold. Its Mayor is a Democrat. All six of its aldermen are Democrats.

So when city elections roll around, it's all about the primary. In the spring of 2009, Canton's Mayor and all of its aldermen were up for election. The issues were like those faced by every city in tough times: education, economic development, public safety. The candidates said what they often say. "We need a change here in Canton, Mississippi. We need a change for ourselves, we need a change for the adults, and we certainly need a change for our children," candidate Dr. William Truly told the audience gathered at Canton High School for the mayoral debate. (Truly won.)

Turnout for the 2009 Canton municipal primary elections hit 32 percent of the voting-age population in the city. One of the voters was Terrance Watts. The thirty-nine-year-old African American Canton man had been recruited to vote by his local alderman, who took him to get his absentee ballot[49] at the charmless, low-slung modern City Hall located on the corner of Peace Street and Shady Lane. Watts's name was on the registered voter rolls. That May, Watts sent in an absentee ballot in the primary election. In June, he sent in an absentee ballot in the general election.

Two years later, Terrance Watts stood before a local judge and pled guilty to voter fraud. Watts had spent all of his life in Canton. He was poor, had a seventh-grade education, and was semi-literate. A few years before he voted, Watts had been convicted of a felony for forging a drug prescription and for selling drugs. He had served about thirteen months in prison and had been released in 2005. But in Mississippi, people with felony convictions are not allowed to vote again, unless they get a bill specific to them passed by the state legislature giving them back the vote. Watts, of course, had never sought to have his voting rights restored. Indeed, between 2000 and 2009, Mississippi restored voting rights via a special legislative bill to only 90 of the 228 people who asked for one—of the more than 145,000 Mississippi citizens with prior felony convictions.

So Watts, indisputably, was not eligible to vote in the Canton elections. And thus he pled guilty. The judge sentenced him to ten years in prison. For voting.

Watts is serving his time in one of Mississippi's largest prisons, a sprawling minimum-to-maximum security complex near the Chickasawhay River, incarcerated with more than 3,000 other men. If he serves his full ten-year sentence, Mississippi likely will have spent more than $175,000 imprisoning him.

---

[49] Twenty-seven states allow absentee voting without requiring the voter to justify the need for the absentee ballot. Mississippi is not one of them. People who want an absentee ballot in Mississippi must provide one of eleven reasons why they need to vote absentee, including that they will be out of town on election day or that they are required to work on election day.

America takes voting very seriously.

How did Watts end up getting caught and prosecuted, two years after voting? Around the time of the election there were diffuse allegations of voter fraud, the sort of rumors that often surround elections. The local district attorney in Mississippi's twentieth judicial district, which includes the county Canton sits in, took up the case. He probably did what any prosecutor would do: pulled the election records and started checking all the names against criminal records, citizenship records (if he could get them), and possibly against residency records to confirm that the voters actually lived where they were registered. When he was through, Watts and five other people were in his crosshairs.

Though Canton is a Democratic bastion, it is only a spot of blue in a sea of Republican red. And the district attorney for the twentieth judicial district of Rankin and Madison Counties is a Republican. There is no reason to believe that Canton voters were placed under the microscope by a Republican prosecutor because they are predominantly Democrats, but there also is no question that throughout the nation both political parties and their affiliated activists push and prod and manipulate the system for maximum partisan advantage. Our election administration system and laws are partisan.

The election system is a complex ecosystem sustained by politicians, judges, prosecutors, administrators, and activists at every level—local, state, and federal. The partisan participants in the election structure have various, distinct tools at their disposal to influence who votes and how. They pass laws making it harder to vote, mandating strict voter identification at polls, reducing early voting days, and imposing tougher registration requirements. They move polling stations or registration sites to inconvenient locales. They understaff polling places or allocate insufficient voting machines to produce delays and long lines. They aggressively purge voter registration lists so that on election day voters who show up discover that they are not registered. They challenge voters at polls. They send out leaflets and make phone calls with misinformation—listing the wrong voting day or polling place or threatening voters with fines and penalties. They pay people to vote. They forge signatures on absentee ballots or registration forms. During recounts, they apply arbitrary rules to ballot counting. They even throw people in jail for honest mistakes or to set an example.

In the last few years, their efforts have escalated.

The Fox Guarding the Chicken Coop

The American election administration system that oversees the nuts and bolts of an election is run largely by partisan officials. In thirty-four states, the top election official, often the Secretary of State, is elected. In another five, the top election official is appointed by partisan politicians, such as the state's Governor. The remaining eleven states and Washington, D.C., have boards, some of which are partisan and some of which are not. The election administration system stretches down into every county and city, and even there the people who run our elections are often partisan. Approximately half of local election officials are either partisan elected officials or appointed by partisans.

The fact that a person in charge of elections also has a party affiliation doesn't condemn him or her to acting unfairly toward members of another party. But it is impossible to take politics out of the politician. Almost all human beings have politics or partisan feelings. The people who run for Secretary of State are typically deeply immersed in their party's structure. When they are appointed to the post, it is usually as a reward for good, loyal service to the party. When they are elected to the post, they usually win by mobilizing party resources. Of course, there are occasional party outsiders who win these posts. And below the secretary of state level, many, probably a very large majority, of election officials are professionals devoted to enforcing the law fairly and impartially. In fact, recently several states have passed laws forbidding election officials from engaging in partisan activity—such as endorsing candidates or campaigning for ballot initiatives. In other states, election officials have taken voluntary pledges to refrain from taking part in campaigns or endorsing candidates. But most states have no such requirements. And in a few of them party politics and partisanship are so paramount that election officials have opened themselves up to charges of hyper-partisanship bordering on venality. Every state has its own political culture and history, and some have climates that tolerate or even nurture treating election administration as an extension of the war between the political parties.

The issue flared dramatically in Florida in 2000, when the co-chair of that state's George W. Bush presidential campaign committee *and* its chief election officer, Katherine Harris, was charged with partisan bias in leading its chaotic recount. Then in 2004, Ohio came under scrutiny. Ohio may be the Buckeye State to some of its residents, but to others it is the "Mother of Presidents." Eight presidents were born in Ohio, more than any other state. The last was Warren G. Harding in the 1920s, so to most contemporary voters Ohio's role in presidential elections is really about its status as a vital swing state. Ohio has voted with the ultimate presidential victor since 1960. In 2004, its prized twenty Electoral College votes were in play, and the John Kerry and Bush campaigns were waging a fierce war for them. The state's elected Republican Secretary of State Ken Blackwell was in charge of the overall election administration. When the ballots were counted after election day 2004, Bush won the state by more than 118,000 votes.

But both before and after the election, Blackwell elicited a string of blistering accusations about his political handling of the election. He served as the co-chair of Bush's reelection campaign. He actively campaigned in support of a ballot initiative barring gay marriage. More worryingly, he issued a series of rulings that Democrats regarded as aimed at helping his party. In early September, with the voter registration deadline looming, he required that all voter registration forms be submitted on a very specific type of paper—eighty-pound stock, white, uncoated. Standard copier and printer paper is twenty-pound stock. And Democrats had been aggressively registering voters using forms printed in newspapers, which was an even lower weight than standard copier paper. They cried foul. Blackwell reversed the ruling three weeks later, but in the interim an unknown number of submitted registration forms were thrown out.

Then Blackwell decided that provisional ballots would be counted only if they were cast in the same precinct in which the voter was registered. Meanwhile, many voters in predominantly Democratic neighborhoods started getting official-looking flyers with misinformation about their polling locations. Finally, Blackwell issued a ruling allowing multiple vote observers and challengers in polling stations. The Republican Party had announced a major initiative to send thousands of observers to polling stations ostensibly to challenge voter eligibility. Democrats worried that the Republican poll challengers would intimidate voters in traditionally Democratic districts. They sued and overturned his ruling, in part.

Kerry lost Ohio in 2004 and also lost the presidency. Blackwell's rulings were not the reason Kerry lost, though they may have played a role. But in the midst of a fierce and high-stakes election, his rulings smacked of partisanship to many. In 2006, Blackwell was once again in charge of the election. He also ran for Governor that year, effectively supervising an election in which he was a candidate. He lost.

Despite public concern about partisanship and election administration, in 2008, the top election officials in Arizona, Kansas, Michigan, Missouri, and Ohio were chairmen of their state's presidential election campaign committees for Senator John McCain.

Moreover, both Democratic and Republican Secretaries of State from Indiana, Arizona, Arkansas, and Rhode Island endorsed candidates in their state's presidential primaries that year.

This kind of behavior certainly does not look good. It does not inspire confidence. But the practical impact of partisanship on election administration is less well understood. Few people believe that a partisan or hyper-partisan Secretary of State can overtly manipulate the system to guarantee that a particular candidate wins. Our system is complex. Partisan administrators can exploit the system at the margins—change a requirement here or there and affect turnout or votes by a particular group of voters by a percentage point or two. Sometimes the election is such a runaway for a particular candidate that the manipulation doesn't change the outcome. Blackwell may have overseen the 2006 Governor's race in which he was a candidate, but he couldn't dictate the outcome and lost.

However, sometimes a small change is all it takes to affect the outcome of an election. In one study, researchers determined that in very close elections, a candidate whose party also controls key state offices like Secretary of State is more likely to win than the statistics would suggest he or she should. They concluded: "Even the closest elections are determined, at least in part, by systematic structural advantages of one party."

The few other studies that have attempted to determine if partisan election officials' behavior can have a quantifiable effect on elections have shown some other impacts. Ballots tend to be better designed in nonpartisan election jurisdictions. Provisional ballots are more likely to be thrown out in districts where the majority of voters belong to one party but the election officials belong to the other.

Registration rolls are purged more aggressively by Republicans than Democrats, with profound impact on people's ability to vote.

America's registration rolls are perennially messy. Addresses are wrong. Dead people are still registered. Names are misspelled.

People who have moved are still on the list. Election officials trying to clean up the lists face a difficult task: excessive pruning may disenfranchise legitimate voters, while inadequate maintenance creates the opportunity for abuse.

Before both the 2000 and 2004 elections, Florida embarked on an effort to clean up its voting lists. In 2000, Florida's then Secretary of State Harris paid an outside data processing firm $4 million to go through the state's voter registration lists and determine whether any of the voters had died or had prior felony convictions, which would render them ineligible to vote in that state. The firm hired to conduct the purge was concerned that some eligible people might be improperly struck from the list. For example, if the name of a convicted felon was similar to the name of a registered voter, what should be done? Florida's election administrators decided to play loose with the name match. And so the Reverend Willie D. Whiting Jr. found his name on the purge list because he was considered the same person as Willie J. Whiting. About twelve thousand people who were eligible to vote were nevertheless put on the list to have their registration eliminated. Florida's voter roll scrub was not fully implemented, so some voters were spared. But not Tampa's Sandylynn Williams, who had voted in every presidential election in the previous sixteen years. She had been confused with her sister, who had a felony conviction, and was turned away at the polls. Ten days after the election, her right to vote was restored. She got a letter of apology.

In 2004, Florida's then Republican Secretary of State Glenda Evans Hood[50] initiated another purge. This time more than 45,000 names were on the list. Once again the purge list was grossly flawed,

---

[50] Katherine Harris was elected to the House of Representatives in 2002. She was Florida's last elected Secretary of State. The state's constitution was amended so that effective 2002, Secretaries of State are appointed by the Governor.

sweeping out people who were actually entitled to vote while failing to catch many who were not.

In 2008, Florida's Republican Secretary of State Kurt Browning went at its registration lists another way. Rather than purging rolls after people had registered, the state instituted strict rules regarding who could be added to the rolls in the first place. Florida went through its recent registrations and cross-checked them against other state or federal databases. But although it had instituted a loose name match requirement in 2000 when it purged voters for prior felony convictions, this time it required a perfect name match between the two records before it would register people. So if a person used a middle initial on his or her driver's license but not on the voter registration form, the voter was at risk come election day. The rule was called "no match, no vote." After laboriously going through and rechecking the records, Florida pared the no-match list down to 12,000 prospective voters. There was no evidence that they were not legitimate voters. Democrats outnumbered Republicans on the list four to one. Four states used "no match, no vote" in 2008.[51]

Finally, in 2012, Florida's latest Republican Secretary of State, Ken Detzner, announced yet another purge. This time the focus was on non-citizens. His office compiled a list of 180,000 people who were registered voters but possibly not citizens. The list was created using an outdated database from the state's Department of Motor Vehicles. A smaller subset of 2,600 people on the list were sent letters demanding that they produce proof of citizenship within thirty days or be struck from the list of registered voters. A number of them believed it was an identity theft scam since the letter asked them to mail in photocopies of sensitive documents. Many more also turned out to be, in fact, citizens whose names were confused with non-citizen's names.

---

[51] They were Florida, Iowa, Louisiana, and South Dakota. Three of the four had Republican Secretaries of State. Iowa had a Democratic Secretary of State.

Election administrators have broad leeway in overseeing elections, but they are only one part of the election ecosystem. The laws they enforce and their budgets are passed by highly political state legislatures where partisan interests are often given free rein. The authors of a study that looked at five Midwestern state legislatures as they passed new election laws were "disconcert[ed] to learn the extent to which the mindset of elected policymakers is not on how to design the voting process for the public's benefit, but rather on how to advance one's candidacy or party."

Of course, no politician would ever publicly support a law, particularly one having to do with voting, because it benefited his or her political party. Instead, politicians can rely on concerns about the integrity of the voting system to justify their votes. And in doing so they tap into a deep, collective, primal memory of election fraud and abuse in American history.

THE GHOSTS OF ELECTIONS PAST

American voting has never been pristine. Politicians from the Revolutionary Era came very close to what could be considered outright vote buying today. Eighteenth- and early nineteenth-century elections were raucous, social, and entirely public affairs. And politicians attracted supporters or would-be supporters to the polls by "treating" them to lavish buffets and drinks. When twenty-three-year-old George Washington ran for the Virginia House of Burgesses[52] in

---

[52] The House of Burgesses was the Virginia Colony's unicameral elected legislative body created in 1618. The colony was ruled by a Governor appointed by the British Crown, but the House of Burgesses had the ability to pass some local laws and engage in limited self-governance. The Governor, however, had veto power. During the Revolutionary Era, the House of Burgesses increasingly asserted itself as the true power in the colony and sent agents to London to seek changes in or to resist royal power.

1755, he failed to "treat" his prospective voters to the customary liquor splurge. He lost and blamed his failure to treat the electorate for his defeat. When he ran again in 1758, he did not make the same mistake. Shortly before his marriage to the wealthy widow Martha Custis, Washington spent £39 for a hogshead and a barrel of punch, twenty-eight gallons of wine, and forty-six gallons of beer, or roughly half a gallon of liquor for every one of the 310 votes he got. He wrote a note to his campaign manager worrying that he had not bought enough liquor. But he had. He won. Washington stayed in the liquor business. In 1799, the last year he was alive, his whiskey distillery at Mount Vernon was one of the largest in the nation and produced eleven thousand gallons of liquor a year.

After the Constitution was adopted, allegations of fraud sprang up immediately. In the first federal election, all five of New Jersey's representatives nearly lost their seats due to charges that the state's elections were incompetently administered. But the first case involving outright election theft came two years later, in 1790, and involved the contest between two Revolutionary War heroes for one of Georgia's three House seats. During the war, James Jackson had served as a colonel under "Mad" Anthony Wayne. Jackson was later promoted to general, and the two became friends and colleagues. By the 1790 House elections, they were bitter political opponents. When Wayne was declared the election's victor, Jackson wouldn't stand for it. He had ample reason to object. He went to Washington, D.C., and complained loudly to the House of Representatives.

During the House's investigation of the election, it found that Wayne had arranged to have ballots diverted from the official count and handed over to him. His partisans inflated the vote count in one county where nine more votes were recorded than there were voters. The election ran rife with "undue and corrupt practices." The House stripped Wayne of his seat, but it refused to hand the election to Jackson. Another man was selected to take the position.

Two years later, Georgia sent Jackson to Washington as its Senator. Mad Anthony Wayne, rebuffed by the House of Representatives, resumed his military career. President Washington appointed him to lead the army in a string of battles against a Native American tribal confederacy led by, among others, the Shawnee leader Tecumseh in the Northwest Territories, mostly in what is now Ohio. After a successful campaign in 1796, Wayne died from gout, a disease often caused by eating rich food and drinking too much alcohol. Fort Wayne, Indiana, was named for him. Fifteen counties scattered throughout the country are named for him. Jackson—who seems to have been a model of rectitude—has been largely forgotten.

America, however, was most decidedly not done with partisan, corrupt, and abusive elections. Two years after one Revolutionary War hero stole an election from another, in 1792 the House of Representatives had to deal with three more contested elections. In Delaware, an election was overturned because the ballots had been improperly counted. In New York, the election results stood even though one county returned more votes for a candidate than there were voters.

The 1792 Virginia election pitting Abraham Trigg against Francis Preston took a more interesting turn. It dissolved into actual fighting. Preston's military brother had stationed soldiers near the polling place. They refused to admit people who wanted to vote for Trigg and hit one of the voting officials. After the polls closed, a riot between the troops and local voters broke out. When Preston came to plead for his seat in the House, he argued that they shouldn't judge the conduct of southern elections by eastern standards. The House agreed that "riots and intimidation were an established custom and quite a matter of course in southern elections." In fact, "the election in question was much less disturbed

than many others in regard to which there was no question."
Preston kept his seat.[53]

Two years later, the number of contested House elections doubled. It has never stopped. By the late nineteenth century, voting
fraud had developed its own vocabulary. "Colonizers" or "pipe-
layers" were voters from another city or state sent in to shore up support in weak areas. In Virginia, they were called "light horsemen"
and rode from county to county casting multiple votes. (Andrew
Jackson was alleged to have sent wagonloads of Tennessee supporters into Kentucky to vote for him in 1828.) "Repeaters" voted
multiple times in the same precinct, often putting on disguises to
avoid being caught. "Floaters" were for sale to the highest bidder and
would roam from polling place to polling place. "Shoulder hitters"
intimidated voters from the opposing party.

Election fraud and abuse reached its peak—at least in popular
imagination—with New York City's Tammany Hall. But almost every city had its political machine, trained in the dark arts of voter
fraud and intimidation. From the mid-nineteenth to early twentieth centuries, Tammany Hall, backed by Irish American immigrants
and insinuated into the city's police and firefighting forces, was a
center of Democratic power in the city. Tammany bosses—William
"Boss" Tweed was just the best known—demanded kickbacks and
siphoned off vast sums from public contracts. And when it came to
corrupt elections, Tammany wrote the book. Tammany supporters
stole or stuffed ballot boxes as needed, paid voters or imported them
from prisons or almshouses, and intimidated rival organizations and
parties.

---

[53] One of Preston's sons became a Senator from South Carolina. The other
was a leader of South Carolina's secessionist movement who later served as a
confederate general in the Civil War. In 1796, Trigg finally won his House seat
and served Virginia in the House of Representatives for another twelve years.

Tammany Hall was formed as a political club in 1788. In the early nineteenth century, the organization backed a number of progressive causes, from universal suffrage to ending debtors prison. By the mid-nineteenth century, the Tammany organization's power and influence surged. In 1852, when a rival group of Democrats tried to mail ballots to every home in the city, a Tammany gang attacked the men guarding the ballots and stole almost half of them. One Tammany boss, Richard Croker, bragged about casting his first ballot in 1864, and then voting sixteen more times that day. In the 1868 election, Tammany Hall ran a repeat voting center on 32nd Street in New York City. More than three hundred repeaters circulated in and out of the building, getting their instructions on where to vote next. The center was run by the city's sheriff, James O'Brien. O'Brien was elected to Congress in 1878.

While Tammany indisputably engaged in colorful voting fraud, the actual scope and impact of its efforts is still a matter of debate. For all its corruption, Tammany Hall also earned the loyalty of a large portion of the city's population. While Tammany bosses lined their pockets, they also distributed considerable financial assistance to struggling families and helped people get jobs. People legitimately and gratefully voted for Tammany-backed candidates in large numbers.

Democrats were not the only ones manipulating the vote. In 1888, Republican-dominated Indiana was determined to do whatever it took to deliver its Electoral College votes to its favorite son, Benjamin Harrison, in his fight for the presidency against New York's Grover Cleveland. Both candidates were renowned for their battles against political corruption. Cleveland, a Democrat, was a well-known opponent of Tammany Hall. Harrison had prosecuted scores of Democrats accused of election fraud, though he only convicted one. During his presidential campaign he called for clean elections. But as election day grew closer and the outcome in his home state was in question, his supporters were not so clean: Harrison almost certainly knew of their plans. One close ally circulated a flyer to party stalwarts instructing them to buy floaters in blocks of five and to supervise them closely. Colonizers were brought in to the state from Pennsylvania to increase Harrison's vote count. Indiana's corrupted Electoral College votes went to Harrison. Cleveland did not even win his home state of New York, and though he almost certainly won the popular vote, he did not win the presidency either, because of the Electoral College. (See Chapter 4 for more on the election of 1888.)

But the tide was turning, and the anti-corruption movement was growing. Cleveland assailed the dishonest election system, railing against the interests "fattened upon corruption and debauched suffrage." By the next presidential election, in 1892, the Australian ballot and lever voting machines were in use widely. (See Chapter 5.) The secret ballot coupled with voter registration systems and the emergence of a semi-professional election system changed the nature of election abuse, though it certainly did not end it.

Big city and even rural machines kept on going. In 1934, Lyndon B. Johnson was working for a Texas Democratic candidate, Maury Maverick, for the House of Representatives. In the days preceding the election, Johnson set up shop in a room in San Antonio's Plaza Hotel. He sat at a desk piled high with five-dollar bills and handed them out to man after man, all of whom came into the room to sell their votes. It was not the last time Johnson would be involved in vote buying or ballot box stuffing. In the 1948 Senate election, the Johnson campaign went on an aggressive hunt for extra votes . . . after election day. They found them in Duval County. And then in Dimmit County. And Cameron County. And Zapata County. And finally in Jim Wells County, where someone changed 765 votes for Johnson into 965 votes for him by adding a loop to the handwritten seven. That gave Johnson 200 more votes. He won the election by 87 votes.

In 1960, when Johnson was John F. Kennedy's vice presidential running mate, Chicago was the locus of fraud allegations. Kennedy's victory in the popular vote over sitting Vice President Richard Nixon was close, only 112,000 votes. But it was Illinois, and its 27 Electoral College votes, that really made the difference. And in that state's popular vote, Kennedy won by fewer than 9,000 votes. Chicago deserved all the credit, providing Kennedy with a suspiciously large 318,000-vote margin of victory over Nixon in just Cook County. Without that margin, Kennedy never would have won Illinois's electoral votes.

Chicago's Democratic Party machine was legendary. And its reputation for voting corruption almost matches Tammany Hall's. In 1960, Nixon's allies alleged that Chicago Mayor Richard J. Daley fixed the city's vote for Kennedy. Nixon allies rushed to Chicago demanding a recount. When they were done, Nixon picked up 943 more votes in the city, but his allies discovered to their chagrin that Nixon's vote tally had actually been inflated in 40 percent of Chicago's precincts. Still, there was no question that some fraud had occurred in Chicago. Almost seven hundred people in the city were later indicted by a special prosecutor for election fraud. But more recent, extensive research into the matter has concluded that the abuse was not so extensive that it in fact cost Nixon the election. Kennedy's margin of victory in Chicago was on par with his margin in most major Democratic-dominated cities. Indeed, his margin in Chicago was lower than the one he obtained in Brooklyn, New York, alone. Daley's machine was effective at getting out the vote, but it was by no means capable of mass-manufacturing thousands of votes. Not in 1960. Still, the story of Mayor Daley stealing the 1960 election for Kennedy persists.

The legacy of Tammany Hall and its latter-day inheritors looms large in modern American discussion about voting fraud. In 2008, when the U.S. Supreme Court was considering the constitutionality of Indiana's law requiring that voters show government-issued photo identification before voting, it cast about for contemporary examples of significant voter fraud in the state and found none. The Court conceded that the comprehensive post-2000 election review of the voting system found "no evidence of extensive fraud in U.S. elections or of multiple voting." But Tammany Hall, which had collapsed into virtual irrelevance in the 1930s, was there to support the Court's concerns about voting fraud. Today, Tammany Hall houses a theater, a deli, a liquor store, and a nail salon.

Fraudulent voting still occurs. But the sort of industrial-scale vote buying and ballot box stuffing of Tammany Hall and Lyndon Johnson would be almost impossible to achieve today. There are simply far too many safeguards in the system, from multiple parties observing ballot counts to prosecutors ready to investigate and indict if they can make a case.

Voting fraud can take many forms and falls into two major categories: fraud committed by individuals and fraud committed by election officials. On the individual level, there is vote buying, in-person voter impersonation, absentee and mail-in ballot fraud, and ineligible voting or registration. In-person voter impersonation occurs when someone goes to the polls and claims to be someone they are not. In absentee ballot fraud, someone forges another person's signature and falsely submits the absentee ballot on his or her behalf. And, finally, ineligible registration and voting occurs when, for example, someone who is not a citizen or who is an ex-felon votes or when someone claims to live in one residence while he or she actually live elsewhere. Election official fraud occurs when results are falsified or when officials wrongly bar people from the polls.

All of these forms of fraud are very rare, although there are certainly recent examples of every single one. The most recent systematic effort to uncover and prosecute voting fraud was launched by the Bush administration in 2002. In October of that year, about a month before an upcoming election, Attorney General John Ashcroft stood in Washington, D.C.'s Great Hall of Justice and announced the creation of the Department of Justice's Ballot Access and Voting Integrity Initiative. Ashcroft had recently redecorated the Great Hall of Justice, which since its construction in the 1930s had held two ten-foot-tall, partially nude Art Deco aluminum statues. Ashcroft had ordered the department to buy an $8,000 set of blue drapes to cover the exposed breast of the female statue, "the Spirit of Justice." With the new blue drape backdrop in place, Ashcroft declared, "We come together today to renew our democratic compact with the American people. We gather here, in this Great Hall of Justice, to begin a new ethic of enforcement of our voting rights."

One of the key differences between the initiative and previous efforts to pursue voting fraud was its focus on individuals. Before Ashcroft made his announcement, the department had prioritized conspiracies to corrupt the process as a whole. Now, individual voters acting on their own would also feel the weight of the nation's largest criminal investigation and prosecution forces: the FBI and the U.S. Attorney Offices.

The initiative lasted for at least four years. As the 2004 elections drew near, New Mexico's U.S. Attorney David Iglesias, who reported to Ashcroft, started getting e-mails and phone calls from various Republican Party officials and members of Congress. One congresswoman was worried about extensive voter registration fraud in her district. She had recently sent letters to a group of newly registered voters, and many of the envelopes had been returned as undeliverable. Another official complained about a voter registration group, Acorn, fraudulently signing up voters. Iglesias created a complaint hotline and set up a state task force to look into the allegations. Department of Justice officials in Washington held out his task force as a model for other prosecutors to follow. New Mexico–based FBI agents and prosecutors looked into more than a hundred voting fraud complaints but could not find a case they could prosecute. They tracked down the registered voters whose mail had been returned. They were all either returned because of incomplete addresses or because many were college students who had moved after registering.

Two years later, Iglesias was fired. The Department of Justice assailed him as an "underperformer" and an "absentee landlord" when it publicly stated the basis for his dismissal. However, after an extensive internal investigation, the department's inspector general concluded there was no factual basis for these justifications. He was fired because of party anger reaching all the way to the White House at how he had failed to prosecute voter fraud cases, never mind whether the cases were legitimate.[54] Another U.S. Attorney was also fired for similar reasons. Iglesias felt he had done the right thing. "I wasn't going to make up evidence. And at the end of two years, I couldn't find one case I could prosecute," he told a journalist. Still he knew the game. They "had wanted splashy headlines trumpeting voter fraud indictments, and when they didn't get what they wanted, they were only too ready to assign blame."

In Wisconsin, the Ashcroft voting integrity initiative did find people it could prosecute. One of them was Kimberly Prude. In 2004, she went to Milwaukee's spectacular Renaissance revival City Hall to register to vote. Shortly thereafter she sent in an absentee ballot. But four years before, Prude had been convicted for trying to cash a counterfeit check. As a result, she was placed on six years' probation, which had two years left to run in 2004. In Wisconsin, people with criminal convictions can vote, but only after their probation is complete. Prude learned of her mistake and called City Hall to try to rescind her vote. But it was too late.

---

[54] He had also been subject to criticism for his handling of a public corruption case.

Federal prosecutors arrested her. A jury convicted her. She was sentenced to two years in prison.

All told from late 2002 until 2007, the nationwide initiative charged 120 people and convicted eighty-six of them. An analysis of a subset of those cases found a total of twenty-six individual voter—as opposed to officials'—convictions. One person was guilty of registration fraud. Twenty, including Prude, were found guilty of voting while ineligible, and five were guilty of voting more than once. In the 2004 presidential election alone, more than 121 million people voted. If we assume all of the cases occurred during that election, then individual voting fraud occurred about .00002 percent of the time. Another forty-four convictions related to government, party, or election official actions involving relatively small or even petty schemes.

OI NUNU, AUUIIN, 8UULU IU IIIC POLLG, AND FELONG

Despite the failure to uncover extensive fraud, by 2005, efforts to stamp out voting fraud shifted to the states. State legislatures passed a flurry of bills and introduced countless more: voter registration drives were restricted, early voting and absentee ballots were curtailed. But by far the most popular line of attack was voter identification laws. As of early 2012, thirty-two states had passed laws requiring some form of voter identification at the polls. In fifteen of them the identification had to include a photo; a utility bill or a Social Security card would not pass muster. (See Table 5.) In the meantime, fourteen more states were considering imposing identification requirements for the first time. Ten of the states that already had laws were debating legislation to tighten the requirement, and another nine were pondering amendments to their laws.

Indiana took the lead in 2005 when it passed the strictest law in the nation, requiring that prospective voters present current government-issued photo identification at polls on election day. Other states had passed identification requirements before then, but they were looser and allowed voters to show employee or student identification or to use a utility bill or bank statement. The Indiana law was immediately subject to litigation. But after the U.S. Supreme Court upheld its constitutionality in 2008, the law went into effect. Voter identification laws like Indiana's began to spread throughout the country.

Voter identification requirements can only address one particular form of fraud: in-person impersonation of another voter at the poll on election day. When pressed to demonstrate the need for the strict new laws, Indiana legislators could not produce evidence of a single arrest or prosecution for voter impersonation. There were, of course, other kinds of voting fraud in Indiana's history. But the law it passed would have addressed none of those.

In South Carolina, legislators passed a voter identification requirement spurred on by the state Attorney General's claim that 900 dead people had voted in recent elections. Presumably, someone else had showed up at the polls on election day and claimed to be the dead person. The State Elections Commission decided to take a close look at the issue and found 207 potential dead voters in a 2010 election. Closer examination found that more than half the problems stemmed from clerical errors. In more than a quarter of the cases the person was actually alive. Ten percent were outright errors—the dead person did not vote. And in three cases an absentee ballot was cast by someone who then died before election day. All told, after its exhaustive hunt for dead voters, the commission could not find a single verifiable case.

Kansas's Secretary of State backed his state's voter identification bill, citing the case of a person dead since 1996 who had voted in 2010. The Wichita, Kansas, newspaper found the "dead" voter in front of his house raking leaves. "I don't think this is heaven," he said. The newspaper looked into the other examples cited to support

TABLE 5. STATE REQUIREMENTS FOR VOTER IDENTIFICATION

States that Request or Require Photo Identification

STRICT PHOTO IDENTIFICATION		PHOTO IDENTIFICATION	
Georgia	**South Carolina[1]	**Alabama[1]	Louisiana
Indiana	Tennessee	Florida	Michigan
Kansas	**Texas[1]	Hawaii	South Dakota
*Mississippi[1]	*Wisconsin[1]	Idaho	
Pennsylvania			

States that Require Identification (Photo Not Required)

Alaska	Delaware	Oklahoma[1]
Arizona	Kentucky	Rhode Island[1]
Arkansas	Missouri	Utah
Colorado	Montana	Virginia
Connecticut	North Dakota	Washington
	Ohio	

Source: National Conference of State Legislatures, May 2012.

* New voter identification law has not yet been implemented; state currently has no voter identification law in effect.

** New voter identification law has not yet been implemented, an older voter identification law remains in effect.

1. In Alabama, South Carolina and Texas, current non-photo voter identification laws stay in effect for the time being. The new photo voter identification requirements will take effect after receiving pre-clearance under Section 5 of the Voting Rights Act. South Carolina and Texas were denied pre-clearance in December 2011 and March 2012, respectively. Alabama's new photo identification law has a 2014 effective date, and the state has not yet applied for pre-clearance.

Wisconsin's voter identification law was declared unconstitutional on March 12, 2012. A state judge issued a permanent injunction barring enforcement of the law, which the state has appealled.

Some call Oklahoma a photo voter identification state, because most voters will show a photo identification before voting. However, Oklahoma law also permits a voter registration card issued by the appropriate county elections board to serve as proof of identity in lieu of photo identification.

Rhode Island's voter identification law takes effect in two stages. The first stage, requiring a non-photo identification, took effect on January 1, 2012. On January 1, 2014, a photo identification requirement will replace the non-photo identification law.

Alabama's new photo identification requirement takes effect with the 2014 statewide primary election. The new law also requires pre-clearance. The delayed implementation date was intended to ensure that the timing of pre-clearance did not occur between the primary and general elections of 2012, thus creating voter confusion.

Mississippi's new voter identification law was passed via the citizen initiative process. It takes effect 30 days after the certification of results, a date that will likely fall in late December 2011 or early January 2012. However, the language in constitutional amendment passed by Mississippi voters is very general, and implementing legislation will be required before the amendment can take effect. The Mississippi provision will also require pre-clearance under Section 5 of the Voting Rights Act before it can take effect.

that legislation and found that the "incidents look more like honest mistakes than voter fraud—ballot applications signed by well-meaning relatives, mail-in ballots with signatures that didn't match those on file, a parent trying to vote for a student off at college—and, in the end, the ballots went uncounted."

In Texas, the state Attorney General said he had received five complaints of voter impersonation for the 2008 and 2010 elections. But he did not indicate how any of the cases were resolved or whether the investigators had found merit in the complaints. More than 13 million Texans voted in those two election years.

Voter impersonation at the polls is incredibly rare for a few obvious reasons. Perpetrating it takes a fair amount of effort. The reward is minimal—just one vote. The risks of getting caught are high. And the penalties are severe.

Legislators were swatting at gnats with a bazooka, and millions of eligible voters without identification were catching the shrapnel. In South Carolina, almost 9 percent of the state's registered voters lacked identification. In Texas anywhere from 603,000 to 795,000 registered voters lacked the newly required identification, or 5 to 6 percent of the population. Nationwide, estimates are that 10 percent of the voting-age population or about 21 million people do not have government-issued photo identification. Certain groups of voters were less likely to have the identification: the poor, the elderly, and minorities. (And those groups of voters are regarded as more likely to vote Democratic.) In Texas, Latinos were twice as likely to lack the required identification as were non-Latinos. In South Carolina, seven of the counties with the largest minority voter bases also had the highest portion of their residents without the requisite identification. Nationwide, 19 percent of people over the age of sixty-five lacked government identification.

Students often felt the brunt of the laws. Student voting has been a contentious issue in states. Students are often regarded as transient and not "real" residents of a state. And they are regarded as reliable voters for one political party—Democrats—rather than the other. Numerous techniques have been developed to discourage them from voting in the state where they go to school, from distributing letters warning them about violating the law, to posting poll watchers who challenge their residency, to launching investigations into their eligibility, as Maine did. But since many students lack driver's licenses, particularly licenses from the state where they go to school, the voter identification requirement was a new way to impede student voting. In Texas, a student identification card issued by a state university would not count for voting purposes. A state-issued gun license would, however. In Wisconsin, the state imposed requirements on what types of university cards would be accepted. But no university card met the requirements.

Many states passing the strict new identification laws sought to mitigate the impact of the requirement. Fearful that requiring people to pay for identification before they would be allowed to vote was perilously akin to the poll tax, they offered free identification. But the supporting documents required to acquire the free identification still cost money. In Texas one of the cheapest supporting documents—a birth certificate—costs $22. And almost a quarter of the state's counties did not have operational driver's license offices. In one of them, prospective voters would need to travel 176 miles round trip to reach a driver's license office.

Opponents of the laws launched a counteroffensive, furious at what they decried as the sharp, partisan nature of the laws. In fact, one law professor analyzed the legislative votes between 2005 and 2007 and found that 95.3 percent of Republican legislators called on to take a stance on the issue voted for the identification laws while only 2 percent of the Democratic legislators did. There were notable exceptions to the fierce partisanship. In Ohio, the Republican Secretary of State opposed a voter identification proposal backed by his party and with the support of several other prominent Republicans scuttled an identification law in that state. Democrats voted for a mild identification requirement in Rhode Island. But elsewhere, Democrats turned to the courts when they could. They sued in Arizona, Georgia, Indiana, Missouri, and Wisconsin. They won some; they lost some. In Texas and South Carolina, where changes to election practices are subject to review under the Voting Rights Act, the U.S. Department of Justice objected to the voter identification provisions and blocked their implementation.

Why all the fury about voter identification laws? By the time all the laws have been litigated, the not-entirely-free identifications are issued, the special DMV branches are opened, and the voter education efforts are implemented, the laws will have cost untold millions of dollars—to prevent something that is barely a problem. Supporters of the laws argued that public confidence in the integrity of the system was paramount. They worried that the mere potential for abuse could cause voters to lose faith in elections. Oddly, though, voters did not seem to have been concerned about the impersonation problem until legislators started passing laws to fix it.

In the meantime, votes indisputably will be lost. It is almost impossible to tell how many people will simply not go to the polls and how many will try to get identification and fail. In 2008, Indiana saw the tip of the iceberg. At least 1,039 people showed up at the polls without identification. Indiana's law required that the poll workers offer them a provisional ballot. Then, if the voter wanted the ballot to count, he or she had to travel in person within ten days of the election to the county election board and provide the necessary documents.[55] In the end, 137 people managed to get their provisional ballots counted.

---

[55] People who are indigent or have religious objections to photo identification can also travel to the elections board and be exempt from the requirement.

Twelve octogenarian and nonagenarian nuns from St. Mary's Convent, located in a complex across the street from the University of Notre Dame in South Bend, Indiana, were not as lucky when they tried to vote during the state's spring primary. One of their fellow nuns, Sister Julie McGuire, was working at the poll that day. The nuns did not have driver's licenses since they did not drive. A few had expired passports. But Sister McGuire had to turn them away. She offered them provisional ballots, but they declined, feeling it would be impossible to apply for and get a driver's license and then to go to the county board of elections within ten days. "You have to remember that some of these ladies don't walk well. They're in wheelchairs or on walkers or electric carts," Sister McGuire told reporters.

Even as legislators were attacking the voter impersonation phantom, other politicians and political groups were launching a ferocious attack on one particular voter registration group: the Association of Community Organizations for Reform Now, or Acorn. The group was founded in 1970 in Arkansas. A product of the counterculture of the late 1960s and early 1970s, Acorn was unabashedly dedicated to liberal, anti-poverty causes: a living wage, affordable housing, health care for the poor. The group had numerous affiliates throughout the nation and received substantial government funding for many of its initiatives. It also conducted extensive voter registration drives.

Voter registration drives have become commonplace throughout the United States in the last thirty years. In 2008, approximately 2 million voter registration forms were submitted by civic voter registration groups like the League of Women Voters or Rock the Vote— about 4 percent of all forms. In October of that year, Acorn claimed to have registered 1.3 million people employing more than 13,000 part-time workers to do so. A few weeks later it sheepishly admitted the number of people it registered was closer to 450,000.

Acorn was a major force in voter registration drives. But there were troubling cases involving the group, cases where people hired by the organization to canvass neighborhoods for new voters falsified forms. In 2007, seven people whom Acorn had hired part time for $8 an hour were charged with felonies in King County, Washington, which includes Seattle. The seven had submitted 1,800 registration forms in late 2006. Election officials were suspicious about the forms and investigated. Only six registrations were legitimate. The seven Acorn workers had flipped through phone and baby name books and submitted voter registration forms using a random assortment of names and addresses. That same year, eight other Acorn workers were indicted in Missouri, also for submitting fraudulent registration forms.

So in 2008, Acorn's voter registration drives were under the microscope. And the mistakes piled up, from submitting a registration for Mickey Mouse in Florida to filing one for a seven-year-old girl in Connecticut. In many instances Acorn workers themselves had pointed out the problems to election officials. Under most state laws, registration groups are required to submit all the forms they gather. The requirement was imposed after reports that registration groups were tossing out forms from people belonging to rival political parties. Republican groups threw out Democratic forms and vice versa. As a result of laws passed to prevent that form of abuse, when a prankster filled out a form as a joke, Acorn had to submit it anyway.

But Acorn's problems went deeper. After the election was over, Nevada's Attorney General moved in on the group. Two of its Nevada affiliate's employees and the group itself were indicted and charged with violating a state law that prohibited groups from paying bounties for registrations. In Clark County, Nevada, which includes Las Vegas, the Attorney General said, Acorn had submitted 91,002 registration forms, including the names of the starting lineup of the Dallas Cowboys. Only 23,186 were valid. An Acorn supervisor had offered the registration workers a $5 bonus for bringing in more than twenty-one registration forms. She named the program "jackpot." Poorly paid workers decided to inflate their bonuses by filling out scores of false forms.

Not surprisingly, paying workers for generating registrations is barred in many states because of the perverse incentives it creates. In 2008, in California, where payment per registration is legal, the local Republican Party hired a voter registration firm to sign up new voters. It paid the firm up to $12 per new voter. The firm collected its reward, but its tactics were questionable. Workers for the firm set up tables in front of grocery stores and asked people to sign a petition increasing penalties for child molesters. But in mid-October dozens of voters were startled to discover that their registration status had been changed. The form they signed also changed their party affiliation from Democratic to Republican.

But Acorn did not survive the scrutiny. Its voter registration errors combined with financial mismanagement and a hidden camera sting operation of a non-voting-related program brought the forty-year-old community organization down. Congress voted to eliminate funds to the group.[56] Acorn filed for bankruptcy in 2010.

Although the Acorn controversy illustrated how third-party voter registration drives can turn sour, overall, civic groups that sign up voters maintain a high level of quality. Election officials regularly reject voter registration forms. Many are incompletely filled out, or a signature is missing, or a box is not checked. From 2007 to 2008, election officials rejected about 1.7 million registration forms as invalid. The rejection rate for registration forms submitted by civic groups was about 2 percent, the average rejection rate for all registrations, wherever they originate.

---

[56] Acorn did not receive taxpayer money for its voter registration drives.

The good news was that in most cases the bogus registrations were caught by scrupulous election officials. Voter registration fraud rarely has much of an impact. Registration officials weed out most of the flagrant errors. Jokesters who register as Mickey Mouse don't actually show up on election day. But after Acorn, registration efforts had a black eye.

Two states, Florida and Texas, decided to crack down on all voter registration groups. In 2011, Florida decided to swathe voter registration groups in red tape and paperwork and impose fines and penalties if the groups slipped up. Voter registration groups now had to register with the state. Each person registering voters was required to sign an affidavit acknowledging in detail the felony penalties he or she would face for submitting false registrations. All registration forms had to be stamped with the exact time they were filled out. And then all forms had to be submitted within forty-eight hours after they were collected. Finally, each group had to file monthly reports with the state.

Two high school teachers registering their students quickly ran into trouble with the law. At Pace High School—home of the Patriots—social studies teacher Dawn Quarles had regularly organized voter registration drives for students who were of voting age, or who would be on election day. Pace, Florida, is a small town near the Gulf Coast, sitting at the top of the northern branch of Pensacola Bay. In 2010, oil from the Deepwater Horizon oil spill had penetrated the bay. An eight-mile section of Pensacola's sandy white beach on the gulf had been covered with oil tar balls. Oil-soaked dead birds were scattered along the beach. The President visited the area; major television networks broadcast their news reports from the city. Earlier that year, just before the spill, Pace High School had won the state baseball championship in its league.

In the fall of 2011, Quarles got seventy-six students to register. She gathered their registration forms and mailed them to the local registration office, as she had done many times before. But she missed the forty-eight-hour deadline. She was fined $1,000. Around the same time, another teacher in New Smyrna Beach on the state's east coast near Cape Canaveral also faced fines. She was lucky. She had been on maternity leave when the new law passed so had a ready explanation for not knowing the rules. The penalty was rescinded.

Faced with the new requirements and with steep fines for slipping up, major civic groups stopped their registration drives. The League of Women Voters, the Boy Scouts, and Rock the Vote all ceased activity. "Our part-time volunteers simply do not have an attorney on one hand and an administrative assistant on the other to help them navigate these treacherous and complex rules and regulations," the head of the League of Women Voters in Florida wrote. The civic groups sued to overturn the law. They won the first round in court. Their case is pending.

New voter registrations in the state began dropping. Even in areas where the voting-age population was increasing, new registrations plummeted: 39 percent in Miami-Dade County, 20 percent in Orange County. And again, as with the voter identification laws, the effects were likely felt most sharply by minorities. In 2008, Latinos and African Americans were two times more likely than white voters to register via a registration drive. One in eight African Americans registered through voter registration drives. For the time being, that option is virtually extinct in Florida.

When Florida legislators debated the registration laws, many of them knew it would make voting harder for people. In fact, that's exactly what some of them wanted. Florida Republican State Senator Michael Bennett confronted the measure's opponents who worried about the burden it would place on voting: "You say it is inconvenient. Ever read the stories about people in Africa? People in the desert who literally walk 200–300 miles so they could have an opportunity to do what we do? And we want to make it more convenient? Why would we make it any easier? I want 'em [voters] to fight for it. I want 'em to know what it's like. I want 'em to have to walk across town to go over and vote."

In addition to restricting voter registration groups, Florida cut back on its early voting period. In the years before the new law was passed, Florida opened pre-election day voting centers for fourteen days, including the Sunday before the election. After, early voting was cut back to eight days, and the Sunday option was eliminated. Predictably, early voting turnout dropped in the 2012 Florida primary elections and so did overall turnout. And predictably, the voters most affected by the cutback were African Americans and the elderly. In 2008, African Americans comprised 13 percent of the state's voters, but they were 22 percent of the early voters. In some counties up to 50 percent of African American voters cast their ballots via early voting. African American churches had often rallied their members to vote on the Sunday before elections. They called it "Souls to the Polls." That practice was now foreclosed.

In 2011, four other states—Georgia, Ohio, Tennessee, and West Virginia—also passed laws limiting early voting or restricting absentee voting.

Florida wasn't done, though. Like many states in the South, the Sunshine State bars people with felony convictions from voting. But it also has a procedure for restoring those voting rights. In 2007, Republican Governor Charlie Crist changed the state's system in an effort to streamline it. People with nonviolent offenses who had completed their sentences were allowed to restore their voting rights without having to fill out extensive paperwork. If they had a restitution order, they had to prove they had paid it. But otherwise, their voting rights were easily restored. In the year that followed, more than 115,000 people had their voting rights restored. Nevertheless, 80 percent of Floridians with felony convictions were still barred from voting. After the initial surge in voting rights restoration, the numbers dropped. Still, 26,000 people had their voting rights restored in 2009. In 2010, as a result of staffing cuts, the number dipped to 5,700.

But in May 2011, Florida's new Republican Governor, Rick Scott, decided to make it even harder to restore voting rights in the state. Going forward, people with nonviolent convictions would have to wait five years before they could apply to vote again. Others would have to wait seven years and personally appear at a hearing before a board to argue their case.

Florida now has one of the toughest laws in the nation in its treatment of ex-felons who seek to vote. In thirty-eight states and the District of Columbia, most people who have served their felony sentences automatically regain their right to vote. Maine and Vermont even allow people to vote from prison. However, in most of the remaining states, including Florida, Iowa, Kentucky, Mississippi, and Virginia, felons can have their voting rights restored only if they apply to the Governor for the privilege or get a special law passed for them by the state legislature.

Predictably, felon disenfranchisement disproportionately affects African Americans. Nationwide, 5.3 million American voters were unable to vote in the 2008 elections because of felony convictions. More than 2 million of them had already completed their sentences. But African American men are seven times more likely than the average American to have lost their right to vote because of a felony conviction. In Florida, 31 percent of all African American men cannot vote because of its law on felon voting. They number more than 200,000.

America has a long history of denying prisoners and released felons the right to vote. In the late eighteenth century, as states were writing their new constitutions following independence from Great Britain, the vast majority barred felons from voting. However, in the late nineteenth century, as southern states were drafting their new constitutions and crafting their Jim Crow laws, many wrote their felon disenfranchisement laws to specifically target African Americans. Crimes that were predominantly committed by African Americans were disenfranchising. Other crimes, perceived as "white" crimes, were not.

Florida was one of those states. So was Mississippi, whose 1890 constitution gave other states a model for disenfranchising African Americans. Mississippi was so open about its goals that in 1896 its state supreme court acknowledged that the state's new constitution aimed to "obstruct the exercise of the franchise by the negro race. By reason of its previous condition of servitude and dependence, this race['s] criminal members [are] given rather to furtive offenses than to the robust crimes of the whites. Burglary, theft, arson, and obtaining money under false pretenses were declared to be disqualifications, while robbery and murder and other crimes in which violence was the principal ingredient were not." Amazingly murderers could vote in Mississippi, but embezzlers could not. Mississippi did not amend its constitution to include violent crimes until 1968.

More than a hundred years after the 1890 constitution was drafted, Mississippi resident Jarvious Cotton challenged the state's felon disenfranchisement provisions. He sued, arguing it could not withstand scrutiny under the U.S. Constitution's Fourteenth Amendment requiring that laws apply equally. Given the overtly racist origins of the state's laws on felon disenfranchisement, Cotton argued it should be declared invalid. But Cotton lost. Although the section was originally discriminatory, its later amendment and reenactment removed that intent.

Mississippi's history presses down heavily on Cotton's life. The civil rights lawyer Michelle Alexander found and published his story in her book *The New Jim Crow*. Cotton's great-great grandfather was a slave and could not vote. The Ku Klux Klan beat his great-grandfather to death for voting. The Klan intimidated his grandfather from voting. Poll taxes and literacy tests kept his father from the polls. Cotton, because of a felony conviction, cannot vote. Five generations of men in Cotton's family have been kept from voting.

In Minnesota, the bitter 2008 recount in the Senate race between Al Franken and Norm Coleman subjected millions of ballots to unprecedented scrutiny. Minnesota, like its neighbor Wisconsin, allows people with felony records to vote, but only after they have completed their probation or parole. Local county prosecutors, poring over the records, found several incidents of released felons voting in the election. They were arrested. Many of them told prosecutors that they had been honestly unaware that they could not vote. But it didn't matter. They had broken the law. They were going to jail.

A raw mathematical calculation lies at the heart of the debate about felon disenfranchisement. Conventional wisdom holds that the former felons would disproportionately vote Democratic if allowed. And large new blocs of Democratic voters could change the outcome of some elections. So the discomfort people feel about ex-felons coupled with palpable political calculations disqualifies ex-felons from voting in large portions of the nation.

Felon disenfranchisement is a fraught issue for voting-rights advocates. Felons are not sympathetic people. And standing up for ex-felons' ability to vote post-sentence can get politicians in deep trouble. In January 2012, Republican presidential primary candidate Rick Santorum learned how. Ten years before, on Valentine's Day 2002, Santorum had been one of three Republican senators to vote for the Martin Luther King Jr. Equal Protection of Voting Rights Act. The proposal—which was never enacted—would have restored voting rights in federal elections to former felons who had completed their sentences. A political group backing Santorum's opponent for the Republican nomination, Mitt Romney, was running ads in South Carolina castigating Santorum for the vote. It showed a man in an orange jumpsuit wearing an "I Vote" sticker and said that Santorum supported letting felons vote. (In fact, he voted to let ex-felons, not prisoners, vote, but to most that was a distinction without a difference.)

Santorum didn't take the attack lying down. During a candidate debate in South Carolina, Santorum noted: "This is Martin Luther King Day. This is a huge deal in the African American community because we have very high rates of incarceration, disproportionately higher rates, particularly with drug crimes in the African American community." He took Romney to task for running false attack advertisements. And he noted that in Romney's own home state ex-felons automatically have their voting rights restored. But the ad and the issue had hurt Santorum's fortunes.

MY INDIANA HOME

American elections and voters are facing unprecedented levels of scrutiny from prosecutors. In the past, prosecutors tended to focus on extensive, systematic efforts to corrupt the voting system. And they found, and likely will continue to find, such efforts. Indeed, if any part of our voting system could be said to be prone to abuse, it is absentee voting. In the past decade, prosecutors have found scattered rings of party officials and activists who forged signatures and submitted batches of fraudulent absentee ballots. The fraudulent absentee ballot batches rarely exceed a few dozen and rarer still could they be said to affect election outcomes. But they are nevertheless concerted efforts to manipulate the system. Still, almost none of the activity and passion devoted to preserving the integrity of voting in America in the last five years has dealt with that issue. Perhaps this is so because everyone uses absentee ballots—all races, all ages, all parties, all income groups. They are enormously convenient, and each party uses them to drive turnout on its behalf. No party knows how to crack down on absentee ballot problems without also severely inconveniencing its own voters.

Instead, prosecutors now also concentrate on individual mistakes. Any serious slip-up, and the police may appear at the voter's doorstep.

In 2011, Indiana's Republican Secretary of State, Charlie White, was spared the indignity of a ride in the back of a police car. He was allowed to turn himself in for booking at the Hamilton County Jail. White, who was in charge of overseeing Indiana's elections, was indicted on three counts of voter fraud. Prosecutors alleged he had lied about his address when he registered and then voted in the 2010 Republican primary. The year before, White had moved voting districts, from his ex-wife's house in Fischer, Indiana, to a condominium in another part of Hamilton County. But he maintained his voter registration at his ex-wife's house. Prosecutors said he did so in order to keep drawing a salary from a job based in Fischer. In early 2012, a jury convicted him. He was sentenced to one year's house arrest, lost his job supervising Indiana's elections, and had his law license suspended. His life was in tatters because he listed the wrong address on his registration form.

One of Indiana's sitting U.S. Senators was treated more gently. Richard Lugar had served Indiana in the U.S. Senate since 1976. With a reputation for bipartisanship and thoughtfulness, Lugar, however, did not seem to have an actual residence in Indiana. He had sold his house in Indiana's Marion County in 1977 and bought a house in the Washington, D.C., area. But in 2012, he was still registered to vote using the address of the house he had sold more than forty years before. Under Indiana law, since he was out of the state on business for the state, he still was entitled to be considered a resident of the state, in much the same way that someone in military service would be treated. But the Marion County Election Board ruled he was not entitled to registration at his old house. Lugar was a homeless Indiana voter with no way to register. He eventually reached a compromise allowing him to register from a family farm. Someone else lives in the house on the farm.

No voting system is perfect. We should never stop trying to eliminate voting abuse and fraud. Fraudulent votes are an affront to our democracy. But they are not the end of our democracy. Yet in the quest to rid the system of every flaw, many recently have lost a sense of proportion and balance. Intense investigations and attacks on voting rights have convulsed the system. Meanwhile, poor management, limited resources, inconsistency, and mean-spirited rules are greater threats to the system than the occasional misinformed voter who uses the wrong address or the former felon who votes before his or her probation is over.

Neither party holds a monopoly on voting integrity. Both Republicans and Democrats have their histories of scandal and abuse. And both parties are perfectly capable of doing the math to see how changes in the election system can be parlayed to their advantage.

Some people want to blame one party and to absolve the other. Or they want to say that today one party is worse than the other. But that's really not the point. Both parties are at war. Voting is one of their battlegrounds.

Voters are caught in the crossfire. The vast majority of them just want to vote, to have that vote counted, and to be treated respectfully by the system. And they want our democracy to thrive. It can do so only when the voter is paramount, not the games we play in the quest for power.

*CHECKING VALIDITY OF ABSENTEE BALLOTS IN RIPLEY COUNTY, INDI-
ANA, 2008. Republican Rachel Edwards (second from left) and Democrat Mary Ann
Warnken (far right) are going through absentee ballots and checking their validity,
determining whether the signatures on the ballots match the voters' signatures on file.
Edwards and Warnken were selected for the task by their respective local political party
chairmen to ensure bipartisanship in the process. The elected Republican County Clerk
Ginger Bradford (far left) and Mo Rocca look on. **Photo Credit:** Trio Pictures*

SIGN POSTED IN 1939 IN MINEOLA, TEXAS, URGING VOTERS TO PAY THEIR POLL TAXES. By 1904, every former Confederate state had instituted a poll tax. In 1939, twenty-three states had either a poll tax in place or restricted voting in some elections to taxpayers. By the mid-1960s, in the wake of the Twenty-fourth Amendment and a Supreme Court decision, the poll tax had been eliminated. **Photo Credit:** Library of Congress/Farm Security Administration

AFTERWORD

THINK BACK TO THE DAY you turned sixteen and got your driver's license, especially that picture of you with your trendy haircut, greasy forehead, and brace-covered teeth.

Flash forward five years to the time you bought your first (legal) beer at twenty-one, by which point you thankfully had learned to brush your hair, wash your face, and wear your retainer.

But what about that teenage year that falls so quietly in between? Nothing on your license changes when you turn eighteen, but it should really be a far more celebratory occasion. You can get into an eighteen-and-over concert or buy a rated-M video game. And more importantly, you now have the right to vote.

Nearly twelve thousand Americans turn eighteen every day. But there is no "driver's ed" for citizenship, no birthday card from Uncle Sam celebrating your new status as a voter. We have fought hard for this right to vote, and our democracy depends on an informed citizenry that participates. Yet only about half of eligible eighteen to twenty-nine year olds are registered to vote today. We can do better.

Only white, male, landowners were allowed to vote when our country was founded, but we have come a long way in expanding

the definition of "We" in We the People. Ask your grandparents if
either of them ever paid a poll tax. Or if they had to wait until they
turned twenty-one to vote, even though they had fought the Nazis
on D-Day. Chances are at least one of them did or knew someone
who did.

Look at the photograph that precedes this afterword. It seems
inconceivable and outrageous today that anyone would ask someone
to pay a tax before he or she was allowed to vote. Makes you think
that even after expanding the franchise to citizens regardless of race,
these new voters weren't all that welcome! Signs like the one in the
picture used to be posted in polling places all over America, well
within the living memory of many, many people.

The thing about America, though, is that we don't let injustices
like the poll tax stand in our way. It often takes a long time—too
long for many—to overcome barriers to voting. But decade after
decade, century after century, the American people have insisted on
their right to vote. And every time we insisted, we succeeded.

We can do it again. It's easier than you think. A twenty-first-
century voting system that makes it easier for all voters—and young
voters in particular—to register to vote and removes barriers to the
ballot box is not just possible today. It is necessary. And at Rock the
Vote we're trying to build at least one simple tool everyone can use
to figure out if his or her state's voting system is making the grade.

Day after day, from college campuses to high school classrooms,
at Rock the Vote, we hear stories about needless bureaucratic barriers that prevent young people from voting.

For young Americans, the greatest barrier to participation is often the outdated process itself. In 2008, six million Americans reported that they did not vote because they did not know how to
register or because they missed their state's voter registration deadline. Our complicated registration process varies state by state, and
our country's antiquated, paper-based electoral system is riddled

with restrictive rules and red tape that don't reflect advances in technology or meet the needs of modern life.

In 2011, we published our first Voting System Scorecard. We evaluated state laws and practices that increase access and foster participation, and we developed a twenty-one-point scale to assess how well states are serving young voters.

We looked at three broad categories of election administration:

- **Voter registration**, including automatic registration, permanent and portable registration, same-day registration, online voter registration, and restrictions on third-party registration drives.
- **Casting a ballot**, including whether votes can be cast on days other than the traditional election day, voter identification requirements, residency laws, the absentee ballot processes, and laws affecting military and overseas voters.
- **Young voter preparation**, including state requirements about civics education and evaluation and the ability of young people to "pre-register" to vote before they turn eighteen.

We found some states that are really trying hard. States like Washington, where people can register online and where voting is conducted by mail. Or states like Montana, where voters can register on election day and where they are committed to high school civics education. There are some other states that need to try harder—like South Carolina and Connecticut.

A chart showing how all the states ranked appears at the end of this afterword, and the full report is available at the Rock the Vote website (www.rockthevote.com). Since the report was first prepared in 2011, many states have passed laws moving toward a more accessible voting system, and others have moved backwards.

Updates to the report will be made regularly. So be sure to check out how your state is doing, and join us in calling for a better elections system.

As voters we need to understand our election system and demand that it work for us, not against us.

Rock the Vote started more than twenty years ago. Our first revolutionary act was to create a telephone voter registration system—1-800-REGISTER. It seems sort of quaint now, but I promise it was innovative at the time.

Since then, we've moved online and to the mobile phone, and we've helped register more than five million people. In 2008, almost 2½ million people downloaded a registration form from Rock the Vote.

The people who work for Rock the Vote—and our thousands of amazing young volunteers—spend our time talking to young people about voting. We don't care whether they're Republicans or Democrats, Independents or Greens. And what we hear over and over again is that they care about voting.

Americans are eager to vote. Those who say young people don't care are wrong. There are 46 million eligible young voters between the ages of eighteen and twenty-nine. They are civically engaged in our communities, passionate about issues, and politically aware.

Unfortunately, not all of them end up voting. Take the 2008 elections. More young people voted than in any other previous U.S. election, but it was only 51 percent of them. This is not necessarily due to apathy. Young people's engagement in politics and causes on Facebook, Twitter, and on campus shows us that they are concerned.

In fact, the Millennial Generation is changing the face of politics. It is the largest generation in history and represents nearly one-quarter of the electorate. It is also the most diverse generation, as more than fifty thousand American Latinos turn eighteen each month.

Millennials possess a unique, socially conscious worldview that has been shaped in the wake of September 11, the wars in Iraq and Afghanistan, and the events surrounding Hurricane Katrina. These moments of national crisis forced all of us to turn to our elected officials for leadership, and the decisions those leaders made directly impacted Millennials' lives. Everything in Millennials' experiences has taught them a fundamental truth: deciding our leaders means deciding our future.

Young voter turnout was one of the top headlines of 2008. Turnout doubled and tripled in early 2008 contests. But their story has been percolating:

- In 2004, 20.1 million eighteen to twenty-nine year olds voted—a 4.3 million jump over 2000. The turnout increase among the youngest voters was more than double that of any other age group.
- In 2006, the turnout of eighteen to twenty-nine year olds grew by nearly 2 million over 2002 levels. Turnout among the youngest voters grew by 3 percentage points over 2002 levels, twice the turnout increase of older voters.

On March 23, 1971, students and educators across the country finally made Congress listen to them with the introduction of the Twenty-sixth Amendment to lower the voting age to eighteen.

So what if we took one day—say March 23—and on that day, once a year, in every high school in America we spoke with students about the history of voting rights and their participation in our democracy? What if we inspire a new generation of students to carry on the legacy of students from forty years ago? We'll engage thousands of young people from across the country, from big cities to little towns, from class presidents to star athletes, from every corner of every state, and register them to vote and teach them about the power that comes with participation.

It's not always a major election year, but every day is someone's eighteenth birthday. Our work encouraging each newly eligible voter to make a lifelong commitment to participate in every election is vital to ensuring that members of America's next generation are heard and that they are able to shape their own destinies. Let's create a voting system that fosters this participation.

Heather Smith
Washington, D.C.
June 2012*

---

* A portion of this afterword previously appeared in the *Huffington Post*.

ROCK THE VOTE'S VOTING SYSTEM SCORECARD[1]

(See following Table for explanation of factors going into scores.)

State	Registration Score	Voting Score	Preparation Score	Overall Score	Rank
Best Possible Score	11	7	3	21	
Alabama	1	2.3	2	5.3	45
Alaska	1	4.5	0	5.5	43 - tie
Arizona	5	4.9	0	9.9	17
Arkansas	2	4.9	0	6.9	35 - tie
California	2	6.8	3	11.8	10 - tie
Colorado	4	5.1	0	9.1	21 - tie
Connecticut	1	3.2	0	4.2	48
Delaware	6	3	3	12	7 - tie
D.C.	6	6.8	1	13.8	3
Florida	1	5.3	1	7.3	34
Georgia	2	4.2	2	8.2	27
Hawaii	1	4.6	1	6.6	38 - tie
Idaho	5	4.8	0	9.8	18 - tie
Illinois	0	6.9	0	6.9	35 - tie
Indiana	4	3.8	0	7.8	28
Iowa	5	6.9	2	13.9	2
Kansas	5	4.9	2	11.9	9
Kentucky	2	3.7	2	7.7	29
Louisiana	4	5.4	2	11.4	12
Maine	5	7	0	12	7 - tie
Maryland	2	6.8	3	11.8	10 - tie
Massachusetts	1	4.8	0	5.8	42
Michigan	2	2.6	2	6.6	38 - tie
Minnesota	5	4.8	0	9.8	18 - tie
Mississippi	1	4.4	2	7.4	33
Missouri	1	2.5	2	5.5	43 - tie
Montana	5	5.9	2	12.9	4

ROCK THE VOTE'S VOTING SYSTEM SCORECARD[1] (CON'T)

State	Registration Score	Voting Score	Preparation Score	Overall Score	Rank
Nebraska	0	6.9	2	8.9	24
Nevada	4	6.4	0	10.4	15
New Hampshire	4	4.7	0	8.7	25
New Jersey	2	4.7	0	6.7	37
New Mexico	0	6.4	2	8.4	26
New York	1	4.6	2	7.6	30 - tie
North Carolina	6	5.8	1	12.8	5 - tie
North Dakota*	N/A	5.4	N/A	N/A	*
Ohio	2	5.1	2	9.1	21 - tie
Oklahoma	1	3.8	0	4.8	46 - tie
Oregon	5	6.8	1	12.8	5 - tie
Pennsylvania	2	4.3	0	6.3	40 - tie
Rhode Island	2	3.3	1	6.3	40 - tie
South Carolina	2	1.8	0	3.8	49 - tie
South Dakota	3	5.3	2	10.3	16
Tennessee	1	3.8	0	4.8	46 - tie
Texas	1	4.5	2	7.5	32
Utah	4	5.5	0	9.5	20
Vermont	1	6.6	0	7.6	30 - tie
Virginia	1	2.8	0	3.8	49 - tie
Washington	6	6.2	2	14.2	1
West Virginia	1	6.1	2	9.1	21 - tie
Wisconsin	5	4.1	2	11.1	13
Wyoming	4	6.8	0	10.8	14
AVERAGE	2.7	5.0	1.1	8.7	

[1] Chart data from March 2011. Data will be regularly updated on the Rock the Vote website.

* North Dakota does not have voter registration. Applying only the non-voter registration metrics —such as all of the voting metrics and the civics score—the state receives 60 percent of the possible points (5.4 out of 9). If North Dakota is given 11 points available for voter registration and 1 point for pre-registration, its total score would be 17.4 out of 21 or the highest in the country.

SCORECARD ELEMENTS AND WEIGHT GIVEN TO EACH ELEMENT

Voter Registration	Best Score
Automatic registration	3
Permanent and portable	1
Same day registration	3
Online voter registration	3
Third-party registration drives	1
Registration Subtotal	11

Casting a Ballot	Best Score
Convenience Voting	2
Voter ID	2
Residency Requirements	1
Absentee laws	1
Military and overseas votes	1
Voting Subtotal	7

Young Voter Preparation	Best Score
Civics education	2
Pre-registration	1
Preparation Subtotal	3
Overall Best Score	**21**

CONSTITUTIONAL PROVISIONS RELATING TO VOTING

(Underlined provisions were later amended)

THE U.S. CONSTITUTION *(ratified 1788)*

THE ELECTION OF REPRESENTATIVES AND THE THREE-FIFTHS CLAUSE

ARTICLE 1, SECTION 2, CLAUSE 3. Representatives and direct taxes shall be apportioned among the several States which may be included within this Union, according to their respective numbers, <u>which shall be determined by adding to the whole number of free persons, including those bound to service for a term of years, and excluding Indians not taxed, three-fifths of all other persons.</u>

THE ELECTION OF SENATORS

ARTICLE 1, SECTION 3, CLAUSE 1. The Senate of the United States shall be composed of two Senators from each State, chosen by the Legislature thereof, for six years; and each Senator shall have one vote.

THE ELECTIONS CLAUSE

ARTICLE 1, SECTION 4, CLAUSE 1. The times, places, and manner of holding elections for Senators and Representatives, shall be prescribed in each State by the Legislature thereof, but the Congress may, at any time, by law, make or alter such regulations, except as to the places of choosing Senators.

PRESIDENTIAL ELECTIONS AND THE ELECTORAL COLLEGE
ARTICLE 2, SECTION 1, CLAUSES 1–4. The executive power shall be vested in a President of the United States of America. He shall hold his office during the term of four years, and, together with the Vice President, chosen for the same term, be elected as follows:

Each State shall appoint, in such manner as the Legislature thereof may direct, a number of electors, equal to the whole number of Senators and Representatives to which the State may be entitled in the Congress; but no Senator or Representative, or person holding an office of trust or profit under the United States, shall be appointed an elector.

The electors shall meet in their respective States, and vote by ballot for two persons, of whom one at least shall not be an inhabitant of the same State with themselves. And they shall make a list of all the persons voted for, and of the number of votes for each; which list they shall sign and certify, and transmit sealed to the seat of the Government of the United States, directed to the President of the Senate. The President of the Senate shall, in the presence of the Senate and House of Representatives, open all the certificates, and the votes shall then be counted. The person having the greatest number of votes shall be the President, if such number be a majority of the whole number of electors appointed; and if there be more than one who have such majority, and have an equal number of votes, then the House of Representatives shall immediately choose, by ballot, one of them for President; and if no person have a majority, then from the five highest on the list the said House shall, in like manner, choose the President. But, in choosing the President, the votes shall be taken by States, the representation from each two-thirds of the States, and a majority of all the States shall be necessary to a choice. In every case, after the choice of the President, the person having the greatest number of votes of the electors shall be the Vice President. But if there should remain two or more who have equal votes, the Senate shall choose from them, by ballot, the Vice President.

The Congress may determine the time of choosing the electors, and the day on which they shall give their votes; which day shall be the same throughout the United States.

AMENDMENTS TO THE CONSTITUTION

THE ELECTORAL COLLEGE

THE TWELFTH AMENDMENT (ratified 1804)

(REPLACED ARTICLE 2, SECTION 1, CLAUSE 3). The electors shall meet in their respective states and vote by ballot for President and Vice-President, one of whom, at least, shall not be an inhabitant of the same state with themselves; they shall name in their ballots the person voted for as President, and in distinct ballots the person voted for as Vice-President, and they shall make distinct lists of all persons voted for as President, and of all persons voted for as Vice-President, and of the number of votes for each, which lists they shall sign and certify, and transmit sealed to the seat of the government of the United States, directed to the President of the Senate; The President of the Senate shall, in the presence of the Senate and House of Representatives, open all the certificates and the votes shall then be counted—the person having the greatest number of votes for President, shall be the President, if such number be a majority of the whole number of electors appointed; and if no person have such majority, then from the persons having the highest numbers not exceeding three on the list of those voted for as President, the House of Representatives shall choose immediately, by ballot, the President. But in choosing the President, the votes shall be taken by states, the representation from each state having one vote; a quorum for this purpose shall consist of a member or members from two-thirds of the states, and a majority of all the states shall be necessary to a choice. And if the House of Representatives shall not choose a President whenever the right of choice shall devolve upon them, before the fourth day of March next following, then the Vice-President shall act as President, as in the case of the death or other constitutional disability of the President. The person having the greatest number of votes as Vice-President, shall be the Vice-President, if such number be a majority of the whole number of electors appointed, and if no person have a majority, then from the two highest numbers on the list, the Senate shall choose the Vice-President; a quorum for the purpose shall consist of two-thirds of the whole number of Senators, and a majority of the whole number shall be necessary to a choice. But no person constitutionally ineligible to the office of President shall be eligible to that of Vice-President of the United States.

RACE AND VOTING, EQUAL PROTECTION
THE FOURTEENTH AMENDMENT (ratified 1868)
SECTION 1. All persons born or naturalized in the United States, and subject to the jurisdiction thereof, are citizens of the United States and of the state wherein they reside. No state shall make or enforce any law which shall abridge the privileges or immunities of citizens of the United States; nor shall any state deprive any person of life, liberty, or property, without due process of law; nor deny to any person within its jurisdiction the equal protection of the laws.
SECTION 2. Representatives shall be apportioned among the several states according to their respective numbers, counting the whole number of persons in each state, excluding Indians not taxed. But when the right to vote at any election for the choice of electors for President and Vice President of the United States, Representatives in Congress, the executive and judicial officers of a state, or the members of the legislature thereof, is denied to any of the male inhabitants of such state, being twenty-one years of age, and citizens of the United States, or in any way abridged, except for participation in rebellion, or other crime, the basis of representation therein shall be reduced in the proportion which the number of such male citizens shall bear to the whole number of male citizens twenty-one years of age in such state.

SECTION 5. The Congress shall have power to enforce, by appropriate legislation, the provisions of this article.

RACE AND VOTING
THE FIFTEENTH AMENDMENT (ratified 1870)
SECTION 1. The right of citizens of the United States to vote shall not be denied or abridged by the United States or by any state on account of race, color, or previous condition of servitude.
SECTION 2. The Congress shall have power to enforce this article by appropriate legislation.

DIRECT ELECTION OF SENATORS
THE SEVENTEENTH AMENDMENT (ratified 1913)
The Senate of the United States shall be composed of two Senators from each state, elected by the people thereof, for six years; and each Senator shall have one vote. The electors in each state shall have the qualifications requisite for electors of the most numerous branch of the state legislatures.

When vacancies happen in the representation of any state in the Senate, the executive authority of such state shall issue writs of election to fill such vacancies: Provided, that the legislature of any state may empower the executive thereof to make temporary appointments until the people fill the vacancies by election as the legislature may direct.

This amendment shall not be so construed as to affect the election or term of any Senator chosen before it becomes valid as part of the Constitution.

SEX AND VOTING
THE NINETEENTH AMENDMENT (ratified 1920)
The right of citizens of the United States to vote shall not be denied or abridged by the United States or by any state on account of sex.

Congress shall have power to enforce this article by appropriate legislation.

WASHINGTON, D.C., ELECTORAL COLLEGE VOTES
THE TWENTY-THIRD AMENDMENT (ratified 1961)
SECTION 1. The District constituting the seat of government of the United States shall appoint in such manner as the Congress may direct: A number of electors of President and Vice President equal to the whole number of Senators and Representatives in Congress to which the District would be entitled if it were a state, but in no event more than the least populous state; they shall be in addition to those appointed by the states, but they shall be considered, for the purposes of the election of President and Vice President, to be electors appointed by a state; and they shall meet in the District and perform such duties as provided by the twelfth article of amendment.
SECTION 2. The Congress shall have power to enforce this article by appropriate legislation.

THE POLL TAX
THE TWENTY-FOURTH AMENDMENT (ratified 1964)
SECTION 1. The right of citizens of the United States to vote in any primary or other election for President or Vice President, for electors for President or Vice President, or for Senator or Representative in Congress, shall not be denied or abridged by the United States or any state by reason of failure to pay any poll tax or other tax.
SECTION 2. The Congress shall have power to enforce this article by appropriate legislation.

VOTING AGE
THE TWENTY-SIXTH AMENDMENT (ratified 1971)
SECTION 1. The right of citizens of the United States, who are 18 years of age or older, to vote, shall not be denied or abridged by the United States or any state on account of age.
SECTION 2. The Congress shall have the power to enforce this article by appropriate legislation.

TIMELINE OF MAJOR EVENTS IN AMERICAN VOTING

1787   The Constitution is drafted in Philadelphia.

1788   The Constitution is ratified. George Washington is elected first President of the United States.

1790   Ten states have property requirements for voting (Connecticut, Delaware, Maryland, Massachusetts, New Jersey, New York, North Carolina, Rhode Island, South Carolina, and Virginia).

1790   The Naturalization Act of 1790 is passed. Citizenship rights for immigrants are limited to whites.

1800   In the presidential election, the Electoral College vote between Thomas Jefferson and Aaron Burr is tied. Jefferson becomes President after the House of Representatives breaks the tie.

1801   Massachusetts creates the nation's first voter registration system.

1804   The Twelfth Amendment to the Constitution is adopted in the wake of the 1800, tied presidential election. The Electoral College is modified.

1807   New Jersey eliminates its provision allowing some women with property to vote.

1824   In the presidential election, Andrew Jackson leads the popular vote but loses the election when it is sent to the House of Representatives, which selects John Quincy Adams.

1828   Andrew Jackson runs for President again and wins.

1848   Seneca Falls Convention organized by Lucretia Mott and Elizabeth Cady Stanton calls for giving women the vote.

1855   Connecticut adopts the nation's first literacy test for voting. Massachusetts follows suit in 1857.

1856   North Carolina is the last state to eliminate property ownership as a requirement to vote.

1868   Fourteenth Amendment to the Constitution is adopted. States that deny voting rights to men will have their representation in Congress reduced proportionately.

1870   Fifteenth Amendment to the Constitution is adopted. The right to vote cannot be denied or abridged on the basis of race.

1870   Mississippi Republican Hiram Revels becomes the first African American to be elected a U.S. Senator.

1872 Susan B. Anthony and eleven other women are arrested in Rochester, New York, for voting in the presidential election.

1876 In the presidential election, Samuel Tilden wins the popular vote against Rutherford B. Hayes, but confusion over the Electoral College votes from three states sends the election to the House of Representatives.

1877 The Tilden-Hayes election is decided by a small group of members of Congress in the Compromise of 1877. Hayes is sworn in as President.

1882 Congress passes the Chinese Exclusion Act barring Chinese immigration and denying citizenship and voting rights to Chinese immigrants.

1887 A federal court rules that a Chinese immigrant of Mongolian descent is not eligible for citizenship under the naturalization laws because he is not white.

1887 Congress passes the Dawes Allotment Act granting citizenship only to Native Americans who give up tribal affiliation.

1888 In the presidential election, Grover Cleveland wins the popular vote, but Benjamin Harrison wins the Electoral College vote.

1888 Australian ballot is first used in the United States in Kentucky.

1890 Second post–Civil War Mississippi constitution is adopted. It imposes a poll tax and a literacy test on voters and bars selected felons from voting.

1890   Wyoming is admitted to the United States. It is the first
              state to allow women to vote since New Jersey rescinded
              their right to vote in 1807.

1890   The Indian Naturalization Act grants citizenship to Native
              Americans by an application process.

1892   With the widespread adoption of the Australian ballot, se-
              cret voting is in place in thirty-eight states.

1892   First lever voting machine is used in Lockport, New York.

1892   Grover Cleveland wins the popular and Electoral College
              vote and becomes President, four years after losing the elec-
              tion due to the college.

1913   More than five thousand women participate in a wom-
              en's suffrage march in Washington, D.C., the day before
              President Woodrow Wilson's inauguration.

1913   Seventeenth Amendment to the Constitution is adopted.
              Going forward, senators are elected by popular vote instead
              of selected by state legislatures.

1920   Nineteenth Amendment to the Constitution is adopted. The
              right to vote cannot be denied or abridged on the basis of sex.

1922   The U.S. Supreme Court holds that a person of Japanese
              origin is barred from naturalization under the statute limit-
              ing eligibility to "free white persons and to aliens of African
              nativity and to persons of African descent."

1923   The U.S. Supreme Court rules that "high caste Hindus" from India are not eligible for citizenship because they do not qualify as white under the naturalization law.

1924   The Indian Citizenship Act of 1924 declares all non-citizen Native Americans born within the United States to be citizens, giving them the right to vote.

1937   The Supreme Court upholds the constitutionality of the poll tax in *Breedlove v. Stuttles.*

1943   The Magnuson Act passes, repealing the Chinese Exclusion Act and for the first time in U.S. history giving Chinese immigrants the right to citizenship and the right to vote.

1952   Walter-McCarran Act grants all people of Asian ancestry the right to become citizens.

1961   Twenty-third Amendment to the Constitution is adopted. Washington, D.C., residents are able to elect electors to the Electoral College.

1963   The March on Washington brings hundreds of thousands of civil and voting rights protesters to the capital.

1964   Twenty-fourth Amendment to the Constitution is adopted. The poll tax is barred.

1964   In *Reynolds v. Sims*, the Supreme Court announces the principle of "one man, one vote."

1965   Voting rights marchers are accosted by police as they attempt to cross the Edmund Pettus Bridge in Selma, Alabama. One man is killed.

1965   The Voting Rights Act is enacted. (See Chapter 2 for details.)

1970   Amendments to the Voting Rights Act of 1965 bar literacy tests nationwide.

1971   Twenty-sixth Amendment to the Constitution is adopted. The age at which people can begin to vote is lowered to eighteen.

1975   The Voting Rights Act is amended to include language assistance to minority voters.

1990   Americans with Disabilities Act is enacted and requires full access to voting facilities for people with disabilities.

1993   National Voter Registration Act is passed. (See Chapter 5 for details.)

2000   In the presidential election, Al Gore wins the popular vote but loses the Electoral College vote to George W. Bush.

2002   Help America Vote Act is passed. (See Chapter 5 for details.)

APPENDIX C

ILLUSTRATIONS

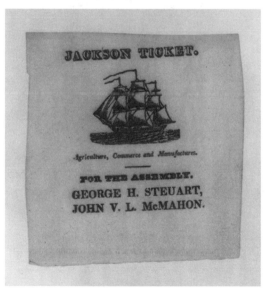

1828 BALLOT FOR THE "JACKSON" DEMOCRATIC CANDIDATES RUNNING FOR THE MARYLAND STATE ASSEMBLY. John V.L. McMahon and George H. Steuart won the race and were elected to the assembly to represent Baltimore. During the 1820s, McMahon was an active supporter of the "Jew Bill," the law to remove the requirement that all elected officials in Maryland swear to "a belief in the Christian religion." After serving in the assembly, Steuart commanded a division of the Maryland Volunteer Militia. His son served as a Confederate general in the Civil War and fought with Robert E. Lee in the last battle of the Civil War, Appomattox. **Source:** *Library of Congress*

1828 MARYLAND STATE ASSEMBLY BALLOT FOR THE WHIG PARTY CANDIDATES ASSOCIATED WITH SITTING PRESIDENT JOHN QUNICY ADAMS. Luke Tiernan and George Richardson lost the election to McMahon and Steuart. Tiernan was a wealthy Irish-born merchant in Baltimore and had served as an elector for Adams in the 1824 presidential election. His grandson, like Steuart's, served as a Confederate general in the Civil War. Rich ardson later went on to serve as the state's Attorney General and was considered one of the best criminal defense attorneys of his day. **Source:** *Library of Congress*

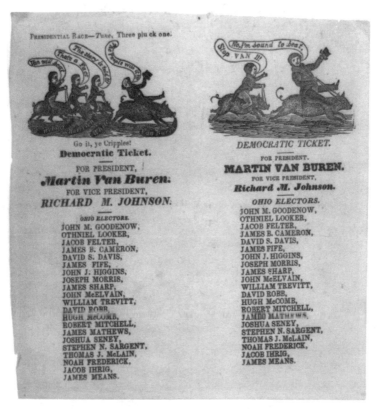

1836 OHIO BALLOT FOR THE DEMOCRATIC CANDIDATES FOR PRESIDENT AND VICE PRESIDENT, MARTIN VAN BUREN AND RICHARD M. JOHNSON. Van Buren won the election but did not win the Ohio vote. Born into a Dutch New York family, he was the first President of non-British or Irish descent. He was also the first born after the Revolutionary War. During the election, Virginia's Electoral College members refused to vote for Van Buren's running mate Richard Johnson of Kentucky, despite the fact that the two candidates had won the Virginia popular vote. Virginia's "faithless" electors were offended by Johnson's open relationship, and children, with a black woman. Because of the action by the Virginia electors, Johnson did not receive enough votes in the college to be elected Vice President. Under the Twelfth Amendment, the decision was sent to the Senate, which voted Johnson into office. Four years later, he was dropped from the ticket. Source: Library of Congress

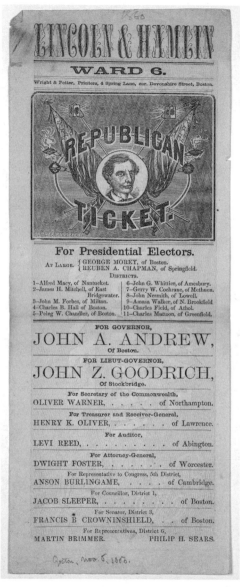

1860 MASSACHUSETTS BALLOT FOR THE REPUBLICAN CANDIDATES FOR PRESIDENT AND VICE PRESIDENT. The 1860 election was deeply fractured. Four men ran for President, and Abraham Lincoln won the presidency with less than 40 percent of the national popular vote. **Source:** *Library of Congress*

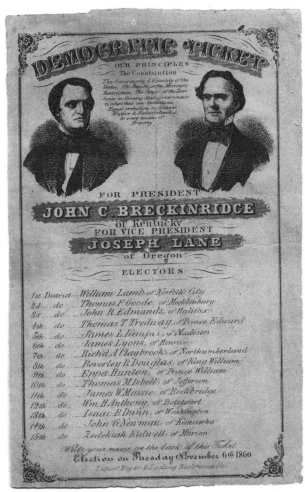

1860 Virginia ballot for the Democratic candidates for President and Vice President. John Breckinridge of Kentucky was the sitting Vice President and was running as the southern Democrats' pro-slavery candidate for President. He won Virginia's popular vote and all of the deep South. He lost the election but in 1861 was sent to Washington, D.C., by Kentucky to serve in the Senate. The Civil War broke out in the spring of 1861, but Kentucky voted to stay in the Union. So Breckinridge remained in the capital until the fall, when he fled to the Confederacy. He was declared a traitor by the Senate. He served as a general in the Confederate Army. After the war ended, he fled the nation but ultimately returned under a grant of amnesty. **Source:** *Cornell University Collection of Political Americana*

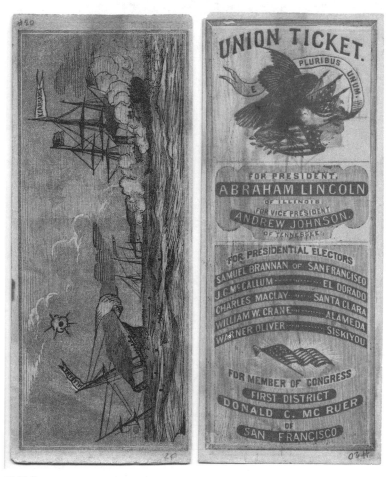

1864 CALIFORNIA BALLOT (FRONT AND BACK) FOR THE REPUBLICAN CANDIDATES FOR PRESIDENT AND VICE PRESIDENT. Abraham Lincoln won reelection handily. He never visited California but wrote friends before his assassination that he wanted to travel to the state once the transcontinental railroad was completed. He was assassinated six weeks after his inauguration. **Source:** *Cornell University Collection of Political Americana*

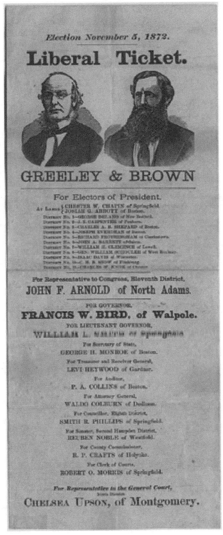

1872 MASSACHUSETTS BALLOT FOR THE LIBERAL REPUBLICAN CANDIDATES FOR PRESIDENT AND VICE PRESIDENT. The presidential candidate, Horace Greeley, was the anti-slavery, crusading newspaper editor of the New York Tribune. In 1872, Greeley led a splinter group of Republicans who denounced the party's sitting President, Ulysses S. Grant. He accepted the support of Democrats, a party he had long criticized. Greeley lost the election and died before the Electoral College votes were counted. Source: Cornell University Collection of Political Americana

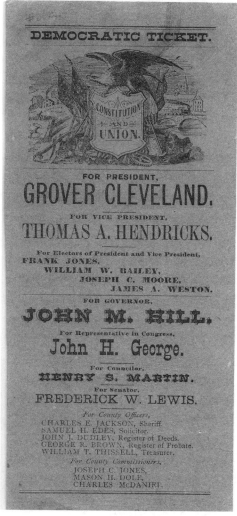

1880 New Hampshire ballot for the Democratic candidates for President and Vice President. New York's Grover Cleveland won the election, though not New Hampshire, and became the first Democratic President since 1856. Cleveland had made a name for himself as a good government reformer and was a bitter enemy of his own state's Democratic machine at Tammany Hall. Cleveland was America's only bachelor President. During the campaign he was smeared by true allegations that he had fathered a child out of wedlock. Four years later, Cleveland lost his reelection bid due to the workings of the Electoral College. **Source:** *Cornell University Collection of Political Americana*

1896 NEW YORK AUSTRALIAN BALLOT FOR PRESIDENT AND VICE PRESIDENT. This was one of the first ballots produced at public expense and distributed to all voters, listing all candidates for office. The Australian ballot initiated an era of secret voting in America. This ballot contains party symbols at the top of the columns, helping illiterate voters to vote the "party line." **Source:** *Smithsonian*

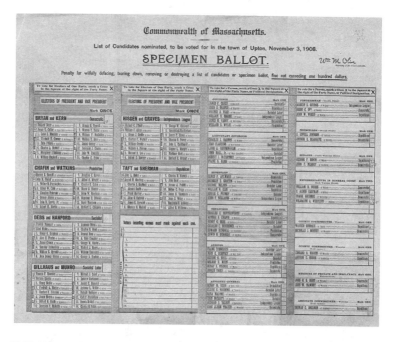

1908 MASSACHUSETTS AUSTRALIAN BALLOT FOR ALL OFFICES. Massachusetts was the first state to use the Australian ballot statewide, beginning in 1892. (It had been used before in a few individual cities.) On this ballot, party symbols have been eliminated. Many regarded the Australian ballot as an underhanded literacy test. By the early twentieth century, U.S. white literacy approached 90 percent. But black and immigrant literacy was much lower. Source: Smithsonian

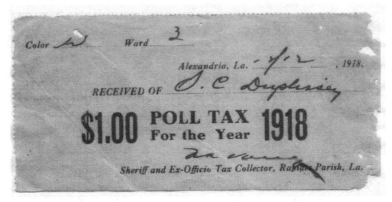

1918 POLL TAX RECEIPT FROM LOUISIANA. By the mid-1890s, most southern states imposed a poll tax that had to be paid before a person could vote. The poll tax was not limited to the South. Nationwide, the average income for an American worker was less than $500. It was far lower in Louisiana. Paying $1 to vote was a significant economic hardship for many. Voting rates among blacks plunged throughout the South. **Source:** *Private collection*

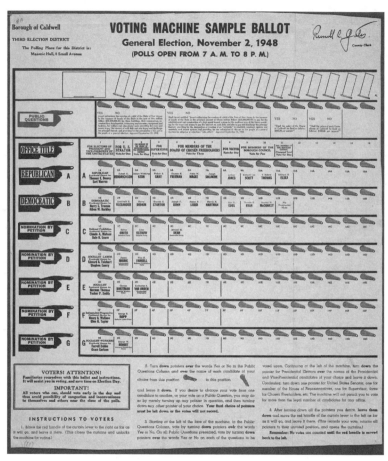

1948 New Jersey Presidential Election Ballot. By the mid-twentieth century, large numbers of Americans in urban areas were voting using lever machines. **Source:** *Cornell University Collection of Political Americana*

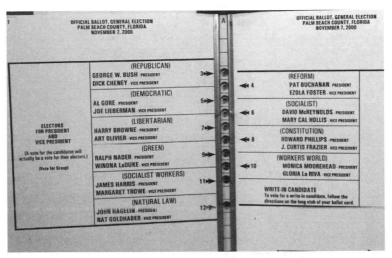

2000 "BUTTERFLY" BALLOT FOR PRESIDENT AND VICE PRESIDENT FROM PALM BEACH COUNTY, FLORIDA. The Palm Beach official in charge of ballot design was concerned that the county's large population of the elderly would have trouble reading a ballot with smaller print. To allow a larger font size, she spread the candidate names across both sides of the "hole punch." However, many voters were confused about where the arrows lined up with the holes, and evidence indicates a substantial number of mistaken votes were cast for Reform candidate Pat Buchanan due to the confusing ballot design.
Source: *Brennan Center for Justice*

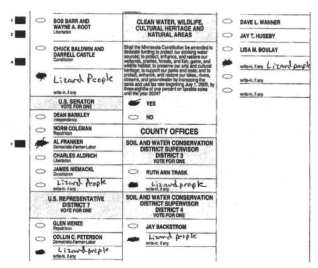

*IMAGES ON THIS PAGE AND FOLLOWING PAGES: SELECTION OF CHALLENGED BALLOTS FOR THE 2008 MINNESOTA SENATE ELECTION. The ballot that included "Lizard People" was not counted as it was judged to be an "over-vote." The "Flying Spaghetti Monster" and "would like Norm Coleman" ballots were counted. **Source:** Office of the Secretary of State of Minnesota*

○ **CHUCK BALDWIN AND DARRELL CASTLE** Constitution	**SOIL AND WATER CONSERVATION DISTRICT SUPERVISOR DISTRICT 1** VOTE FOR ONE
○	○ WADE BASTIAN
write-in, if any	● *Flying Spaghetti Mon*
U.S. SENATOR VOTE FOR ONE	**SOIL AND WATER CONSERVATION DISTRICT SUPERVISOR DISTRICT 4** VOTE FOR ONE
○ **DEAN BARKLEY** Independence	
○ **NORM COLEMAN** Republican	○ BERNIE THOLE
● **AL FRANKEN** Democratic-Farmer-Labor	● *ESM* write-in, if any
○ **CHARLES ALDRICH** Libertarian	**SOIL AND WATER CONSERVATION DISTRICT SUPERVISOR DISTRICT 5** VOTE FOR ONE
○ **JAMES NIEMACKL** Constitution	
○ write-in, if any	○ CHUCK RAU
U.S. REPRESENTATIVE DISTRICT 6 VOTE FOR ONE	● *ESM* write-in, if any
○ **BOB ANDERSON** Independence	**SPECIAL ELECTION FOR SOIL AND WATER CONSERVATION DISTRICT SUPERVISOR DISTRICT 3** To fill vacancy in term expiring January 3, 2011 VOTE FOR ONE
○ **MICHELE BACHMANN** Republican	
● **EL TINKLENBERG**	

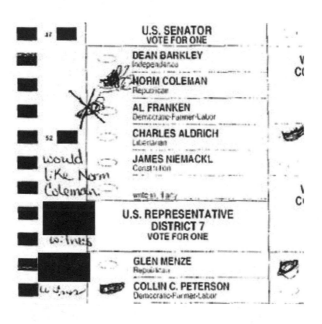

ADDITIONAL RESOURCES

PEOPLE WHO WANT TO FIND out more about various voting requirements in their states can often visit their state's Secretary of State website. In several states, elections are run by boards, and a quick Internet search will help find its website. Many of these sites also help voters

- establish the registration deadline
- get registration forms
- confirm whether they are registered
- determine where their polling station is
- apply for an absentee ballot
- determine if their absentee ballot has been received and proccsscd

Two third-party organizations also maintain websites to help prospective voters.

> Rock the Vote's website gathers information of upcoming elections in all states and includes registration deadlines and helpful information for finding polling locations. It

also allows visitors to post questions, which are usually answered promptly and accurately.

The National Conference on State Legislatures' section on elections and campaigns also generates regular reports and updates on state election laws, including voter identification requirements, early and absentee voting, registration requirements, military voting, felon voting, and numerous other issues.

A number of other groups are dedicated to the study or reform of particular aspects of voting in America. People interested in learning more about voting rights can visit these groups' websites. They are listed in alphabetical order.

The Advancement Project
Brennan Center for Justice
DC Vote
Demos
Fair Elections Legal Network
FairVote
Lawyers Committee for Civil Rights Under the Law
League of Women Voters
National Popular Vote
The Sentencing Project
Why Tuesday?

Many other groups also tackle the issue of voting in America on a local basis or as part of other missions.

Several organizations also systematically study election issues. Voters interested in such research can find extensive data and analysis at the websites of the following organizations:

California Institute of Technology/Massachusetts Institute of Technology Voting Technology Project

Center for Democracy and Election Management (at
  American University)
Center for Information and Research on Civic Learning
  and Engagement (CIRCLE at Tufts University)
Center for the Study of Politics and Governance, Program
  for Excellence in Election Administration (at the
  University of Minnesota)
Election Administration Commission
Election Law @ Moritz (at Ohio State University)
Pew Center on the States

The Electoral Dysfunction website, www.electoraldysfunction.org, contains additional material, including a selection of original source material relating to voting rights. For example, readers interested in learning more about the Voting Rights Act of 1965 will find the text of President Lyndon B. Johnson's address to Congress calling for its passage. Readers interested in the women's suffrage movement will find a full copy of the 1872 sentencing hearing of Susan B. Anthony for illegal voting. And a copy of Frederick Douglass's speech calling for black voting rights in April 1865 within days of the Lincoln assassination is also available. Other material includes letters from John Adams and Thomas Jefferson relating to the franchise and copies of key *Federalist Papers*.

ACKNOWLEDGMENTS

FIRST AND FOREMOST, I WOULD like to thank my mother and father, both of whom brought me to the polls when I was a child and let me pull the lever with them. It was thrilling. They voted Democratic and Republican at various times and taught me to respect the ideals articulated by both parties.

This book would not have been possible without Bennett Singer's generosity of spirit and tenacious determination. I owe him and the members of the *Electoral Dysfunction* documentary team my deepest thanks. They are David Deschamps, Leslie D. Farrell, Mridu Chandra, and Benjamin Kramer. The film's extended family includes Maura May and Alison Oliver. Two law school students deserve thanks (and good grades) for helping me research the issues surrounding felon disenfranchisement and the Terrance Watts case: Maureen McDonald and Lauren Barlow. Finally, Mo Rocca has been dedicated to the film and to voting issues for years. Neither this book, nor the documentary, would have come to pass without his wit and commitment.

The New Press team was incredible, pulling this together on an expedited schedule. Thanks to Diane Wachtell for taking a gamble on me, her skillful editing, and her steadfast commitment to creating this book. Thanks also to Tara Grove for her patience, support, and help. I also could not have written this book without the assistance of the staff of the Brooklyn Public Library, the New York Public Library, and the Library of Congress. The staff at the Carroll Gardens branch of the Brooklyn Public Library deserves a special award for maintaining a library that cheerfully hosts everyone from age zero to one hundred. Several friends were enormously helpful and supportive, providing comments, insight, and moral support: Theresa Amato, Caroline Fredrickson, Dan Gerstein, Susan Kraham, Kathy O'Connor, Jill Straus, Mary Lynne Werlwas, and Nathaniel Wice. Two people deserve to be singled out. Blake Cornish gave me a home in Washington, D.C., as I researched and worked on this project. He has been an extraordinary friend. My cousin Ellen Baird read, edited, and commented on almost all of the chapters, even as she cheered me on and helped keep me going many days.

SELECT BIBLIOGRAPHY

BOOKS

Acemoglu, Damon, and James Robinson. *Why Nations Fail.* New York: Crown Business, 2012.

Alexander, Michelle. *The New Jim Crow: Mass Incarceration in the Age of Colorblindness.* New York: The New Press, 2012.

Amar, Akhil Reed. *America's Constitution: A Biography.* New York: Random House, 2008.

Bartels, Larry M. *Unequal Democracy: The Political Economy of the New Gilded Age.* Princeton, NJ: Princeton University Press, 2008.

Beekman, Richard. *Plain, Honest Men: The Making of the American Constitution.* New York: Random House, 2009.

Berkin, Carol. *A Brilliant Solution: Inventing the American Constitution.* Orlando, FL: Harvest Books, 2002.

Bishop, Bill. *The Big Sort.* Boston: Houghton Mifflin Company, 2008.

Brennan, Jason. *The Ethics of Voting.* Princeton, NJ: Princeton University Press, 2011.

Butler, Jon. *Becoming America: The Revolution Before 1776.* Cambridge, MA: Harvard University Press, 2001.

CalTech/MIT Voting Technology Project Voting. "What Is, What Could Be." July 2001. http://vote.caltech.edu/drupal/files /report/voting_what_is_what_could_be.pdf.

Campbell, Tracy. *Deliver the Vote: A History of Election Fraud, An American Political Tradition—1742–2004*. New York: Carroll & Graf Publishers, 2005.

Caplan, Brian. *The Myth of the Rational Voter: Why Democracies Choose Bad Policies*. Princeton, NJ: Princeton University Press, 2007.

Caro, Robert A. *The Years of Lyndon Johnson: The Path to Power*. New York: Vintage Books, 1982.

Caro, Robert A. *The Years of Lyndon Johnson: Means of Ascent*. New York: Alfred A. Knopf, 1990.

Caro, Robert A. *The Years of Lyndon Johnson: Master of the Senate*. New York: Alfred A. Knopf, 2002.

Chernow, Ron. *Alexander Hamilton*. New York: The Penguin Press, 2004.

Clarke, M. St. Clair, and David A. Hall. *Contested Elections in Congress from the Year 1789 to 1834, Inclusive*. Washington, DC: Gales and Seaton, 1834.

Craig, Stephen C., and Michael D. Martinez. "Voter Competence." In *The Electoral Challenge: Theory Meets Practice*, edited by Stephen C. Craig and David B. Hill. Washington, DC: CQ Press, 2011.

Crigler, Ann N., Marion R. Just, and Edward J. McCaffery, eds. *Rethinking the Vote: The Politics and Prospects of American Election Reform*. Oxford: Oxford University Press, 2004.

Crozier, Michel, Samuel P. Huntington, and Joji Watanuki. *The Crisis of Democracy: Report on the Governability of Democracies to the Trilateral Commission*. New York: New York University Press, 1975.

Dahl, Robert. *On Democracy*. New Haven, CT: Yale University Press, 1998.

Dahl, Robert. *Democracy and Its Critics*. New Haven, CT: Yale University Press, 1989.

Dinkin, Robert J. *Voting in Revolutionary America: A Study of Elections in the Original Thirteen States, 1776–1789*. Westport, CT: Greenwood Press, 1982.

Dinkin, Robert J. *Campaigning in America: A History of Election Practices*. Westport, CT: Greenwood Press, 1989.

Donnell, Ryan. *Behind the Curtain: A Look at Philadelphia's Unique Polling Places*. Philadelphia: Blurb, 2011.

Downs, Anthony. *An Economic Theory of Democracy*. New York: Harper & Row, 1957.

Dworkin, Ronald, ed. *A Badly Flawed Election: Debating Bush v. Gore, the Supreme Court, and American Democracy*. New York: The New Press, 2002.

Dyer, Frank Lewis, and Thomas Commerford Martin. *Edison, His Life and Inventions*. New York: Harper Brothers, 1929.

Ellis, Joseph J. *American Creation: Triumphs and Tragedies at the Founding of the Republic*. New York: Alfred A. Knopf, 2007.

Ely, John Hart. *Democracy and Distrust*. Cambridge, MA: Harvard University Press, 1980.

Ewald, Alec C. *The Way We Vote: The Local Dimension of American Suffrage*. Nashville, TN: Vanderbilt University Press, 2009.

Fiorina, Morris P. "Extreme Voices: A Dark Side of Civic Engagement." In *Civic Engagement in American Democracy*, edited by Theda Skocpol and Morris P. Fiorina, 395–426. Washington, DC: Brookings Institution Press, 2002.

Fitrakis, Robert J., Steven Rosenfeld, and Harvey Wasserman. *What Happened in Ohio?* New York: The New Press, 2006.

Fortier, John C., ed. *After the People Vote: A Guide to the Electoral College*. Washington, DC: AEI Press, 2004.

Fortier, John C. *Absentee and Early Voting.* Washington, DC: AEI Press, 2006.

Fox Piven, Frances, Lorraine C. Minnite, and Margaret Groarke, eds. *Keeping Down the Black Vote.* New York: The New Press, 2009.

Fox Piven, Frances, and Richard A. Cloward. *Why Americans Still Don't Vote and Why Politicians Want It That Way.* New York: Beacon Press, 2000.

Fund, John H. *Stealing Elections: How Voter Fraud Threatens Our Democracy.* San Francisco, CA: Encounter Books, 2004.

Gelman, Andrew. *Red State, Blue State, Rich State, Poor State: Why Americans Vote the Way They Do.* Princeton, NJ: Princeton University Press, 2009.

Gerken, Heather K. *The Democracy Index: Why Our Election System Is Failing and How to Fix It.* Princeton, NJ: Princeton University Press, 2009.

Griffith, Benjamin E., ed. *America Votes! A Guide to Modern Election Law and Voting Rights.* Chicago, IL: ABA Books, 2008.

Gumbel, Andrew. *Steal This Vote: Dirty Elections and the Rotten History of Democracy in America.* New York: Nation Books, 2005.

Gutmann, Amy, and Dennis Thompson. *Why Deliberative Democracy?* Princeton, NJ: Princeton University Press, 2004.

Haidt, Jonathan. *The Righteous Mind: Why Good People Are Divided by Politics and Religion.* New York: Pantheon Books, 2012.

Hasen, Richard J. "The Fraudulent Fraud Squad." In *The Voting Wars: From Florida 2000 to the Next Election Meltdown* by Richard J. Hasen. New Haven: Yale University Press, 2012.

Hernson, Paul S., Richard G. Niemi, Michael J. Hanmer, Benjamin B. Bederson, Frederick C. Conrad, and Michael W. Traugott. *Voting Technology: The Not So Simple Act of Casting a Ballot.* Washington, DC: Brookings Institution Press, 2008.

Hill, David. *American Voter Turnout: An Institutional Perspective.*
Boulder, CO: Westview Press, 2006.

Hofstadter, Richard. *The American Political Tradition.* New York:
Vintage Books, 1974.

Jefferson, Thomas. *Writings.* New York: The Library of America,
1984.

Kaufmann, Karen M., John R. Petrocik, and Daron R. Shaw.
Unconventional Wisdom: Facts and Myths About American Voters.
Oxford: Oxford University Press, 2008.

Key, V.O., Jr. *The Responsible Electorate: Rationality in Presidential
Voting 1936–1960.* New York: Vintage Books, 1966.

Keyssar, Alexander. *The Right to Vote: The Contested History of
Democracy in the United States.* New York: Basic Books, 2000.

Koza, John R., Barry Fadem, Mark Grueskin, Michael S. Mandell,
Robert Richie, and Josph F. Zimmerman. *Every Vote Equal: A
State-based Plan for Electing the President, Third Edition.* Los Altos,
CA: National Popular Vote Press, 2011.

Lakoff, George. *The Political Mind.* New York: Viking, 2008.

Lears, Jackson. *Rebirth of a Nation: The Making of Modern America,
1877–1920.* New York: HarperCollins, 2009.

Lepore, Jill. "A World of Paine." In *Revolutionary Founders: Rebels,
Radicals, and Reformers in the Making of the Nation*, edited by Alfred
F. Young, Ray Raphael, and Gary Nash, 87–96. New York:
Alfred A. Knopf, 2011.

Lepore, Jill. *The Whites of Their Eyes.* Princeton, NJ: Princeton
University Press, 2010.

Levendusky, Matthew. *The Partisan Sort.* Chicago, IL: The
University of Chicago Press, 2009.

Lewis-Beck, Michael S., William G. Jacoby, Helmut Norpoth, and
Herbert Weisberg. *The American Voter Revisited.* Ann Arbor, MI:
The University of Michigan Press, 2008.

Lupia, Arthur, and Mathew D. McCubbins. *The Democratic Dilemma: Can Citizens Learn What They Really Need to Know?* Cambridge: Cambridge University Press, 1998.

Maier, Pauline. *Ratification: The People Debate the Constitution, 1787–1788.* New York: Simon & Schuster, 2010.

McCullough, David. *John Adams.* New York: Simon & Schuster, 2001.

Minnite, Lorraine C. *The Myth of Voter Fraud.* Ithaca, NY: Cornell University Press, 2010.

Morris, Roy, Jr. *Fraud of the Century: Rutherford B. Hayes, Samuel Tilden and the Stolen Election of 1876.* New York: Simon & Schuster, 2003.

Munck, Gerardo L. *Measuring Democracy: A Bridge Between Scholarship and Politics.* Baltimore: The Johns Hopkins University Press, 2009.

National Commission on Federal Election Reform. *To Assure Pride and Confidence in the Electoral Process.* Washington, DC: Brookings Institution Press, 2002.

Nelson, Craig. *Thomas Paine.* New York: Penguin Books, 2006.

Neuman, Russell W., George E. Marcus, Michael MacKuen, and Ann N. Crigler, eds. *The Affect Effect: Dynamics of Emotion in Political Thinking and Behavior.* Chicago, IL: University of Chicago Press, 2007.

Niemi, Richard G., Herbert F. Weisberg, and David C. Kimball, eds. *Controversies in Voting Behavior.* Washington, DC: CQ Press, 2011.

Okrent, Daniel. *Last Call: The Rise and Fall of Prohibition.* New York: Scribner, 2010.

Oppenheimer, Danny, and Mike Edwards. *Democracy Despite Itself: Why a System That Shouldn't Work At All Works So Well.* Cambridge, MA: Massachusetts Institute of Technology Press, 2012.

Overton, Spencer. *Stealing Democracy: The New Politics of Voter Suppression*. New York: W.W. Norton & Company, 2006.

Paine, Thomas. *Collected Writings*. New York: The Library of America, 1995.

Patterson, Thomas E. *The Vanishing Voter: Public Involvement in an Age of Uncertainty*. New York: Alfred A. Knopf, 2002.

Popkin, Samuel L. *The Reasoning Voter*. Chicago, IL: University of Chicago Press, 1991.

Poundstone, William. *Gaming the Vote: Why Elections Aren't Fair (and What We Can Do About It)*. New York: Hill and Wang, 2008.

Rahn, Wendy M., John Brehm, and Neil Carlson. "National Elections as Institutions for Generating Social Capital." In *Civic Engagement in American Democracy*, edited by Theda Skocpol and Morris P. Fiorina, 111–62. Washington, DC: Brookings Institution Press, 2001.

Raphael, Ray. *Mr. President: How and Why the Founders Created a Chief Executive*. New York: Alfred A. Knopf, 2012.

Rorabough, W.J. *The Alcoholic Republic: An American Tradition*. New York: Oxford University Press, 1979.

Rowell, Chester H. *A Historical and Legal Digest of All the Contested Election Cases in the House of Representatives of the United States from the First to the Fifty-sixth Congress, 1789–1901*. Washington, DC: Government Printing Office, 1901.

Schlesinger, Arthur M., Jr. *The Cycles of American History*. Boston: Mariner Books, 1999.

Schlozman, Kay Lehman, Sidney Verba, and Henry Brady. "Civic Participation and the Equality Problem." In *Civic Engagement in American Democracy*, edited by Theda Skocpol and Morris P. Fiorina, 427–60. Washington, DC: Brookings Institution Press, 1999.

Schumpeter, Joseph A. *Capitalism, Socialism and Democracy.* New York: Harper & Row, 1950.

Sherr, Lynn. *Failure Is Impossible: Susan B. Anthony in Her Own Words.* New York: Times Books, 1995.

Skocpol, Theda. "How Americans Became Civic." In *Civic Engagement in American Democracy,* edited by Theda Skocpol and Morris P. Fiorina, 27–80. Washington, DC: Brookings Institution Press, 2000.

Skocpol, Theda. "Advocates without Members: The Recent Transformation of American Civil Life." In *Civic Engagement in American Democracy,* edited by Theda Skocpol and Morris P. Fiorina, 461–510. Washington, DC: Brookings Institution Press, 2003.

Stewart, David O. *The Summer of 1787.* New York, Simon & Schuster, 2007.

Tribe, Laurence H. *The Invisible Constitution.* New York: Oxford University Press, 2008.

Waldstreicher, David. *Slavery's Constitution: From Revolution to Ratification.* New York: Hill and Wang, 2009.

Wayne, Stephen J. *Is This Any Way to Run a Democratic Election?* Washington, DC: CQ Press, 2007.

Weiner, Jay. *This Is Not Florida: How Al Franken Won the Minnesota Senate Recount.* Minneapolis: University of Minnesota Press, 2010.

Westen, Drew. *The Political Brain.* New York: Public Affairs, 2007.

Wolfinger, Raymond E., and Steven J. Rosenstone. *Who Votes?* New Haven, CT: Yale University Press, 1990.

Wood, Gordon S. *The Radicalism of the American Revolution.* New York: Alfred A. Knopf, 1992.

Woodward, C. Vann. *The Strange Career of Jim Crow.* New York: Oxford University Press, 2002.

ARTICLES AND REPORTS

Aldrich, John H., Jacob M. Montgomery, and Wendy Wood. "Turnout as Habit." *Political Behavior* 4 (2011): 535–63.

Alvarez, R. Michael. "Voter Registration: Past, Present and Future." Testimony before the Commission on Federal Election Reform, Washington, DC, June 15, 2005.

Alvarez, R. Michael, and Thad E. Hall. "Resolving Voter Registration Problems: Making Registration Easier, Less Costly and More Accurate." Voting Technology Project Working Paper. August 2009. http://vote.caltech.edu/drupal/node/292.

Alvarez, R. Michael, Stephen Ansolabehere, and Catherine H. Wilson. "Election Day Voter Registration in the United States: How One-Step Voting Can Change the Composition of the American Electorate." Voting Technology Project Working Paper. June 2002. http://vote.caltech.edu/drupal/node/16.

Alvarez, R. Michael, Stephen Ansolabehere, Adam Berinsky, Gabriel Lenz, Charles Stewart III, and Thad Hall. "2008 Survey of the Performance of American Elections: Final Report." Voting Technology Project Working Paper. March 1, 2009. http://vote.caltech.edu/drupal/node/231.

Ansolabehere, Stephen. Testimony Before the Senate Committee on Rules and Administration, Washington, DC, March 11, 2009. http://vote.caltech.edu/drupal/http%3A/%252Frules.senate.gov/public/index.cfm%3FFuseAction%3DInNews.MajorityNews%2526ContentRecord_id%3Df72bc608-5056-8059-76f6-97bcc0202f3d.

Ansolabehere, Stephen. "Is There Racial Discrimination at the Polls? Voters' Experiences in the 2008 Election." Voting Technology Project Working Paper. March 2009. http://vote.caltech.edu/node/241.

Ansolabehere, Stephen, and David Konisky. "The Introduction of Voter Registration and Its Effect on Turnout." *Political Analysis* 14 (2006): 83–100.

Ansolabehere, Stephen, and Nathaniel Persily. "Measuring Election System Performance." *NYU Journal of Legislation and Public Policy* 13 (2010): 445–69.

Ansolabehere, Stephen, and Nathaniel Persily. "Vote Fraud in the Eye of the Beholder: The Role of Public Opinion in the Challenge to Voter Identification Requirements." *Harvard Law Review* 121 (2008): 1737–774.

Ansolabehere, Stephen, Nathaniel Persily, and Charles Stewart III. "Race, Region, and Vote Choice in the 2008 Election: Implications for the Future of the Voting Rights Act." *Harvard Law Review* 123 (2010): 1385–436.

Burns, Alexander. "How Much Do Voters Know?" *Politico*, March 13, 2012. http://www.politico.com/news/stories/0312/73947.html.

Center for Democracy and Election Management. "The State of Elections in the Fifty States: Evaluating the Process Where It Counts." July 15, 2009. http://www1.american.edu/ia/cdem /pdfs/CDEM%20Final%20Rpt%20of%20the%20States%20 -%20July%2015%2009.pdf.

Center for Democracy and Election Management. "Election Administration Profiles of All Fifty States." July 15, 2009. http://www1.american.edu/ia/cdem/pdfs/CDEM%20 Rpt%20Supplemental-%20State%20Profiles%20-%20July%20 15%2009.pdf.

Citizens for Election Integrity Minnesota. "Facts About Ineligible Voting and Voter Fraud in Minnesota." November 2010. http:// www.ceimn.org/sites/default/files/Facts%20About%20 Ineligible%20Voting%20and%20Voter%20Fraud%20in%20 Minnesta%20(2010).pdf.

Citrin, Jack, Erik Schickler, and John Sides. "What if Everyone Voted? Simulating the Impact of Increased Turnout in Senate Elections." *American Journal of Political Science* 47 (2003): 75–90.

Commission on Federal Election Reform. "Building Confidence in U.S. Elections." September 2005. http://www1.american.edu /ia/cfer/report/full_report.pdf.

Cox, Cathy. Testimony before the National Commission on Federal Election Reform, Atlanta, GA, March 26, 2001. http://tcf.org /publications/pdfs/pb506/hearing1_p1.pdf.

Dawes, Christopher T., and James H. Fowler. "Partisanship, Voting and the Dopamine D2 Receptor Gene." *Journal of Politics* 71 (2009): 1157–71.

Demos. "Voters Win with Same Day Registration: 2010 Midterm Elections Fact Sheet." May 2011. http://www.demos.org /publication/factsheet-voters-win-same-day-registration.

Dionne, Jr., E.J. "If Nonvoters Had Voted: Same Winner, but Bigger." *New York Times*, November 21, 1988.

Electionline. "Election Reform: What's Changed, What Hasn't and Why 2000–2006." February 2006. http://www.pewtrusts.org /uploadedFiles/wwwpewtrustsorg/Reports/Election_reform /electionline_022006.pdf.

Feddersen, Timothy, Sean Gailmard, and Alvaro Sandroni. "Moral Bias in Large Elections: Theory and Experimental Evidence." *American Political Science Review* 103 (2009): 175–92.

File, Thom, and Sarah Crissey. "Voting and Registration in the Election of November 2008." U.S. Census Bureau. 2010. http:// www.census.gov/prod/2010pubs/p20-562.pdf.

Fiorina, Morris P., and Samuel Abrams. "Political Polarization in the American Public." *Annual Review of Political Science* 11 (2008): 563–88.

Fischer, Eric A., and Kevin J. Coleman. "CRS Report for Congress: Election Reform and Local Election Officials: Results of Two National Surveys." February 7, 2008. http://www.fas.org/sgp/crs/misc/RL34363.pdf.

Fowler, James H., and Christopher T. Dawes. "Two Genes Predict Voter Turnout." *Journal of Politics* 70 (2008): 579–94.

Fowler, James H., Laura A. Baker, and Christopher T. Dawes. "Genetic Variation in Political Participation." *American Political Science Review* 102 (2008): 233–48.

Funk, Patricia. "Theory and Evidence on the Role of Social Norms in Voting." 2005. http://www.pubchoicesoc.org/papers2005/Funk.pdf.

Gelman, Andrew. "What Difference Would It Make if Everybody Voted?" December 1, 2007. http://andrewgelman.com/2007/12/what_difference/.

Grimmer, Justin, Eitan Hersh, Brian Feinstein, and Daniel Carpenter. "Are Close Elections Random?" January 28, 2011. http://www.stanford.edu/~jgrimmer/CEF.pdf.

Guess, George. "Dysfunctional Decentralization: Electoral System Performance in Theory and Practice." Center for Democracy and Election Management Working Paper. April 20, 2009. http://www1.american.edu/ia/cdem/pdfs/Dysfunctional%20Decentralization%204-20.pdf.

Highton, Benjamin, and Raymond Wolfinger. "The Political Implications of Higher Turnout." *British Journal of Political Science* 31 (2001): 179–223.

Hoke, Candice, Ronald B. Adrine, and Tom J. Hayes. *Final Report of the Cuyahoga County Election Review Panel*. January 1, 2006. http://engagedscholarship.csuohio.edu/scholbks/41.

Huefner, Steven F., Daniel P. Tokaji, Edward B. Foley, and Nathan Cemenska. "From Registration to Recounts: Developments in the Election Ecosystems of Five Midwestern States." 2007. http://moritzlaw.osu.edu/electionlaw/projects/registration-to -recounts/book.pdf.

Huefner, Steven F., Nathan A. Cemenska, Daniel P. Tokaji, and Edward B. Foley. "From Registration to Recounts Revisited: Developments in the Election Ecosystems of Five Midwestern States." 2011. http://moritzlaw.osu.edu/electionlaw/projects /registration-to-recounts/2011edition.pdf.

Inspector General of the U.S. Department of Justice. *An Investigation into the Removal of Nine U.S. Attorneys in 2006*. September 2008. http://www.justice.gov/oig/special/s0809a/final.pdf.

Jenkins, Jeffrey A. "Partisanship and Contested Election Cases in the House of Representatives, 1789–2002." *Studies in American Political Development* 18 (2004) 112–35.

Kaplan, Robert D. "Was Democracy Just a Moment?" *The Atlantic*, December 1997. http://www.theatlantic.com/magazine/archive /1997/12/was-democracy-just-a-moment/6022/.

Kimball, David C., Martha Kropf, and Lindsay Battles. "Helping America Vote? Election Administration, Partisanship, and Provisional Voting in the 2004 Election." *Election Law Journal* 5 (2006): 447–61.

Krauthammer, Charles. "In Praise of Low Voter Turnout." *Time*, May 21, 1990.

Krugman, Paul. "Stop Making Sense." *New York Times*, November 5, 2002.

Leighley, Jan, and Jonathan Nagler. "Who Votes Now? And Does It Matter?" Paper presented at the 2007 Annual Meeting of the Midwest Political Science Association, Chicago,

Illinois, March 7, 2007. http://www.nyu.edu/gsas/dept /politics/faculty/nagler/leighley_nagler_midwest2007 .pdf.

Lopez, Mark Hugo. "The Latino Electorate in 2010: More Voters, More Non-Voters." Pew Hispanic Center. April 26, 2011. http:// www.pewhispanic.org/2011/04/26/the-latino-electorate-in -2010-more-voters-more-non-voters/.

Minnite, Lorraine. "Election Day Registration: A Study of Voter Fraud Allegations and Findings on Voter Roll Security." November2007. http://www.demos.org/publication/election -day-registrationstudy-voter-fraud-allegations-and-findings -voter-roll-security.

Mlodinow, Leonard. "A Facial Theory of Politics." *New York Times*, April 21, 2012. http://www.nytimes.com/2012/04/22/opinion /sunday/a-facial-theory-of-politics.html.

Moretti, M. Mindy. "Doing a Nonpartisan Job in a Hyper-partisan World." *Electionline Weekly*, February 9, 2012. http:// www.electionline.org/index.php/2012/726-electionline weekly-february-9-2012.

Mulligan, Casey B., and Charles Hunter. "The Empirical Frequency of a Pivotal Vote." NBER Working Paper Series. November 2001. http://www.nber.org/papers/w8590.

Norden, Lawrence. "Brennan Center for Justice: Voting System Failures: A Database Solution." September 2010. http:// www.brennancenter.org/content/resource/voting_system_ failures_a_database_solution/.

Norden, Lawrence. "Brennan Center for Justice: The Machinery of Democracy: Voting System Security, Accessibility, Usability, and Cost." June 28, 2006. http://www.brennancenter.org /content/resource/machinery_of_democracy_protecting _elections_in_an_electronic_world/.

Norden, Lawrence, Aaron Burstein, Joseph Lorenzo Hall, and
Margaret Chen. "Brennan Center for Justice: Post-Election
Audits: Restoring Trust in Elections." August 1, 2007. http://
www.brennancenter.org/content/resource/post_election
_audits_restoring_trust_in_elections/.

Norden, Lawrence, and Sundeep Iyer. "Brennan Center for
Justice: Design Deficiencies and Lost Votes." December 2011.
http://www.brennancenter.org/content/resource/design
_deficiencies_and_lost_votes/.

Norden, Lawrence, David Kimball, Whitney Quesenbery, and
Margaret Chen. "Brennan Center for Justice: Better Ballots." 2008.
http://www.brennancenter.org/content/resource/better_ballots/.

Pearson, Helen. "Personality Predicts Politics: Pollsters
May Be Aided by Test of How Judgmental Voters Are."
Nature, September 22, 2004. http://www.nature.com
/news/2004/040920/full/news040920-8.html.

Perez, Myrna. "Brennan Center for Justice: Voter Purges."
September 30, 2008. http://brennan.3cdn.net/5de1bb5cbe
2c40cb0c_s0m6bqskv.pdf.

Perez, Thomas. Letter from U.S. Department of Justice Civil Rights
Division to Office of the Texas Secretary of State. March 12, 2012.

Perez, Thomas. Letter from U.S. Department of Justice Civil
Rights Division to the Assistant Deputy Attorney General of
South Carolina. December 23, 2011.

Pew Center on the States. "Inaccurate, Costly, and Inefficient."
February 2012. http://www.pewstates.org/research/reports
/inaccurate-costly-and-inefficient-85899378437.

Pew Center on the States. "Revisiting Dead Voter Allegations in
South Carolina." March 13, 2012. http://www.pewstates.org
/research/analysis/revisiting-dead-voter-allegations-in-south
-carolina-85899377124.

Pew Center on the States. "Election Administration by the
Numbers." February 9, 2012. http://www.pewstates.org/
research/reports/election-administration-by-the-numbers
-85899377331.

Pew Center on the States. "Data for Democracy: Improving
Elections Through Metrics and Measurement." December 3,
2008. http://www.pewstates.org/research/reports/data-for
-democracy-85899372163?p=1.

Pew Center on the States. "Being Online Is Still Not Enough:
Reviews and Recommendations for State Election Websites."
December 6, 2011. http://www.pewstates.org/research
/reports/being-online-is-still-not-enough-85899376525.

Pew Center on the States. "Upgrading Democracy: Improving
America's Elections by Modernizing States' Voter Registration
Systems." November 2010. http://www.pewstates.org/up
loadedFiles/PCS_Assets/2010/Upgrading_Democracy_re
port.pdf.

Pew Center on the States. "Provisional Ballots: An Imperfect
Solution." July 2009. http://www.pewstates.org/research
/reports/provisional-ballots-85899379307.

Pew Center on the States. "The Cost of Statewide Recounts: A
Case Study of Minnesota and Washington." November 2010.
http://www.pewtrusts.org/uploadedFiles/Recount_brief.pdf.

Pew Research Center for People and the Vote. "Who Votes, Who
Doesn't and Why: Regular Voters, Intermittent Voters, and
Those Who Don't." October 18, 2006. http://www.people
-press.org/files/legacy-pdf/292.pdf.

Pew Research Center for the People and the Press. "Mixed
Reactions to Republican Midterm Win." November 11, 2010.
http://www.people-press.org/2010/11/11/mixed-reactions
-to-republican-midterm-win/.

Pew Research Center for the People and the Press. "The Party of Nonvoters." October 29, 2010. http://pewresearch.org/pubs/1786/who-are-nonvoters-less-republican-educated -younger.

Pintor, Rafael Lopez, and Maria Gratschew. "Voter Turnout Since 1945: A Global Report." International IDEA Report. 2004.

Pitts, Michael J., and Matthew D. Neumann. "Documenting Disenfranchisement: Voter Identification During Indiana's 2008 General Election." *Journal of Law & Politics* 25 (2009): 329–73.

Ponoroff, Christopher. "Brennan Center for Justice: Voter Registration in a Digital Age." July 2010. http://www.brennan center.org/content/resource/voter_registration_in_a_digital _age/.

Portney, Kent, Richard C. Eichenberg, and Richard G. Niemi. "Gender Differences in Political and Civic Engagement among Young People." Paper presented at the meeting of the American Political Science Association, Toronto, Ontario, September 2009. http://ase.tufts.edu/polsci/faculty/eichenberg/Niemi PortneyEichenbergAug26.pdf.

Rasmussen. "Are Our Elections Rigged?" Rasmussen Poll. May 12, 2011. http://usa.goooh.com/2011/05/12/2012-election/are-our -elections-rigged-rasmussen-poll/.

Robert, Eve. "Voter Registration: An International Perspective." FairVote Report. April 21, 2009. http://www.fairvote.org /universal-voter-registration-an-international-perspective# .T76R2I7CFiw.

Rogers, Estelle. "The National Voter Registration Act at Fifteen." Project Vote Report. 2008. http://projectvote.org/images /publications/NVRA/THE%20NVRA%20at%20FIFTEEN --A%20Report%20to%20Congress.pdf.

Somin, Ilya. "When Ignorance Isn't Bliss: How Political Ignorance Threatens Democracy." Cato Institute Policy Analysis. September 22, 2004. http://www.cato.org/pubs/pas/pa525.pdf.

Stanton, Steven J., Jacinta C. Beehner, Ekjyot K. Saini, Cynthia M. Kuhn, and Kevin S. LaBar. "Dominance, Politics, and Physiology: Voters' Testosterone Changes on the Night of the 2008 United States Presidential Election." *PLoS ONE* 4 (2009): e7543. doi:10.1371/journal.pone.0007543. http://www.plosone.org/article/info:doi%2F10.1371%2Fjournal.pone.0007543.

Stewart III, Charles. "What Hath HAVA Wrought? Consequences, Intended and Not, of the Post-Bush v. Gore Reforms." Voting Technology Project Working Paper. April 7, 2011. http://vote.caltech.edu/drupal/node/366.

Talukdar, Monideepa, Rob Richie, and Ryan O'Donnell. "Fuzzy Math: Wrong Way Reforms for Allocating Electoral College Votes." FairVote Policy Perspective. September 2011. http://www.fairvote.org/fuzzy-math-wrong-way-reforms-for-allocating-electoral-college-votes#.T8fviI7CFiw.

Task Force on Inequality and American Democracy, American Political Science Association. "American Democracy in an Age of Rising Inequality." 2004. http://www.apsanet.org/imgtest/taskforcereport.pdf.

Teixeira, Ruy, and John Halpin. "The Path to 270: Demographics versus Economics in the 2012 Presidential Election." November 2011. http://www.americanprogress.org/issues/2011/11/path_to_270.html.

Thompson, Clive. "Can You Count on Voting Machines?" *New York Times Magazine*, January 6, 2008.

Tokaji, Daniel P. "Partisan and Nonpartisan Election Administration." Report presented at the Election Reform

Agenda Conference, Iowa City, Iowa, May 2009. http://www
.myweb.uiowa.edu/bhlai/reform/papers/tokaji.doc.

U.S. Census Bureau. *Statistical Abstract of the United States: 2011.*
2011. http://www.census.gov/prod/2011pubs/11statab/stloc
gov.pdf.

U.S. Election Assistance Commission. *The Impact of the National
Voter Registration Act of 1993 on the Administration of Elections
for Federal Office 2009–2010.* June 30, 2011. http://www.eac
.gov/assets/1/Documents/2010%20NVRA%20FINAL%20
REPORT.pdf.

U.S. Election Assistance Commission. *The Impact of The National
Voter Registration Act of 1993 on the Administration of Elections
for Federal Office 2007–2008.* June 30, 2009. http://www
.eac.gov/assets/1/AssetManager/The%20Impact%20of%20
the%20National%20Voter%20Registration%20Act%20on%20
Federal%20Elections%202007-2008.pdf.

U.S. Election Assistance Commission. *2010 Election Administration
and Voting Survey: A Summary of Key Findings.* December 2011.
http://www.eac.gov/assets/1/Documents/990-281_EAC
_EAVS_508_revised.pdf.

U.S. Election Assistance Commission. *2008 Election Administration
and Voting Survey: A Summary of Key Findings.* November 2009.
http://www.eac.gov/assets/1/Documents/2008%20Election
%20Administration%20and%20Voting%20Survey%20
EAVS%20Report.pdf.

U.S. Election Assistance Commission. *Election Crimes: An Initial
Review and Recommendations for Future Study.* December 2006.
http://www.eac.gov/assets/1/workflow_staging/Page/57.PDF.

U.S. Election Assistance Commission. *The Electoral College.* January
2011. http://www.eac.gov/voter_resources/the_electoral_col
lege.aspx.

Wallace-Wells, Benjamin. "The Oblivious Voter." Hoover Institution Policy Review. April 1, 2003. http://www.hoover.org /publications/policy-review/article/7093.

Weigel, David. "Stupid Voters Are People, Too." Slate, March 19, 2012. http://www.slate.com/articles/news_and_politics/politics /2012/03/the_media_shouldn_t_apologize_for_reporting _what_voters_actually_say_.html.

Weiser, Wendy R. "Are HAVA's Provisional Ballots Working?" Paper presented at the Center for Democracy and Election Management, HAVA Conference, Washington, DC, March 29, 2006. http://www1.american.edu/ia/cdem/usp/hava_papers /Weiser.pdf.

Weiser, Wendy R., and Vishal Agraharkar. "Brennan Center for Justice: Ballot Security and Voter Suppression." October 2010. http://www.brennancenter.org/content/resource/ballot _security_and_voter_suppression/.

Weiser, Wendy R., and Lawrence Norden. "Brennan Center for Justice: Voting law Changes in 2012." October 2011. http://www.brennancenter.org/content/resource/voting _law_changes_in_2012/.

Weiser, Wendy, ed. "Brennan Center for Justice: Voter Registration Modernization: Collected Reports and Papers." October 2009. http://www.brennanceter.org/content /resource/voter_registration_modernization_collected _reports_and_papers/.

Wilkinson, Will. "Thank You for Not Voting." Ottawa Citizen, October 22, 2008. Reprinted at http://www.cato.org/publica tions/commentary/thank-you-not-voting.

"The Psychology of Voting: Flagging Up Bias." The Economist, August 6, 2011. http://www.economist.com/node /21525362.

COURT CASES

Breedlove v. Suttles, 302 U.S. 277 (1937).

Bush v. Gore, 531 U.S. 98 (2000).

Crawford v. Marion County Board of Elections, 553 U.S. 181 (2008).

Harper v. Virginia Board of Elections, 383 U.S. 663 (1966).

In re Ah Yup, 1 F. Cas. 223 (C.C.D. Cal. 1878).

Marbury v. Madison, 5 U.S. 137 (1803).

Reynolds v. Sims, 377 U.S. 533 (1964).

Storer v. Brown, 415 U.S. 724 (1974).

Weinschenk v. State of Missouri, 203 S.W.3d 201 (MO. 2006).

INDEX